Study **&** *Master*

Study Guide 11
English

Jeanne Maclay-Mayers

CAMBRIDGE
UNIVERSITY PRESS

CAMBRIDGE UNIVERSITY PRESS
Cambridge, New York, Melbourne, Madrid, Cape Town, Singapore, São Paulo, Delhi

Cambridge University Press
The Water Club, Beach Road, Granger Bay, Cape Town 8005, South Africa

www.cambridge.org
Information on this title: www.cambridge.org/9780521695169

© Cambridge University Press 2008

First published 2008

Printed in South Africa by Paarl Print

ISBN   978-0-521-69516-9 paperback

Editor: Kathy Sutton
Designer: Graham Arbuckle
Typesetter: Jenny Wheeldon
Illustrators: Beverley de Meyer, James Whitelaw, Lyn De La Motte, Robin McBride, Sandy Lightley
. . . .

If you want to know more about this book or any other Cambridge University Press
publication, phone us at (021) 412-7800, fax us at (021) 419-8418 or send an e-mail
to capetown@cambridge.org

Contents

Learning Outcome 4: Language

The learner is able to use language structures and conventions appropriately and effectively.

We know this when the learner is able to:

Assessment Standard 1

identify and explain the meanings of words and use them correctly in a wide range of texts:
- apply knowledge of important spelling patterns, rules and conventions for new and/ or complex words and compile a personal spelling list
- use common abbreviations and acronyms correctly
- use dictionaries and a thesaurus effectively for different purposes such as researching meanings and pronunciation
- apply knowledge of roots, prefixes and suffixes to determine the meaning of new words
- use gender, plurals and diminutives of nouns correctly
- use the comparative and superlative degrees of adjectives and adverbs correctly
- identify how languages borrow words from one another
- distinguish between commonly confused polysemes, homophones and homonyms and use them correctly
- use one word for a phrase and a range of synonyms and antonyms correctly.

Assessment Standard 2

use structurally sound sentences in a meaningful and functional manner:
- identify and use parts of speech such as nouns, verbs, pronouns, adjectives and adverbs in a range of texts accurately and meaningfully
- use verb forms and auxiliaries to express tense and mood in familiar contexts with increasing accuracy
- use negative forms correctly
- use subject, object and predicate correctly
- use simple sentences appropriately and correctly and construct acceptable compound and complex sentences by using clause, phrases and conjunctions
- recognise and use different sentence types such as statements, questions, commands and instructions correctly
- use active and passive voice appropriately
- use direct and indirect speech correctly and for required effect
- use correct word order in sentences with growing accuracy and understand how word order can influence meaning
- use concord with increasing accuracy
- use punctuation correctly and for a range of purposes such as to clarify meaning, show grammatical relationships and add emphasis
- use a range of figurative language such as idioms, idiomatic expressions and proverbs appropriately
- translate sentences from target language in to home language and visa versa.

Assessment Standard 3

develop critical language awareness:
- explain denotation and connotation
- explain how the implicit and explicit messages, values and attitudes reflect the position of the speaker/receiver/reader/viewer
- identify and challenge bias and stereotyping, and emotive, persuasive and manipulative language, and explore alternative ways of expression.

Introduction

Dear learners

This book covers all the language rules for Learning Outcome 4 that the National Curriculum Statement requires Grade 11 First Additional Language learners to know. It is also a very thorough guide to how to use English.

Language rules are presented in small, easy-to-understand pieces, in a logical order. You are taught the rules you need to know and given plenty of chances to practise using these rules. You might have a fuzzy understanding of grammatical rules when you start working through this book, but you will have a clear understanding of English grammar when you finish.

Because English is a verb-based language, I have given a lot of attention to verbs in this book. This is necessary. English teachers often do not spend as much time on verbs as they should, therefore learners have to learn the rules about verbs subconsciously, which can be slow and frustrating. This book will help you to learn the rules about verbs in a clear and logical way that you can use immediately.

Every exercise offers important rules and then makes you practise using these rules. However, sometimes learning rules can seem boring, so this book has lots of magazine articles and other extracts for you to read. These form part of the activities that follow each section of exercises. You will use the information you have just learned to answer questions about the language used in the articles and other extracts. The answers to all the exercises and activities are in the back.

Just before the answer section, there is also a section showing some important texts you could be asked to write. It is not possible to offer a format for every text you might be asked to write, but the ones that are included are very likely to come up in examinations and you should learn how to set them out and become familiar with specific phrases to use in particular places in these texts.

Do not start reading this book the night before your exams. There are 130 exercises and 13 activities to do, as well as 20 model formats to revise. If you work through one exercise, activity or model format every evening, it will take you 163 evenings to finish working through this book! (However, if you have started reading this the night before an exam, skim through the contents page and choose to focus on those areas that you do not know well.)

When you work through the book, try not to jump around between exercises. They have been carefully ordered so that they build on each other. This means that the complicated concepts seem quite simple, if you get to them after doing all the exercises beforehand. This is not a bundle of hints and tips. It is a systemic approach to mastering the English language.

I hope that you find it useful and enjoyable.

Jeanne Maclay-Mayers

Language knowledge and skills

Breaking a sentence into its parts of speech

Here is a short introduction to the eight different parts of speech. Every word in a sentence can be put into one of these categories. Throughout this book we will be using these categories, and discussing in more detail what they mean.

nouns – words for people, places, things and ideas, such as 'Thembi', 'Boom Shaka', 'Sun City', 'parties' and 'love'
pronouns – little words such as 'he', 'she' or 'it' that stand in the place of the full names of people, places and things

Boom Shaka's members were Thembi Seete, Junior Sokhela, Theo Nhlengethwa, and Lebo Mathosa.

determiners – little words such as 'the' and 'a' that come in front of some nouns
adjectives – words that describe nouns, such as 'big' and 'new'
verbs – words that describe actions, such as 'sing' and 'learn', or show that something exists, such as 'is' and 'was'
adverbs – words that give more information about a verb – how it happened, when it happened or where it happened, such as 'carefully', 'yesterday' and 'there'
prepositions – little words that show where things are in relation to each other, such as 'on' and 'from'
conjunctions – words that join different ideas in a sentence, such as 'and' and 'therefore'

1   Divide the following sentences up into individual words and write the words in the appropriate place in the table. (Don't worry if you find this difficult. We will be looking at each part of speech again later.)
   a   The band was popular in South Africa.
   b   Junior, Theo, Thembi and Lebo learned the new song carefully.
   c   Thembi and Lebo danced beautifully.
   d   They liked Sun City.

Parts of speech	Sentence a	Sentence b	Sentence c	Sentence d
nouns				
pronouns				
determiners				
adjectives				
verbs				
adverbs				
prepositions				
conjunctions				

2   Now write a sentence of your own by using some of the words from the table you have filled in. Circle each word and label it according to what part of speech it is.

Types of nouns

Nouns are words that refer to people, places, things or ideas. Nouns are usually categorised in the following way.

Concrete nouns		Abstract nouns
Proper nouns	**Common nouns**	

In this table there are two main sections: concrete nouns and abstract nouns. Concrete nouns are nouns you can sense (touch, smell, hear, taste or see). Abstract nouns, such as 'love' or 'hate', cannot be sensed with the five senses yet we know that they still exist.

Concrete nouns are further divided into proper nouns and common nouns. Proper nouns are usually the names of people, places and important things, such as religions and events. The first letter of a proper noun is written as a capital letter to show respect. Common nouns are simply things, and there is no reason to spell them with a capital letter.

1   Categorise the following list of nouns according to the table above.

people	Thembi	victory
North Sea Jazz Festival	car	pride
Boom Shaka	music	Nike
church	friend	performance
kindness	fashion	Johannesburg
Christianity	Greeks	grief
religion	believer	Islam

When we use the word 'God' with a capital letter this shows we are talking about the god that we believe in and respect. When we talk about other gods (or goddesses) we use a small 'g'.

2   Rewrite the following sentence, inserting capital letters where appropriate.

The greeks worshipped nike, a goddess of victory, before they converted to christianity.

A statue of Nike

Plural nouns

Regular plural nouns

Some singular nouns can be made into plurals to show that there is more than one of them. The word 'song' is a singular noun that can be made into the plural noun 'songs'. Adding 's' is the most common way of changing a singular noun into a plural noun. This is the regular pattern we should follow unless there is a reason not to.

1   Change these singular nouns into plural nouns by adding 's'.
   a   girl
   b   believer
   c   length

If a singular noun ends in 's' already, we have to add 'es' to the end of it to change it into a plural. Otherwise, when we said this word, we would not be able to hear that it was now a plural noun. For example, say 'actress' aloud. Now say 'actresss' and 'actresses' aloud. When we say 'actresses' aloud we can hear it is a plural because it sounds different from the singular form 'actress'. But 'actresss' would sound the same as 'actress', and so would not let us show that it was a plural.

   If a singular noun ends in 'ch' or 'sh', we usually also add 'es' to the end of it to make it a plural. If a singular noun ends in 'f', we have to remove the 'f' and add 'ves' to the end of it to make it a plural.

> These rules all help us to pronounce the plural nouns more easily.

2   Change these singular nouns into plurals nouns by adding 'es'.
   a   wife
   b   brooch
   c   manageress
   d   splash

Irregular plural nouns

A few nouns are made into plurals in different ways. Sometimes we have to follow strange old English rules when we make a singular noun into a plural (for example, 'man' must change to 'men'). In other cases the noun may come from a different language, so when we make it into the plural we follow the rule from that language (for example, the Latin word 'memorandum' changes to the plural form 'memoranda'.) We call plural nouns that do not follow the normal rules 'irregular plural nouns', and some of the most important ones are shown in the table that follows.

Singular noun	Plural noun
woman	women
sheep	sheep
medium	media
criterion	criteria
phenomenon	phenomena
stigma	stigmata
bacterium	bacteria
axis	axes
die	dice

3 Complete the following sentences by changing the words in brackets into plural nouns.
   a The (learner) looked at the (bacterium) under the (microscope).
   b We can continue playing only when you throw the two (die).
   c The (planet) rotate on their (axis).

Uncountable nouns

The above examples of nouns can all be counted. We can see if there is one of them or more than one of them, which is why we call them countable nouns.

Sometimes nouns cannot be counted, such as 'pride' or 'air'. We call this kind of noun an uncountable noun, and we never change it into a plural.

4 Complete these sentences by putting uncountable nouns from the list on page 11 into the spaces.
   a When I listen to their _____ I always want to go out and have fun.
   b After their deaths I was filled with _____.

Collective nouns

Collective nouns are singular nouns that refer to a group of things. When we use a collective noun we often use a plural noun in the same phrase. For example, the phrase 'a regiment of soldiers' contains the collective (singular) noun 'regiment' and the plural noun 'soldiers'.

5 Complete the following phrases by using one of the collective nouns in the box for each.

herd	flock	pride	library

   a a _____ of lions
   b a _____ of sheep
   c a _____ of cattle
   d a _____ of books

Nouns showing gender or size

Sometimes we use nouns that indicate whether something is male or female, or full-grown or still small. We usually do this in relation to animals.

Nouns that give extra information about animals			
Plural form	Adult male	Adult female	Young form
cattle	bull	cow	calf
sheep	ram	ewe	lamb
pigs/swine	boar	sow	piglet
horses	stallion	mare	foal
antelope/deer	buck/stag/hart	doe	foal
dogs	dog	bitch	puppy
cats	cat/tomcat	cat	kitten
chickens	cock	hen	chick
geese	gander	goose	gosling
ducks	drake	duck	duckling
swans	swan	swan	cygnet
lions	lion	lioness	cub
tigers	tiger	tigress	cub
bears	bear	bear	cub
fish	fish	fish	fry
whales	bull	cow	calf

1 Complete the following sentences by inserting an appropriate word from the table.
   a To avoid fights we keep only one _____ in our chicken coop. However, we have many _____, so that they lay many eggs.
   b When whales breed, the _____ gives birth to only one _____.
   c The bears had only one young _____, and it was still unsteady when it tried to walk.
   d As I watched the adult cattle being branded, I was glad that I was not a _____ or a _____.

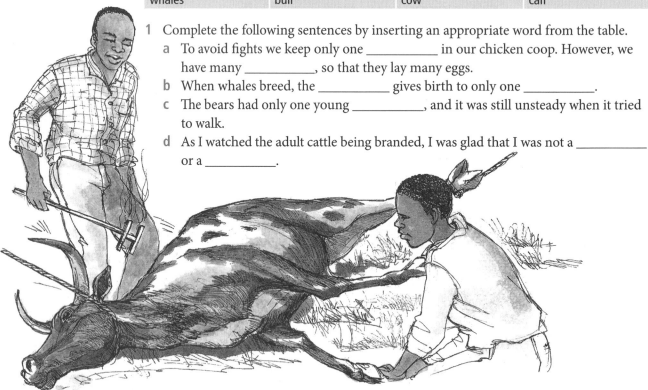

Sometimes we also use different nouns to refer to men and women. For example, we use the word 'waiter' to refer to a man and 'waitress' to refer to a woman, but we use the word 'caretaker' to refer to a man or a woman. The following table shows some nouns where there is a different form for the male version and the female version.

Nouns to do with titles, jobs or special roles that show gender	
Masculine version	**Feminine version**
king	queen
prince	princess
count	countess
actor	actress
director	directress (or 'director' in modern English)
manager	manageress (or 'manager' in modern English)
poet	poetess (or 'poet' in modern English)
chairman	chairwoman
god	goddess
priest	priestess
prophet	prophetess
monk	nun
waiter	waitress

These days, people often use the masculine form to refer to both men and women, particularly when referring to directors of films. The restaurant industry now uses the slang term 'waitron' to refer to a waiter or waitress. However, one of the few feminine forms that we never drop is 'actress'.

2 Complete the following sentences by inserting an appropriate noun.
  a Angelina Jolie is a famous _____, but many people find her unattractive although she is beautiful.
  b I was surprised to find out that the violent film's _____ was a woman.
  c The advertisement did not specify whether the restaurant was looking for a _____ or a _____; it simply said 'Waitron needed', so I think they would be happy for a man or a woman to apply for the job.

Many languages have word endings that show that a speaker is talking about a small version of something. We call the new nouns that are created this way 'diminutives'. Apart from the terms use to describe young animals, English does not usually use diminutives. Normally, English speakers put the word 'small' in front of a noun instead. However, a few nouns that do have diminutive forms are shown below.

flat – flatlet
flower – floweret
sweet – sweetie

As well as expressing the idea that something is physically small, diminutives can also be used to express affection or to be rude.

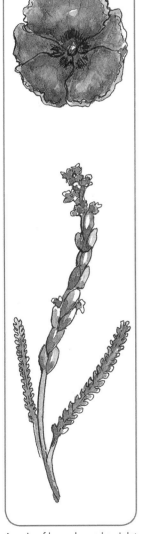

A sprig of lavender and a violet

3 Why is a diminutive used in the following paragraphs?
  a You cannot marry a man who rents a flatlet! How would you be able to have a family?
  b Her husband apologised immediately, saying 'I'm sorry sweetie! I never meant to hurt you.'
  c Unlike violets, if you look closely at a lavender 'flower', you will see that it is actually made up of many small flowerets.

Ordering adjectives

Adjectives are words that describe nouns. They can come before nouns or after verbs and nouns. We often use adjectives to show our opinions of something. For example, in the following two sentences 'good' is an adjective that describes the noun 'singer'.

She was a *good* singer.
The singer was *good*.

We can use the following adjectives to show our opinion of something or someone.

Adjectives that show we like something	Adjectives that show we do not like something
good	bad
excellent	terrible
brilliant	awful
fantastic	horrible
outstanding	substandard
meritorious	poor
wonderful	shocking

1   Use an appropriate adjective from the table in each of the following sentences:
   a   My friend is an _____l singer but I cannot bear to tell her that she has a bad voice.
   b   The concert featured many excellent performers, but Brenda Fassie was the most _____g.
   c   I bought a T-shirt from the market at the station but the quality of it was really _____r, one armhole was smaller than the other and the stitching started coming undone as soon as I put it on.
   d   I worked hard on my biology project and my teacher gave me a high mark and wrote '_____t' next to the mark.

If you like, you can use lots of adjectives before or after one noun, but the different types must be arranged in the following order. Examples are given of each type.

Opinion	Size	Age	Shape	Colour	Origin	Material
good	small	young	square	red	Zulu	wooden
perfect	medium	middle-aged	flat	gold	Malawian	iron
excellent	large	old	cylindrical	white	European	paper
lucky	tall	elderly	round	orange	German	bead/beaded

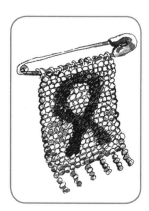

2   For each of these sentences, insert the words in brackets in the correct places.
   a   The _____ _____ boy was adopted by the American superstar named Madonna. (Malawian, small)
   b   The _____ _____ tube had a _____ lipstick inside. (red, cylindrical, gold)
   c   Because _____ _____ cities are so full of traffic, many people cycle to work or take the train. (large, European)
   d   The AIDS symbol had been used on the _____ _____ brooches. (square, Zulu)
   e   We use a _____, _____, _____ pot to make potjiekos in. (iron, large, black)

Adjectives of degree

We can use adjectives to show degree. For example, Lance might be *tall*, but Ashwell may be *taller*, and Mpisholo could be the *tallest* person you have ever met. The comparative degree is used when two people or things are being compared. The superlative degree is used when more than two people or things are being compared.

The following table shows how short, regular adjectives are changed in order to show a difference in degree.

The absolute form of a short, regular adjective	The comparative form of a short, regular adjective	The superlative form of a short, regular adjective
short	shorter	shortest
old	older	oldest
lucky	luckier	luckiest

If an adjective has more than two syllables we consider it a long adjective. The following table shows how we insert an adverb in front of long, regular adjectives to show a difference in degree. We do this instead of adding a suffix to the end of the adjective.

The absolute form of a long, regular adjective	The comparative form of a long, regular adjective	The superlative form of a long, regular adjective
virtuous	more virtuous	most virtuous
fantastic	more fantastic	most fantastic
sophisticated	more sophisticated	most sophisticated

Some adjectives with two syllables are categorised as short adjectives (for example, 'lucky'), and some are categorised as long adjectives (for example, 'famous').

A few adjectives change completely when we change them into their comparative or superlative form. These are called irregular adjectives. (Luckily there are not many irregular adjectives to learn.) The following table shows how the two most common irregular adjectives are changed in order to show a difference in degree.

The absolute form of an irregular adjective	The comparative form of an irregular adjective	The superlative form of an irregular adjective
good	better	best
bad	worse	worst

Some adjectives cannot be changed to show degree. For example, 'wooden' cannot be changed. A thing either is wooden or it is not.

1   Complete the following sentences with adjectives of the correct degree.
   a   Naledi is (short), but Jeff is (short) and Natalie is the (short) of them all.
   b   Lance Armstrong is the (fast) cyclist in the world.
   c   Lebo Mathosa was (famous), but Brenda Fassie was (famous).
   d   Of all the teachers at the school, Mr Khumalo is the (tall).
   e   She was chosen to act the main part in the film. I think she is the (lucky) girl alive.
   f   I am (old) than my sister, but she dresses up in such formal clothing that she seems (sophisticated).

Similes and metaphors

We often compare the things we are talking about to other things, in order to describe them more effectively. For example, we often describe bad news that surprises people as a 'bombshell'. Bombshells are actually the containers for bombs, which soldiers use to blow up their enemies. When we call a piece of news a bombshell we are saying that, compared to other bits of news, this piece of news was worse, and has a bigger effect on the emotions of the people that heard it. We make this kind of comparison to emphasise what we are saying.

I'm pregnant.

Kate dropped a bombshell that evening when she told her parents that she was pregnant.

Similes and metaphors are types of comparison. They are very similar. Look at these examples where different things are compared to a bomb explosion, for different reasons.

Simile: When my brother's band practises their music in our garage it sounds *as if* a bomb is going off – but unfortunately it lasts much longer.
Simile: When she got angry she exploded *like* a nuclear bomb.
Simile: She is more explosive *than* a pile of fireworks on a hot day.
Metaphor: Once my beautiful sister had peroxided her hair, her boyfriend called her 'the blonde bombshell'.
Metaphor: The young band exploded onto the South African music scene.
Metaphor: When my mother found out we had finished all the bread she blew up at us.
Metaphor: We were blown away by their kwaito music.

The first three of the above examples are called similes, because they are comparisons that use a comparing word ('like', 'as' or 'than'). Because similes use one of these three words they are easier to spot than metaphors, which do not.

Metaphors are comparisons that do not use a comparing word. They simply say, for example, 'she is a blonde bombshell' and we are left to work out that she attracts as much attention as a bombshell when it explodes, rather than she is a heavy metal container with a fuse attached. Metaphors are even harder to understand when only the verb gives us a clue that a comparison is being made, as happens in the last three examples on the previous page. The terms 'exploded', 'blew up' and 'blown away' are normally used to describe bombs or what happens to people near to a bomb explosion, but here they are used to describe people and music instead. Metaphors are a more sophisticated way of making a comparison than similes.

Old-fashioned bombs had a strong shell with explosive material inside. They also had a fuse made of rope that someone needed to light. When the fire burnt along the rope and reached the bomb, it exploded.

Modern bombs have a timer that someone sets. When the timer reaches zero, the bomb goes off.

Hand grenades are small bombs that go off a short while after you pull out the trigger. During this time the soldier is meant to throw the hand grenade at the enemy and then run away.

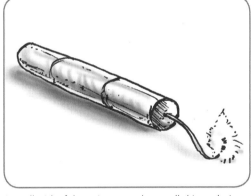

A small stick of dynamite can make a really big explosion.

1   What is being compared to what in the following similes? Say why the writer is doing this.
    a   After she found out about his many lies, Tumi was as cold as ice towards her husband.
    b   Rikki was always a big baby, and now he looks like a giant when he is next to his friends.
    c   Christopher was grumpier than a bear with a sore head.
    d   He thinks he will be able to keep the murder a secret, but actually it is a timebomb waiting to go off.

2   What is being compared to what in the following metaphors? Say why the writer is doing this.
    a   Bandile has a short fuse.
    b   Teachers try to keep learners on track until their final examinations.
    c   When Mthunzi arrived to apologise, he was bombarded with insults by his girlfriend.
    d   The dancer is dynamite on stage.

When we use similes and metaphors we are using figurative language. When what we say is exactly what we mean we are using literal language.

Abbreviations and acronyms

Abbreviations

'Abbreviate' means 'shorten'.

Sometimes we shorten words so they are quicker to say. The shorter words we create are called abbreviations. We can abbreviate many different parts of speech, but the examples below are all of commonly abbreviated nouns. When we abbreviate we use only part of the original word or phrase.

tel – telephone

fax – facsimile

pop – popular

bike – bicycle

tech – technology

fan – fanatic

ad – advertisement

Beemer – a car made by BMW

cell – cellular telephone

email – electronic mail

Jo'berg/Jozi – Johannesburg

trike – tricycle

lab – laboratory

fort – fortification

Merc – a car made by Mercedes Benz

± short symbol used to mean 'plus' or 'and'

1 Use the correct abbreviations in the following sentences.
   a I prefer sending information by _____ than by _____, because even if the receiver's machine is not switched on the message will wait in his/her inbox.
   b When I was old enough to ride a _____ I gave my little sister my old red _____.

Alternatively, we can use the first letter of each word in a phrase to make an abbreviation and say the name of each letter aloud.

ANC (pronounced 'ay-en-see') – African National Congress

ANCYL (pronounced 'ay-en-see-wy-el') African National Congress Youth League

YCL (pronounced 'wy-see-el') – Young Communist League

DA (pronounced 'dee-ay') – Democratic Alliance

R&B (pronounced 'ar-and-bee') – rhythm and blues

SMS (pronounced 'ess-em-ess') – short message service

VW (pronounced 'vee-double-yu') – Volkswagen

BMW (pronounced 'bee-em-double-yu') – Bavarian Motor Works

PSL (pronounced 'pee-es-el') – Premier Soccer League

HIV (pronounced 'aych-eye-vee') – Human Immunodeficiency Virus

UK (pronounced 'you-kay') – United Kingdom

SA (pronounced 'es-ay') – South Africa

SABC (pronounced 'ess-ay-bee-see') – South African Broadcasting Association

USA (pronounced 'you-ess-ay') – United States of America (This sometimes abbreviated to just 'United States' or 'US'.)

V&A (pronounced 'vee-en-ay') – Victoria and Albert (a past English queen and her husband)

HQ (pronounced 'aich-ku') – headquarters

LLB (pronounced 'el-el-bee') – *legum baccalaureus* (Latin phrase for educational qualification meaning 'bachelor of laws')

We can also abbreviate words by using numbers. For example, the nineties are often written as the '90s' (and pronounced 'nineties'). The twentieth century (1900–2000) is often written as the '1900s' (and pronounced 'the nineteen hundreds').

An unusual abbreviation is to use '@' to mean 'at'. This abbreviation is used in email addresses and has now become fashionable amongst people who use computers and cell phones.

2   Use the correct abbreviation in the following sentences.
   a   Young soccer stars dream of playing in the _____.
   b   The _____ won the first democratic elections in South Africa and has governed the country ever since. The _____ is the official opposition party.
   c   Germany produces three famous brands of cars: _____s, _____s and _____s.

We can also abbreviate people's titles, such as when we use 'Mrs' instead of 'Mistress'. These abbreviations become part of proper nouns, which is why they start with a capital letter. When the last letter of the abbreviation is not the last letter of the original word, then it is traditional to put a full stop after the abbreviation.

Mr – Mister (for a married man or an unmarried man)
Mrs – Mistress (for a married woman)
Miss – Mistress (for an unmarried woman)
Ms – Mistress (for a woman who refuses to be titled according to whether she is married or unmarried)
Dr – Doctor (a person who has a medical degree or a person who has the highest university degree in any learning area)
Rev. – Reverend (for the leader of a Christian congregation)
Prof. – Professor (for a high-ranking person in a university)

3   Use the correct abbreviations in the following sentences.
   a   My parents are _____ Mabena and _____ Mabena.
   b   At university my sister is taught by _____ Finlayson, who has a doctorate degree, and _____ Mlipha, who is the head of department.

Acronyms

You have looked at the kind of abbreviations that use the first letters of words from the original phrase, writing them as capitals and then sounding out each individual letter. But sometimes people take the first letters and make a new word that is written in capitals, but that can also be pronounced as if it was a real word. (For example, COSATU is not pronounced 'see-oh-es-ay-tee-yu'; it is pronounced 'cosatu'.) Such words are called acronyms. When people create acronyms they try to make them easy to pronounce.

COSATU – Council of South African Trade Unions
SWAPO – South West African People's Organisation
SAMA – South African Music Awards
AIDS – Acquired Immunodeficiency Syndrome

4   Use the correct abbreviation in the following sentence.
   _____ is an organisation that looks after the rights of South African workers.

Exercise 9

Synonyms

Synonyms are words that have similar meanings to each other. The nouns 'noise' and 'sound' are an example of a pair of synonyms.

1 Match the nouns in column A with their synonyms in column B.

Some of these pairs of synonyms have other synonyms. For example, the nouns 'stress' and 'tension' also have 'anxiety' as a synonym. In the table below, the adjectives 'special' and 'unusual' also have 'distinctive' as a synonym.

Column A	Column B
a place	sorrow
b vocalist	degree
c aeroplane	singer
d clothing	jet
e sneaker	area
f level	pedestal
g base	age
h device	trainer
i fragrance	perfume
j explosion	blast
k form	gadget
l era	serpent
m confidence	shape
n grief	dedication
o stress	self-esteem
p commitment	apparel
q snake	tension

2 Match the adjectives in column A with their synonyms in column B.

Some of these words can be used as different parts of speech, and when used in a different way they would no longer be part of this pair of synonyms. For example, we can use 'core' as a noun, but then the adjective 'inner' would no longer be a synonym.

Column A	Column B
a real	breakable
b provocative	trendy
c core	flawless
d fragile	gifted
e fashionable	minute
f virtuous	funny
g tiny	basic
h abstract	gentle
i tender	fortunate
j likely	inner
k lucky	persuasive
l witty	genuine
m simple	controversial
n perfect	probable
o talented	good
p convincing	theoretical

3   Match the verbs in column A with their synonyms in column B.

Column A	Column B
a enhance	educate
b move	strike
c express	perform
d act	alter
e want	protest
f change	transfer
g complain	rupture
h make	fire
i leave	control
j teach	construct
k allow	desire
l govern	think
m retrench	gaze
n incorporate	let
o suppose	quit
p hit	improve
q look	include
r tear	tell

Some synonyms differ in degree, for example, to 'gaze' at something means that you look longer and harder at it than if you simply 'look' at it.

Some synonyms are used in more formal situations than others, for example, 'educate' is more formal than 'teach'.

Some synonyms have more positive connotations than others, for example, 'govern' is a more positive word than 'control' when it refers to ruling a country.

Some synonyms allow people to make small but important distinctions, for example, if a company 'retrenches' a person this shows the person is not losing his/her job because of the quality of his/her work. If a company 'fires' someone, then this implies that person was not good at his/her job.

Often you can use either one of a pair of synonyms in a sentence. In this case we say the synonyms are 'interchangeable'. But synonyms are not always interchangeable.

4   Match the adverbs in column A with their synonyms in column B.

Column A	Column B
a solo	immediately
b frequently	promptly
c constantly	just
d quickly	carefully
e simply	alone
f now	worldwide
g also	always
h tenderly	often
i internationally	too

Using one word for a phrase

Often we can choose to use many simple words to describe something, or we can choose one special word to say the same thing. For example, we can say 'a ceremony organised to respectfully bury a dead person' or we can use the word 'funeral', which means the same thing.

1   Match the phrases in column A with the words in column B that mean the same thing.

Column A		Column B
a	fantastic to watch	traditional
b	say it does not exist, will not happen or is not true	icon
c	friends and acquaintances of a similar age	obituary
d	not at a good time	generation
e	based on the old ways of doing things	controversy
f	to begin something enthusiastically; to set something into motion	amulet
g	suggest someone by name for a particular title	limousine
h	ongoing public argument about provocative subject	spectacular
i	drops of water left outside after a cool night	launch
j	an almost godlike person that is so well-known that he/she starts to represent a particular era	deny
k	religious object or lucky object	cynic
l	huge group of similarly aged people who do not necessarily know each other but experience the same era	nominate
m	an article that announces the death of someone and summarises their life	peers
n	possible to get	hearse
o	easily breakable	fragile
p	expensive car that is so long it contains a little room so that passengers can sit facing each other and have a party	available
q	a person who expects the worst from other people	untimely
r	long car for transporting coffins	dew

2   Which of the above words describes each of the objects in the illustrations below?

a

b

Activity A

Read the obituary on pages 26 and 27, which was published on the *Mail & Guardian*'s website. Then answer the questions below.

1   Who was this obituary written about?
2   Brenda Fassie is called a 'pop icon' in this obituary.
   a   What word has been abbreviated in the term 'pop icon'?
   b   What does the word 'icon' mean when it is used in this context?
3   Give a synonym for the following words from the text:
   a   vocalist (line 11)
   b   grief (line 38)
4   Why are the first letters of the words Boom Shaka written in capital letters?
5   Explain the meaning of the following extract from the text: 'She launched her solo career in 2000 …'
6   What acronym is commonly used for the phrase 'South African Music Award'.
7   The following abbreviations are used in the text. Write them out in full.
   a   R&B (line 24)
   b   ANCYL (line 38)
   c   YCL (line 42)
8   Lebo Mathosa's last album was called 'Lioness'.
   a   Is this word a noun or an adjective?
   b   Is this word masculine or feminine?
9   The *Star Tonight* called a 2004 performance by Lebo Mathosa the 'most outstanding performance of the year'. Who was the *Star Tonight* comparing her to when it used the superlative degree in this statement?
10 Danny K said that Lebo Mathosa 'just blew everyone off the stage'. What is the singer being compared to in this metaphor?
11 Did Lebo Mathosa seriously mean to suggest that, during a tour, people who woke up late would be left behind? How do you know this?
12 Select the best explanation from the following for what the last sentence of the obituary means:
   a   Although the writer had tried hard to find out about the funeral nobody would tell her what had happened there.
   b   The funeral had not been held when this obituary was published so the writer could not say what had been said during this ceremony.
   c   When this obituary was published the writer had not been able to find out when or where the funeral would be.

'You can't deny death, you can't fear it'

Hila Bouzaglou | Johannesburg, South Africa

23 October 2006

In November 2004, after the death of pop icon Brenda Fassie, singer Lebo Mathosa told the *Mail & Guardian* in an interview: 'You can't deny death, you can't fear it. I'm sure God has a better place for us, if you're a believer.'

Two years later, in a twist of fate, 29-year-old Mathosa, like her controversial role model, has
5 moved on to that 'better place'.

The R&B and kwaito singer died in a car accident east of Johannesburg on October 23 when her driver lost control of the car and it overturned, killing Mathosa instantly.

Mathosa, whose music also incorporated elements of African music, dance and funk, was born on July 16 1977 and started singing at the age of seven for her church. She moved to
10 Johannesburg when she was 14 and joined the music industry as a teenager in Hillbrow.

In 1994 she shot to fame as the lead vocalist and dancer for kwaito – or 'bubblegum', as Mathosa called it – group Boom Shaka. As part of Boom Shaka, Mathosa courted controversy in her daring skirt lengths and sexy dance moves, but the group became multi-platinum-sellers and icons of post-apartheid music.

15 She launched her solo career in 2000 with her debut album, *Dream*, which won her three South African Music Awards in 2001.

Her album *Drama Queen*, released in 2004, won best dance album at the South African Music Awards in 2005 and her last album, *Lioness*, dived deeper into traditional and Afro-pop music.

Mathosa was lucky enough to be one of the few South African performers who was constantly
20 in demand on the performance circuit, regardless of whether she had an album on the charts.

She performed at the North Sea Jazz Festival in Cape Town, at the Celebrate South Africa concert in London's Trafalgar Square and at Nelson Mandela's 85th birthday in front of 16 000 people.

Mathosa was also featured on American R&B star Keith Sweat's All Africa Album, acted in
25 South African television shows *Generations*, *Backstage* and *Muvhango* and was nominated as one of Africa's sexiest women by *FHM magazine*.

Described as a fun-loving person by her colleagues in the music industry, Mathosa was a powerful artist who demanded attention on stage and whose live acts were spectacular.

Her performance at the Kora Awards in 2004 was labelled as the 'most outstanding
30 performance of the year' by the *Star Tonight*.

South African pop star Danny K, who toured many times with Mathosa, said that at an MTV base show where they performed together Mathosa 'just blew everyone off the stage'.

Mathosa will not only be missed by the music industry but on all levels of South African society – even on a government level.

35 Minister of Arts and Culture Pallo Jordan said on Monday: 'We will always remember her as a highly gifted, young African "drama queen" who used her life, talent and career to promote pride, respect and appreciation for African music, dance, fashion, heritage, art and culture.'

The African National Congress Youth League (ANCYL) also expressed its grief over her death.

'Lebo Mathosa was a friend and had a special relationship with the ANCYL. Through her
40 music, she will be remembered as an icon, inspirator, artist, entertainer and as part of a
generation that revolutionised our music industry,' said ANCYL spokesperson Zizi Kodwa.

Young Communist League (YCL) secretary Buti Manamela said the YCL was devastated and
shocked to learn about the untimely death of Mathosa, 'a pioneer of cultural revolution and
kwaito music in our country'.

45 A former public relations officer for EMI, Boyce Fiyo, worked closely with Mathosa for three
years. He said she was a 'kind of ambassador for South Africa' and that the South African music
industry has lost an icon.

Fiyo reminisced about a 2005 tour to Port Elizabeth with Mathosa, remembering Mathosa's
'jolliness' and good sense of humour. 'It's always hard to wake people up on tour, so Lebo said,
50 "Let's make a time to meet and if you're not here we'll leave that person behind"',
he said.

Big Boy Mlangeni, marketing manager for Mathosa's first label, Bula Records, said Mathosa
was an artist that everybody loved. 'I believe that anything that happens, there's a purpose.
[Mathosa's death] was from God himself,' he said.

55 Funeral details were not available at the time of going to press.

Antonyms

Antonyms are words that mean the opposite of each other. The words 'noise' and 'silence' are a pair of antonyms.

Noise

1 Match the nouns in column A with their antonyms in column B.

Column A	Column B
a self	subject
b captivity	death
c life	exile
d cause	oppressed
e light	communist
f truth	injustice
g base	responsibility
h atheist	other
i immigrant	darkness
j justice	believer
k victory	opponent
l capitalist	monarchy
m democracy	lie
n comrade	failure
m king	employee
n right	effect
o employer	freedom
p oppressor	top

2 Match the verbs in column A with their antonyms in column B.

Column A	Column B
a give	retreat
b assemble	veto
c come	groan
d construct	lower
e raise	obstruct
f approve	regress
g connect	disperse
h help	disconnect
i progress	receive
j laugh	go
k advance	destroy

Silence

3 Match the adjectives in column A with their antonyms in column B.

Column A		Column B
a	equal	global
b	subtle	false
c	movable	pennypinching
d	convincing	abusive
e	local	unconvincing
f	convenient	unequal
g	recognisable	unexpected
h	genuine	uncertain
i	perfect	unsubtle
j	domestic	unrecognisable
k	certain	unusual
l	expected	unfashionable
m	possible	imperfect
n	fashionable	immovable
o	extravagant	impossible
p	respectful	inconvenient
q	urban	invisible
r	usual	indivisible
s	respectful	present
t	early	rural
u	absent	flippant
v	divisible	late
w	visible	public

4 Match the adverbs in column A with their antonyms in column B.

Column A		Column B
a	here	incompletely
b	well	alternatively
c	largely	rarely
d	yesterday	ironically
e	sincerely	tomorrow
f	verbally	physically
g	commonly	badly
h	full	there
i	extravagantly	metaphorically
j	completely	cheaply
k	similarly	jokingly
l	literally	empty
m	seriously	slightly

Irony and sarcasm

Irony

An ironic statement is a statement that means the opposite of what it seems to mean. We often use ironic statements to make a joke. For example, in the obituary on Lebo Mathosa, Boyce Fiyo remembers that she once said, as an ironic joke, 'It's always hard to wake people up on tour. Let's make a time to meet and if you're not here we'll leave that person behind.' Lebo Mathosa was not actually suggesting that they leave anybody behind, and the people who heard her say this would probably have laughed with her at such a suggestion.

Sarcasm

Sarcastic comments are meant to be nasty or hurtful. Sometimes people use irony in a sarcastic way, and then we should call this 'sarcasm' rather than 'irony'.

How to show that we are being ironic and not sarcastic

Sometimes people who make an ironic statement are scared that the person they are talking to will misunderstand them and be hurt. So they wink an eye at them, or squeeze their mouth to one side of their face and their tongue to the other. This shows the listener that he/she is not meant to understand the statement in a literal (straightforward) way but in an ironic way.

1   Which of these sentences is ironic and which is sarcastic?

a

b

How to show we are being genuinely enthusiastic and not sarcastic

When people are sarcastic they often use intensifying adverbs such as 'really'. But now, when people are very enthusiastic, other people do not know if they are being sincere or if they are just making a nasty joke. If you think your enthusiasm might be misunderstood, say 'seriously' after your comment. Then people will know you meant what you said.

2   Rewrite the following statement so that is sounds more sincere.
    'You look really pretty.'

Exaggerations and rhetorical questions

Exaggerations

An exaggeration is a statement that makes out that something is bigger or better than it truly is. For example, it would be an exaggeration if a mother said to her daughter, 'I have told you a thousand times not to clean the non-stick frying pan with the rough scrubbing brush.' The mother might have told her daughter this many times, but it is very unlikely that she would have told her this a thousand times.

1   Copy down the following sentences and underline the part that is an exaggeration.
    a   'Where have you been,' asked Susie when her mother fetched her from school. 'I've been waiting forever!'
    b   'I've asked you a million times to clean your room,' said Ma Masinga to her son.

A fancy name for an exaggeration is a 'hyperbole'.

Rhetorical questions

Rhetorical questions are questions that the speaker, or writer, does not expect anyone to answer. The person who uses a rhetorical question is using it to make a point, and it is really a statement disguised as a question.

   If your teacher asks you a real question it is rude not to answer it. But if your teacher asks you a rhetorical question then it is rude to answer it. So it is important to be able to tell the difference between a real question and a rhetorical question.

2   Is the following question a real question or a rhetorical question?

Connotations

The meanings of all English words have been defined in a dictionary. But dictionaries do not have enough space to tell you everything about a word. Dictionaries give you the denotative meaning of a word, which is its literal meaning. They often do not give a word's connotative meaning, which is the positive or negative tone that it gives to a sentence. The connotation of a word is the mood that is associated with a word because of how it is usually used.

Some words have good connotations, some have bad connotations, and some words are neutral (having neither good nor bad connotations).

For example, the nouns 'smell' and 'scent' have the same denotative meaning. However, while 'smell' has neutral or negative connotations, 'scent' always has positive connotations.

1   Would you use the words 'smell' or 'scent' in the following speech bubbles?

a

b

When we talk about business we often use words with positive or negative connotations, depending on how we feel about the people and the companies that we are talking about. The following table shows words that we use when we talk about business.

Words that we use in the context of business that have positive or negative connotations		
Denotative meanings	Words with positive connotations	Words and idioms with negative connotations
business (noun)	enterprise	racket
person who runs their own business (noun)	entrepreneur	capitalist
business-like atmosphere in the workplace (adjective)	professional	corporate
advertise and sell (verb)	market	flog
talk about business to other business people	network	wheel and deal

2   Complete the following paragraph with words from the table on the previous page that have negative connotations.

The company had been started by a _____ (a) who was interested in one thing: profit. He paid his employees badly and made them work long hours. His workers never had time to finish the products properly, which frustrated them. The telemarketing division then had to _____ (b) these inferior products over the telephone to unsuspecting consumers. The atmosphere in the office was never fun and relaxed, but always very _____ (c). Meanwhile the owner of the business was out on his private golf course with other businessmen, trying to _____ _____ _____ (d) in order to make more money. The other entrepreneurs knew that he ran a shameful _____ (e), but they enjoyed playing on his golf course so they did not say anything to his face.

When we talk about our own religion we usually use words with positive connotations, because we want to show our good intentions and our respect for God. However, when we see other people worshipping their gods, we sometimes use words with negative connotations to describe what they are doing. This expresses the fact that we are uncomfortable with what they are doing and would prefer that they belonged to the same religion as ourselves. The following table shows some nouns that we use when we talk about religions.

Nouns that we use in the context of religion that have positive or negative connotations		
Denotative meanings	Nouns with positive connotations	Nouns with negative connotations
something that people believe to be true	belief	superstition
small group of people following their own religion or their own version of a major religion	sect	cult
a person who believes in/follows a particular religion	believer	fanatic
adjective used to describe someone who follows religious texts very strictly	orthodox	fundamentalist
strict set of moral rules and ideas	principles	dogma

3   Lebo Mathosa said 'I'm sure God has a better place for us, if you're a believer.' In this quotation, does the word 'believer' have positive or negative connotations?

4   Complete the following sentences using one of the words from the above table.
   a   _____ Jews have two fridges in their houses, because they believe that you cannot keep meat and milk in the same fridge.
   b   According to the _____ of his religion he is not allowed to wear a condom, but I think that is a silly rule when we are fighting an AIDS epidemic.
   c   The buildings were blown up by a religious _____ who was trying to protest about the way the country was governed.
   d   I live my life according to ethical _____ .
   e   My mother never travels on the 13th day of the month because she thinks it is an unlucky day, but I think that is a silly _____ .

Determiners

Determiners are little words that almost always come in front of a noun. We can only put one determiner in front of a noun.

Numerical determiners

Numerical determiners come in front of nouns and show how many of this type of noun there are. For example, the word 'three' is a numerical determiner in the sentence 'Three men are dead.'

A definite determiner

The word 'the' is the definite determiner is English. We put it in front of nouns when we are talking about a specific example of something. For example, we say 'the singer' when we are talking about a specific singer.

Indefinite determiners

When we are not being that specific we use the indefinite determiners 'a' or 'an' instead of 'the'. The words 'a' and 'an' mean the same thing. We use 'a' in front of most words that start with consonants, but we use 'an' in front of words that begin with vowels. We also use 'an' in front of words that begin with a silent consonant, where the first letter that is actually spoken is a vowel.

1   Use 'a', 'an' or 'the' in these sentences.
    a   I'm bored. Let's go for _____ walk.
    b   Could you play _____ CD called *Drama Queen*?
    c   _____ event such as a wedding is rather stressful to organise.
    d   Take the medicine and then wait _____ hour to see whether it has worked.

When we are not sure of the exact amount of something we use 'some' or 'any' in front of the noun. We use the word 'some' in positive sentences and the word 'any' in negative sentences.

2   Use 'some' or 'any' in these sentences.
    a   There is still _____ petrol in the car.
    b   There are not _____ biscuits in the tin.

A negative determiner

When we are showing that there are none of something, we can put 'no' in front of the noun.

3   In the following sentences, replace the existing determiner with 'no'.
    a   There is a cow.
    b   There is some milk.

Pronouns, and the first, second and third person

When you read the following paragraph you will see that using the same noun over and over again makes this paragraph very clumsy.

Gcina Mhlophe is a famous South African writer. Gcina Mhlophe wrote Mazanendaba and the magical story shell. *However, Gcina Mhlope does not write only children's stories but a variety of other texts as well.*

This is why we use pronouns such as 'she' to stand in the place of nouns once we have already used them.

Pronouns are different from determiners, because while determiners come *with* nouns, pronouns are used *instead of* nouns.

Pronouns change their form depending on how or where they are used in a sentence. But there are patterns that will help you remember how to make these changes. To learn these patterns you need to know the concept of first, second and third person.

First, second and third person

When you are talking about yourself you are using the first person. (I, me, etc.)
When you are talking about the person you are talking to you are using the second person. (you)
When you are talking to someone about someone, or something, else you are using the third person. (he, she, it, etc.)

I like to drive. *You* like to drive. But my wife ... eish ... *she* doesn't like to drive. She won't even get her license!

1   Complete each sentence with one of these pronouns: I, you, he, she, it.
    a   The first time that Peter got onto an aeroplane _____ was very nervous.
    b   'Calm down,' said his father, '_____ must understand that aeroplanes have far fewer accidents than cars do. _____ promise you that flying is safer than driving.'

The different kinds of pronouns are discussed further on pages 30, 39, 43, 146, 194 and 197.

Personal pronouns

Personal pronouns that come before the verb

This table shows the singular personal pronouns that come in front of the verb in a sentence (as subjects of the sentence).

	Singular personal pronouns that go before the verb
First person	I
Second person	you
Third person	he, she, it

1   Insert the correct word from this list of pronouns into the speech bubbles below.

We can also use the first, second and third person in plural pronouns.

	Singular personal pronouns that go before the verb	Plural personal pronouns that go before the verb
First person	I	we
Second person	you	you
Third person	he, she, it	they

2   Insert the correct word from the list of plural pronouns into the speech bubbles below.

3 Insert the correct pronoun into each space in the following paragraph.

Amy was in love with Mzi but _____ (a) had never told him this.
_____ (b) did not know if he had special feelings for her. _____ (c) was
always very friendly and thoughtful, but maybe _____ (d) was just a good friend.
That evening Amy, Sara, Mzi and Denis had a great time watching television at Sara's
house, and afterwards _____ (e) had a good conversation about soccer.
    'We should come and watch you guys play tomorrow,' said Amy.
    '_____ (f) would like that,' replied Mzi, 'wouldn't we, Denis?'

Personal pronouns that go after the verb
Different forms of these personal pronouns are used when they come after the verb in the
sentence (as objects of the sentence).

	Singular personal pronouns that go after the verb	Plural personal pronouns that go after the verb
First person	me	us
Second person	you	you
Third person	him, her, it	them

4 Insert the correct pronoun into each space in the paragraph below.

The next day, while Mzi and Denis were playing in the soccer match, Amy and Sara
arrived to watch _____ (a). Mzi could feel Amy's eyes on _____ (b) and he
was determined to score a goal to impress her. Normally comfortable in midfield, he
moved forward so he was closer to the other team's goals.
    When Denis got the ball Mzi called to him, 'Here, pass to _____ (c). I'm free!'
So Denis kicked the ball to _____ (d). Then Mzi ran with the ball, avoided the
goalie and, luckily, he scored.
    'Well done!' said Denis. 'But remember to pass the ball sometimes as well.'
    'OK!' replied Mzi, knowing he had been selfish with the ball. 'I'll pass it to
_____ (e) soon. Just be ready!'
    But although the team continued to play well, that was the only goal of the match.
    'Thanks for coming to support _____ (f),' Mzi said to the girls afterwards.
    'Oh, we enjoyed watching both of _____ (g),' said Amy. 'Your team played very
well – passing a lot to each other, most of the time.'
    'Is that a criticism of _____ (h)?' Mzi wondered.

Possessive determiners

Possessive determiners show who owns something. Like all determiners they go in front of a noun.

	Singular possessive determiners	Plural possessive determiners
First person	my	our
Second person	your	your
Third person	his, her, its	their

1   Insert the correct possessive determiner into each of the spaces in the paragraph below.

The four friends were relaxing together at Amy's house.
'It's so hot today!' complained Sara.
'Ja, and I'm hungry,' grumbled Denis. 'I forgot to eat _____ (a) breakfast.'
'I know,' said Mzi, 'let's go and get ice creams from a café.'
'Great idea,' replied Amy. 'The one at the end of _____ (b) road has some great flavours.'
'I'm feeling too lazy to move,' said Sara. 'Don't you want to buy me one and bring it back?'
'Mmm,' said Denis. 'For me too. One of those double chocolate ones. You know, with chocolate on the inside and chocolate on the outside.'
'Well, we will see what we can find,' said Mzi. 'But first you will both need to give us _____ (c) money.'
Amy and Mzi walked to the café together. Once inside the shop, Amy opened the chest freezer. 'I wonder what flavour Sara wants. I think _____ (d) favourite is choc-mint. What type is _____ (e) favourite, Mzi?'
'Strawberry.'
'Really! That's mine too!'

Possessive pronouns

Possessive pronouns show who owns something. Like all pronouns they are used *instead of* nouns. Many of them are similar to the possessive determiners (which are used *with* nouns), because they are used in such a similar way.

	Singular possessive pronouns	Plural possessive pronouns
First person	mine	ours
Second person	yours	yours
Third person	his, hers, its	theirs

1   Insert the correct possessive pronoun into each of the spaces in the paragraphs below.

'Are these yours?' asked Denis, holding out a pair of socks to Mzi.

'No, why would they be _____ **(a)**?' said Mzi, looking confused.

'Well, my mother found them in our washing basket, and they aren't _____ **(b)**, so she thought maybe they were _____ **(c)**.'

Mzi looked at his friend with a frown. 'I don't wear socks with little mice on them. I'm not that type of guy.'

'Hmm, yes, they are rather uncool. But Amy might like you in them. They would show you had a sensitive side.'

'Why don't you ask her if they are _____ **(d)**? Or Sara's?'

'Well, you are going to see them later. You can ask them if they are either of _____ **(e)**.'

'OK, if I remember,' said Mzi.

Sound devices

People use sound devices to make their language sound interesting. Here are the main six sound devices.

Alliteration
If nearby words have consonants that sound the same we call this alliteration. This is often used in poems.

Assonance
A sentence or a line has assonance if some of the vowels used inside the words sound the same. Poems often use assonance.

Onomatopoeia
Sometimes words sound like the noise they describe, for example the 'plop' of a pebble landing in a pool or the 'swoosh' of air as a cyclist rides past you. These words are examples of onomatopoeia, but there are not many of them in the English language.

Repetition
If a word or a phrase is repeated more than once we call this repetition. It is used for emphasis in political speeches, and is used in songs to make the verses join together. It is also common in poems.

Rhythm
A text has rhythm if there is a pattern to the number of beats (syllables) in each line. Songs usually have rhythm and old-fashioned poems usually do as well.

   Some songs and poems have the same number of syllables (beats) in every single line. This gives a sense of unity to the song or poem. Other poems end on a line that has fewer syllables than the other lines that have come before it. This makes the last line stand out.

Rhyme
A text rhymes if the sounds at the end of the lines sound the same. Songs and poems usually have some lines that rhyme.

   We say that poems that use rhyming sounds at the end of their lines have a rhyme scheme. When we write a rhyme scheme we give each rhyming sound a letter. The poem below has a rhyme scheme of 'abcb'.

Roses are red

Roses are red,
Violets are blue,
Sugar is sweet,
And so are you.

Anonymous

1   What is the rhythm of this poem?
2   Identify an example of alliteration in this poem.

Activity B

Read the following poem and answer the questions that follow.

One Perfect Rose

A single flow'r he sent me, since we met.
    All tenderly his messenger he chose;
Deep-hearted, pure, with scented dew still wet –
    One perfect rose.

I knew the language of the floweret;
    'My fragile leaves,' it said, 'his heart enclose.'
Love long has taken for his amulet
    One perfect rose.

Why is it no one ever sent me yet
    One perfect limousine, do you suppose?
Ah no, it's always just my luck to get
    One perfect rose.

Dorothy Parker

1 The word 'perfect' is used to describe the rose that the woman has received. In this context does the word 'perfect' mean 'finished' or 'flawless'?
2 Do the words in the first two stanzas have positive or negative connotations?
3 a How many syllables are there in the first line of every stanza (verse)?
   b Why does the poetess use the terms 'flow'r' in line 1 and 'floweret' in line 5 instead of the word 'flower'?
4 What parts of speech are the underlined words in the following phrases? (Give as much detail as possible.)
   a since <u>we</u> met
   b <u>my</u> luck to get
5 What sound device is used in line 7?
6 What phrase is repeated in this poem?
7 Identify the rhetorical question that is used in this poem.
8 Which are more expensive: roses or limousines?
9 Is the last stanza meant in a literal way or an ironic way?
10 Write out the rhyme scheme of this poem.

Demonstrative determiners

We usually use demonstrative determiners when we are pointing at something, and they tell the listener to look at where we are pointing. We also use them when we are referring back to something we, or other people, have already said. Like all determiners, demonstrative determiners are used *with* nouns.

This is a table showing the demonstrative determiners.

	Singular demonstrative determiners	Plural demonstrative determiners
Applying to near things	this	these
Applying to things further away	that	those

1   Insert the appropriate determiner into the speech bubbles below.

Demonstrative pronouns

Demonstrative pronouns are often used when people are pointing at something while they are talking. We also use them when we are referring back to something we, or other people, have already said. Like all pronouns, demonstrative pronouns are used instead of nouns.

This is a table showing the demonstrative pronouns, which are the same words as the demonstrative determiners on page 42.

	Singular demonstrative pronouns	Plural demonstrative pronouns
Applying to near things	this	these
Applying to things further away	that	those

1   Insert the correct demonstrative pronoun into each of the spaces in the speech bubbles below.

Using a dictionary

When you do not know the meaning of a word you can look it up in a dictionary. A dictionary contains most of the words in a language in an alphabetical list, and for each one it gives a definition.

For example, if you were trying to understand your school report and your teacher had written that you were 'making progress', you could look up the word 'progress' in a dictionary. If you look up the word 'progress' in the *Cambridge Advanced Learner's Dictionary* you will find these entries.

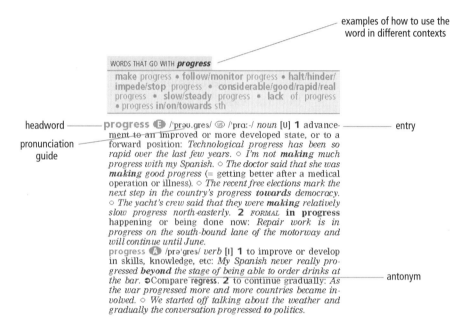

There are two entries for 'progress', under two different headwords, because this word can be used as a noun or a verb. The noun 'progress' usually means 'advancement to an improved state'. The verb 'progress' means 'improve' or 'continue gradually'. As well as giving the possible meanings of the headword and what part of speech this word can be, the dictionary will also tell you how to pronounce this word, which syllables to stress, and in which contexts it is used. Some dictionaries will also give synonyms, antonyms and information on the history of the word.

1 a In the context of your teacher's comment on your school report, namely that you are 'making progress', is the word 'progress' being used as a noun or a verb?

   b In this context, what is the meaning of the word 'progress'?

The *Cambridge Advanced Learner's Dictionary* gives a pronunciation guide for each word. This is the group of funny-looking letters, which belong to the huge International Phonetic Alphabet that has a different symbol for each sound in every language. The relevant symbols are explained at the back of the *Cambridge Advanced Learner's Dictionary*.

2 Compare the symbols given in the two different entries for the word 'progress'.

   a Are they exactly the same?

   b What does this mean?

The stress symbol (') appears on the headword or pronunciation guide before the syllable that must be stressed the most.

3 The word 'progress' has two syllables.

   a When it is pronounced as a noun, is the first syllable or the second syllable stressed?

   b When it is pronounced as a verb, is the first syllable or the second syllable stressed?

4 Give an antonym for the verb 'progress'.

5 The verb 'progress' can also be made into the noun 'progression'. Therefore, from the root word 'progress', there are two nouns: 'progress' and 'progression'. Which of these nouns would you use in each of the following sentences?

   a After taking Computer Studies at school, studying Computer Programming at university was a natural _____.

   b The building of a computer room is now in _____, but the school does not have many computers to go into this room once it is finished.

6 Most of us feel that we should always be making progress towards something better. Explain the problem that the one woman is having in the cartoon below.

Translating, and borrowing words from other languages

Translating

When we rewrite a sentence from one language into another language we are translating it. However, the translated sentence will never mean exactly the same as the original sentence. For example, the French political philosopher Jean-Jacques Rousseau's statement *'L'homme est né libre, et partout il est dans les fers'* can be translated as:

- 'Man is born free but is everywhere in chains';
- 'Man is born free, yet is everywhere in chains'; or
- 'Man is born free and everywhere he is in chains'.

This quotation is not meant to be understood literally; it is meant to be understood figuratively. It emphasises how society restricts the individual.

1 Translate 'Man is born free but is everywhere in chains' into your home language.

Borrowing words from other languages

Many words that we now think of as English have been taken from other languages. In particular, the English language has taken words from French and Latin, which used to be more important languages in Europe than English was.

English has many pairs of synonyms where one word comes from Old English and one comes from French or Latin. An example of this is the pair of synonyms 'freedom' and 'liberty', which are both nouns used in the English language. The noun 'freedom' is based on the adjective 'free', which comes from the Old English adjective *'frēo'*. The noun 'liberty' is based on the French noun *'liberté'*, which is based on the Latin adjective *'līber'*, which means 'free'.

2 What older language does the root of the word 'freedom' come from?
3 Give a synonym for the word 'freedom'. What languages does this come from?

The interesting question is: Why would English-speakers take a noun (namely, *'liberté'*) from the French language when they already had a noun that expressed the same meaning (namely, 'freedom') in their own language? There are a number of possible answers:

- English-speakers sometimes used words from French to sound classy and educated.
- Educated English people were used to writing advanced ideas in French, not English.
- During the French Revolution, when the French people overthrew their king and demanded a democracy, they called for *'Liberté!'*. The English word 'liberty' therefore has connotations of political freedom and is often used in political contexts.

4 Insert the word 'freedom' or the word 'liberty' into the following sentences, as appropriate.
   a After I moved out of my parent's house I had a wonderful sense of _____.
   b Although the French people's dreams of _____ came true, this did not last.

Some other French phrases used in English are:

- *café* (pronounced 'ca-fay') – informal restaurant or small food shop
- *cliché* (pronounced 'clee-shay') – old saying or plot that people are tired of
- *vignette* (pronounced 'vi^{n}yet') – short piece showing typical scenes
- *vogue* (pronounced 'voag') – fashion
- *raison d'être* (pronounced 'rayson detr') – reason for existing
- *à la mode* (pronounced 'a-la-moad') – in fashion
- *savoir-faire* (pronounced 'sa-vwa-fair') – attitude of knowing what to do

Understanding a word by thinking about its root word and other parts

Often when you come across long, unfamiliar words, these words will contain parts that you might already know. For example, the word 'unprogressive' means 'not thinking about improving society'. To make it easy to understand, this word can be divided into three parts.

The prefix is the part at the front. The root is the part in the middle. The suffix is the part at the end.

The most important part is the root. This contains the main meaning of the word. For example, the root 'progress' comes from the Latin word '*prōgressus*' which means 'going forwards'.

The prefix is used to change the meaning of the root in some way. The prefix 'un' means 'not' so we know that 'unprogressive' will have something to do with 'not going forward'.

The suffix influences how the word can be used in a sentence. The suffix 'ive' is added to a root to make an adjective. So we know that 'unprogressive' is an adjective.

When we combine what we have discovered about the word 'unprogressive' we can work out a lot about the word. However, its meaning might have changed since the word became part of the English language, or it could be used in a metaphorical way. In the case of 'unprogressive', the word is not used to describe people who are standing still. It is used in a metaphorical way to describe people who allow society to stay the way it is, with all its many problems and inequalities. So the word 'unprogressive' describes people who do not think about improving society to make it better and fairer for everyone.

1   Complete the following sentence using the adjectives 'progressive' and 'unprogressive'.
    The apartheid government was _____, while the ANC government is _____.

    Here are some words from other languages that are sometimes used as roots in English.

    cyclus (Latin) – circle/wheel
    pēs (Latin) – foot
    centum (Latin) – hundred
    phōnē (Greek) – sound
    stereos (Greek) – solid
    tupos (Greek) – image

2   For each of the following words, give the Latin or Greek word or words that form the root, and write down what these foreign words mean.
    a telephone
    b bicycle
    c pedal
    d century
    e pedestal
    f archetype
    g stereophonic

Prefixes and suffixes

Prefixes

Prefixes are little groups of letters that can be added to the front of a word. A prefix is used to change the meaning of the root in some way. Sometimes we need to use a hyphen between a prefix and the root word.

Here are some common prefixes and their usual meanings:

un/in/im – not	super – bigger/better than normal
mono – one	archi – chief
tri – three	bi – two
trans – across	mille –thousand
motor – using an engine	homo – same
en – to put in/to put on	multi – many
tele – from far away	ex – out of/past
hyper – more than normal/more than is healthy	co – together
	über – bigger/better than normal

The prefix '*über*' comes from the German language and it is only recently that people have started using it in English. Therefore we still write it in italics to show that it is a foreign prefix.

1 Insert the correct prefix from the list into each sentence below.
   a I do not like to see my _____-wife and her new boyfriend.
   b The SABC broadcasts _____vison programmes all over South Africa.
   c I thought your narrative essay was interesting and _____usual.
   d My _____workers are lazy so I end up having to work even harder.
   e Put your letter inside this _____velope.
   f Many people think _____sexuality is unnatural but people cannot help who they are attracted to.
   g When I _____late a text I always need to use a dictionary.
   h Bread is cheaper at the _____market than the bakery, but it is often not as nice.
   i Adolf Hitler, the leader of Germany during the Second World War, believed that German people were the _____*mensch* and should control the world.
   j The person in charge of designing this building is the _____tect.
   k A machine for riding on is called a _____cycle when it has one wheel, a _____cycle when it has two wheels, and a _____cycle when it has three wheels.
   l A _____car has four wheels. You do not need to push it because is has an engine that burns petrol and makes it go.
   m A _____bike has two wheels, so it is like a bicycle with an engine.
   n _____pedes have more legs than caterpillars.
   o A _____-word verb has a verb made up of more than one word.
   p My sister is _____-allergic; she's the kind of person who can hardly eat anything on a menu.

Suffixes

Suffixes are little groups of letters that can be added to the end of a word. A suffix is used to change a word into a different part of speech.

Here are some common suffixes that can be added to roots to make them into adjectives:

y
ble
al
ent/ant
ful
ous/ious
en
an/ian/ean
tic
ive
less
er
est

The suffixes 'er' and 'est' are usually added to words that are already adjectives.

2   Complete the incomplete word in each of the following sentences. Use one of the above suffixes to do this, and change the end of the root word as well if necessary.
   a   The beauti_____ woman became an actress.
   b   I feel happ_____ on sunny days than when it is raining.
   c   My brother is bett_____ at chess than I am.
   d   'Meritorious' means 'good', but 'excell_____' is an even higher compliment.
   e   I cried when I heard the terri_____ news.
   f   Wood_____ chairs are more expensive than plas_____ chairs.
   g   Most Germ_____ people are very sorry that Adolf Hitler was ever elected as the leader of their country.
   h   The victor_____ army returned home proudly, but not without casualties.
   i   The high_____ mountain in the world is Mount Everest.
   j   My sister has flaw_____ skin without any pimples or wrinkles.
   k   Animals that only come out at night are called nocturn_____ animals.
   l   He is a nice teacher most of the time but he is also quite explos_____.

Sometimes the suffixes 'ing' and 'ed', which are normally added to verbs, can be used to form words that are actually used as adjectives. Adjectives that are formed in this way are discussed on page 140.

3   Insert 'ing' or 'ed' into the following sentences.
   a   I think what he did is absolutely shock_____.
   b   This curv_____ piece of wood is part of the chair I am making.
   c   She sprays perfume on her paper so that she can send scent_____ letters to her friends.
   d   My teacher prefers to mark typ_____ essays to handwritten ones.

Prepositions

A preposition usually shows how things are related to each other. A preposition can show a relationship of space, a relationship of possession, or a relationship of time.

Prepositions of place

Here are some prepositions to do with how objects are related within a space:

on   above   over   under   below   to   from   in

We use 'on' when one object is sitting on top of another, we use 'above' when one object is higher than another but not touching it, and we use 'over' when one object is moving across and above another object. However, we can usually use 'under' and 'below' interchangeably.

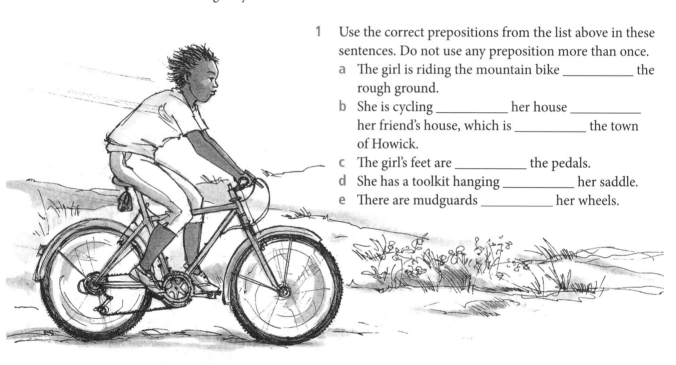

1   Use the correct prepositions from the list above in these sentences. Do not use any preposition more than once.
  a The girl is riding the mountain bike _____ the rough ground.
  b She is cycling _____ her house _____ her friend's house, which is _____ the town of Howick.
  c The girl's feet are _____ the pedals.
  d She has a toolkit hanging _____ her saddle.
  e There are mudguards _____ her wheels.

Prepositions of possession

The word 'of' is also a preposition. Sometimes it has a similar meaning to 'from' as shown in the following sentences. In this case it could be considered a preposition of place.

His family comes *from* Africa.   He is *of* African origin.

However, 'of' is also used in many other ways, such as to show possession, as shown here.

The origin *of* the man is Africa.   The name *of* the man is Zwelethini.

The preposition 'to' is also used to indicate that someone possessed something, as shown in the sentences below.

The house belongs *to* the man.   That name belongs *to* him.

2   Insert a preposition of possession into each of the following sentences.
  a The book belongs _____ that girl.
  b The name _____ that girl is 'Rose'.

Prepositions of time

Here are some prepositions to do with time:

over	throughout	since	between	during
on	after	until	before	in

3 Use the correct prepositions from the list above in these sentences. Use each word only once.

_____ (a) history, humans have been on the move, so that many historians now talk about the 'routes' that people have walked, rather than the 'roots' that people have that tie them to one place. All humans originally come from Africa (which is why this continent is often called the 'cradle of humankind'), but _____ (b) time humans have spread out over the whole world.

Human tribes walked from Africa to Europe and Asia, and, surprising as it may sound, they walked to North America as well. Although North America is now separated from Europe by the Atlantic Ocean, _____ (c) the Ice Ages much of this ocean was frozen in ice caps at the North Pole and the South Pole. Therefore during the Ice Ages there was a 'land bridge' between Europe and North America. Humans walked across this strip of land to North America and then some went on to South America. Then the seas rose _____ (d) the last Ice Age, cutting off the Americas from Europe, Asia and Africa.

However, once humans invented boats they spread out further over the world, populating Australia, New Zealand and many smaller islands, _____ (e) all the areas in the world that were not too hot or too cold had people on them.

The people in Europe started to develop larger and larger boats. _____ (f) the seventeenth century the Europeans have used these boats to travel great distances. Many European countries tried to colonise other areas of the world. For example, many English people sailed to North America. They conquered the American people that had arrived there _____ (g) them, and they settled there, eventually declaring themselves a separate country from England.

Many African countries were also colonised by European countries, but they were not as heavily settled by Europeans as America was. _____ (h) 1900 and 1970 most of these African countries declared themselves independent.

Some smaller areas remain colonised by larger and more powerful countries. However, while some of these colonised people still want to be independent, others have chosen to remain part of the countries that conquered them long ago. For example, _____ (i) 1990 the people on the island of Aruba voted to remain part of the Netherlands instead of becoming independent.

One day everybody might be satisfied with the way that the world has been divided into countries, and _____ (j) that day we might actually have world peace.

Showing possession in singular nouns

An apostrophe looks like a little comma at the top of the line of writing: ʼ. When used with an 's' it can indicate that something is possessed by something else. It probably used to be a preposition that stood as a word in a sentence (like 'se' still does in Afrikaans).

Afrikaans: *die man se naam*
English: *the man's name*

However, in English the possessive apostrophe and the 's' are now always attached to a noun. A noun with the possessive apostrophe and the 's' attached to it does not act like a noun. It either acts like a determiner or an adjective.

When we want to show that something belongs to something else we can do this by adding an apostrophe and an 's' to the noun that owns the other noun, as long as this first noun was a singular noun. The new noun that is formed acts like a possessive determiner or a possessive adjective. We usually place it before the noun that it describes, as in the examples below.

If the apostrophe and the 's' are added to a common noun, this word acts like an adjective and comes between the determiner and the noun that is possessed. If the apostrophe and the 's' are added to a proper noun this word acts like a determiner and comes before the noun that is possessed. (In this case no other determiner can be used as we can only use one determiner before a noun.) In either case, we can still add as many adjectives as we want to between the possessive word and the noun that is possessed, as shown below.

1 Rewrite the following sentences as phrases that use a possessive apostrophe and an 's'.
  a That new CD belongs to my lucky little sister.
  b The wonderful silver bicycle belongs to Jonathan.
  c The chocolate ice cream belonged to the hungry teenager.
  d The black limousine belonged to Cindi September.

We can also change sentences that use the preposition 'of' in a possessive way into sentences that use an apostrophe and 's' to show possession, as shown below.

the book of the man   *the man's book*
the book of Matthew   *Matthew's book*

2 Rewrite the following sentences using a possessive apostrophe and an 's'.
   a The slogan of the American sportswear company is 'Just do it!'
   b The slogan of Nike is 'Just do it!'
3 Rewrite the following sentences so that they are grammatical. Add an apostrophe and an 's'. Do not change the word order.
   a Jeremy bicycle is broken.
   b Ntombi bag is empty.
   c The man car has two flat tyres.
   d The girl hair was braided with beads.

We can also place the noun with the possessive apostrophe and the 's' and the noun it describes later in the sentence, as shown below.

Whose house is that? It is Thembi's house.

4 Answer the following questions based on the information given in 3 a–d above.
   a Whose broken bicycle is that? (It is …)
   b Whose empty bag is this? (It is …)
   c Whose car is that with the flat tyres? (It is …)
   d Whose hair was braided with beads? (It was …)

Sometimes we don't bother to say the noun that follows the noun with the possessive apostrophe and the 's'. But we only do this when it is clear what the noun would be if it were mentioned.

Look at an example of how a noun can be left out after a possessive noun acting as an adjective.

> You can think of this unmentioned noun as an invisible noun that is still there.

We know that the missing noun is 'house'.

> In the questions in 5 c and d, we use 'he' and 'she' rather than 'him' and 'her' because these questions are based on the statements 'He is her husband' and 'She is their daughter', where the pronouns are the subjects of the sentences.

5 What is the missing noun in the answers to each of the following questions?
   a Whose dress is that? It is Marlena's.
   b Whose dog is that? It is Bonnie's.
   c Whose husband is he? He is Rachel's.
   d Whose daughter is she? She is Inge and Kobus's.

Showing possession in plural nouns

The way that we add the possessive apostrophe to a plural noun depends on whether this plural is regular or irregular. In some cases we add the possessive 's', but in some cases it is not needed.

Regular plural nouns always end in an 's'. Therefore, when we make a regular plural noun into a possessive word, we just add an apostrophe, but we add it after the 's'. Look at the examples below.

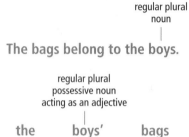

The fact that the word 'boys'' is plural is indicated by the position of the apostrophe.

Irregular plural nouns do not end in an 's'. Therefore, when we make an irregular plural noun into a possessive word, we have to add an apostrophe and an 's'.

Look at the examples below.

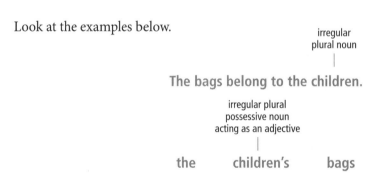

1   The following sentences contain regular and irregular plural nouns that you need to change. Place the possessive apostrophe in the correct place.
    a   In our road all the houses look the same and the houses doors are all the same as well.
    b   Many actresses families hardly see them when they are working on a film.
    c   There is a nurse at the clinic that helps with womens medical problems.
    d   The dices corners have been worn smooth because they have been used so often.
2   The following sentences contain singular and plural nouns that you need to change. Place the possessive apostrophe in the correct place.
    a   The cars left back wheel is flat because it went over a nail on the road.
    b   A womans bag was found in the shop and is being kept at the front desk.
    c   The wheels axes are not perfectly parallel; they need to be aligned.
    d   The bacterias environment was destroyed by the strong detergent.

Words in bold or italics, and underlined words

Normal letters in a book are called 'roman' letters. If we want letters to stand out, then we change the roman letters into italics or bold, or we underline the letters.

Bold

We may write words in bold (**bold**) to show:
- they are being emphasised
- they are a heading or sub-heading
- they are key words or phrases in an explanatory text, which a person might search for when using the Internet.

1 Use the word 'never' in a sentence of your own and make it bold to emphasise it.
2 Which words would you say are key words in the following paragraph? Write them in bold.

Throughout history, humans have been on the move, so that many historians now talk about the 'routes' that people have walked, rather than the 'roots' that people have that tie them to one place. All humans originally come from Africa (which is why this continent is often called the 'cradle of humankind'), but over time humans have spread out over the whole world.

Italics

When we print out a text from a computer we can use italics (*italics*), which is slanted type. We may write words in italics to show:
- they are the title of a book or other long text
- they are stage directions in a play script or a film script
- they are from a different language
- they are being emphasised
- they are being referred to, rather than used in a normal way.

If, for any reason, we write a whole paragraph in italics, we use roman letters for these purposes. See the second paragraph on page 35 for an example of this.

3 Why are some of the words in the following sentences in italics?
    a During the French Revolution the people called for '*Liberté*!'
    b She *never* goes to bed until she has washed up and cleaned the kitchen.
    c Unity Dow wrote *The Screaming of the Innocent* and *Juggling Truths*.

Underlining

When we want to use italics but we cannot because we are writing a text by hand, then we underline the relevant words. In most situations, underlining and italics serve the same purpose. However, we also underline:
- the subject of a business letter
- the words on a web page that will take us to another page if we click on them (hyperlinks).

4 Why are the some words in the following sentence underlined?
   Wesley Snipes acted in <u>Blade</u> and <u>Blade 2</u>.

Activity C

The following text is an abridged extract from an encyclopaedia called *Wikipedia*, which is on the Internet at www.wikipedia.org and is free for everyone to use.

Statue of Liberty

The Statue of Liberty on Liberty Island in New York Harbor.

Liberty Enlightening the World (*La liberté éclairant le monde*), known more commonly as the **Statue of Liberty**, was given to the United States by France in 1885.

The French people had discussed what to give the United States to mark the Centennial of the American Declaration of Independence, and Frederic Auguste Bartholdi was commissioned to design a sculpture. It was agreed upon that the American people were to build the base.

The site chosen for the statue was then called Bedloe's Island, where there was already an early nineteenth-century star-shaped fortification. This became a part of the base for the statue.

However, in France, progress on the project was slow. Bartholdi required the assistance of an engineer to address structural issues associated with designing such a colossal copper sculpture. Gustave Eiffel (designer of the Eiffel Tower) was asked to design the massive iron framework to hold the statue up on the inside.

The statue was completed in France in July, 1884. To prepare for transit across the Atlantic Ocean, the statue was reduced to 350 individual pieces and packed in 214 crates. The statue was re-assembled on the pedestal that the Americans had built four months later.

On October 28, 1886, the Statue of Liberty was dedicated by President Grover Cleveland in front of thousands of spectators. (Ironically, it was Cleveland who, as Governor of the State of New York, had earlier vetoed a bill by the New York legislature to contribute $50 000 to the building of the base.)

The Statue of Liberty was a real lighthouse from 1886 to 1902, and the island on which the statue stands was renamed Liberty Island.

The Statue of Liberty is one of the most recognisable icons of the U.S. worldwide, and, in a more general sense, represents liberty and escape from oppression. The Statue of Liberty was, from 1886 until the Jet Age, often the first glimpse of the United States for millions of immigrants after ocean voyages from Europe.

1 Why is the statue usually called the Statue of Liberty, rather than the Statue of Freedom?

2 Why are words '**Liberty Enlightening the World**' written in bold?

3 Why are words '*La liberté éclairant le monde*' written in italics?

4 Why are many words, such as <u>Frederic Auguste Bartholdi</u>, underlined?

5 What word in the third paragraph can be abbreviated to fort?

6 The word 'progress' is used in paragraph 4. In this context is it:
   a   a noun meaning 'development'
   b   a verb meaning 'improving'
   c   an adjective meaning 'forward-thinking'?

7 The word 'transit' is used in paragraph 5. In this context is it:
   a   a preposition that means the same as 'across'
   b   a verb that means 'carry'
   c   a noun that means 'the process of being carried somewhere'?

8   a   What is the meaning of the Latin root '*pēs*' of the word 'pedestal'?
    b   What is the meaning of the Latin root '*centum*' of the word 'centennial'?

9   a   Identify one preposition of place in the seventh paragraph.
    b   Identify one preposition of possession in the seventh paragraph.
    c   Identify three prepositions of time in the last paragraph.

10 a   What is the meaning of the prefix 're' in the word 're-assembled'?
    b   Why has the word 're-assembled' been used in this context instead of the word 'assembled'?

11 Why is it ironic that President Grover Cleveland was the main speaker at the ceremony held to celebrate the statue in 1886?

12 Suggest a reason why the island might have been called Bedloe's Island before its name was changed to Liberty Island.

13 What synonym for the word 'pedestal' is used in this text?

14 When the Statue of Liberty was first erected, how did most travelers to the USA arrive:
   a   by land
   b   by sea
   c   by air?

15 In the last paragraph the term 'Jet Age' is used to refer to modern times when aeroplanes are used for long-distance travel.
   a   What established historical term has been changed to make this new term?
   b   Give a synonym for the word 'age', as it is used in this context.

16 The Statue of Liberty is called 'one of the most recognisable icons of the U.S. worldwide'. Does this mean it is:
   a   a religious statue worshipped throughout the world
   b   the symbol that most people associate with the United States
   c   a sculpture of a real woman who died and later came to represent a particular time period?

17 What is the full name of the United States?

Verbs and the first, second and third person

Verbs are those words that show action or existence. In other words, they are 'doing words' or 'being words'.

1 Which is the verb in each of the following sentences?
  a I look at my brother.
  b My brother is naughty.
  c He has a new toy.
  d He jumps on it.
  e My naughty brother is jumping on his new toy.

Every verb has a base form. This is the simplest form of the verb. We can change the base form into a variety of other forms when we want to express particular things or match the verb to its subject.

2 What is the base form of the verbs in sentences 1 a and b?

The noun or pronoun that comes in front of the verb is its subject, and the form of the verb changes according to whether that noun or pronoun is in the first, second or third person.

Regular verbs
Regular verbs are those verbs that change their form according to a normal pattern. Regular verbs have a very simple pattern in the present tense, because only the third-person singular form is different from the base form.

   This table shows the different forms of the base verb 'look' when it is in the present tense.

Most verbs are regular verbs so it would be useful to learn this pattern.

The way we write the verb in the title of these tables is called the infinitive form of the verb. When you see the word 'to' in front of the verb like this, you know the word that follows is the base form of the verb.

The verb 'to look' in the present tense		
First person singular:	I	look
Second person singular:	you	look
Third person singular:	he/she/it	looks
First person plural:	we	look
Second person plural:	you	look
Third person plural:	they	look

Irregular verbs

There are irregular verbs that do not follow this common pattern. These irregular verbs are verbs that have been in the language for a very long time, and describe very basic ideas. For this reason it is important to learn the patterns of the irregular verbs, because you will use them often.

The verbs 'be' and 'have' are both irregular verbs. Many people forget these are verbs because they cannot see the action they are describing, but remember that verbs can be either 'doing' or 'being' words, and the various forms of 'be' and 'have' let us describe the way things are.

This table shows the different forms of the verb 'be' when it is in the present tense.

The verb 'to be' in the present tense		
First person singular:	I	am
Second person singular:	you	are
Third person singular:	he/she/it	is
First person plural:	we	are
Second person plural:	you	are
Third person plural:	they	are

This table shows the different forms of the verb 'have' when it is in the present tense.

The verb 'to have' in the present tense		
First person singular:	I	have
Second person singular:	you	have
Third person singular:	he/she/it	has
First person plural:	we	have
Second person plural:	you	have
Third person plural:	they	have

3 Change the base verb in brackets into its present-tense form that matches its subject.
   a I (look) at my big pile of homework.
   b We (look) at the car.
   c You (be) a good soccer player.
   d She (be) a good friend.
   e He (have) his own room.
   f They (have) lots of bicycles.

Remember that we do not always change the verb's form to make it match the verb's subject. In some situations the base form is the same as the form of the verb that matches the subject.

The present tense and the past tense of verbs

The English language allows you to indicate whether an action is happening in the present or whether it happened in the past. To do this you need to use the appropriate form of the verb. Things that are happening now should be described using a verb in the present tense. Things that have happened in the past should be described using a verb in the past tense.

Regular verbs

Regular verbs follow the patterns shown in the table below when they are used in the past tense or the present tense.

The verb 'to look'		Past tense	Present tense
First person singular:	I	looked	look
Second person singular:	you	looked	look
Third person singular:	he/she/it	looked	looks
First person plural:	we	looked	look
Second person plural:	you	looked	look
Third person plural:	they	looked	look

As you can see in the table above, we add the suffix 'ed' to make the past-tense form of a regular verb, whatever the subject is. However, if a regular verb already ends in 'e', we just add 'd'.

If a regular verb ends in 'y' and there is no vowel in front of that 'y' we drop the 'y' and add 'ied'. However, if a regular verb ends in 'y' and there is a vowel in front of that 'y' we add 'ed' after the 'y'.

1 Change the following sentences into the past tense by changing the present-tense verbs into the past tense.
   a   I look for my friend in the crowd.
   b   He looks proudly at his girlfriend.
   c   We dance together.
   d   They party all through the night.
   e   You play soccer well.
   f   She jumps into the dam for a swim.

2 Change the following sentences into the present tense by changing the past-tense verbs into the present tense.
   a   I stated my opinion clearly.
   b   You advertised for a waitress every summer.
   c   It crawled across the kitchen floor.
   d   We played soccer in the afternoon.
   e   She cried with sorrow.
   f   They fried some eggs in a pan.

Irregular verbs

Irregular verbs do not follow the normal pattern for the past and present tenses, so they should be learned individually.

The verb 'to be'		Past tense	Present tense
First person singular:	I	was	am
Second person singular:	you	were	are
Third person singular:	he/she/it	was	is
First person plural:	we	were	are
Second person plural:	you	were	are
Third person plural:	they	were	are

The verb 'to have'		Past tense	Present tense
First person singular:	I	had	have
Second person singular:	you	had	have
Third person singular:	he/she/it	had	has
First person plural:	we	had	have
Second person plural:	you	had	have
Third person plural:	they	had	have

3 Complete the following sentences using the past-tense form of the verb that matches the subject.
   a He (have) a lean body.
   b I (be) very angry.
   c We (be) in the car.
   d You (be) a well-behaved class yesterday.
   e You (have) a wonderful bicycle.
   f She (have) a happy childhood.

4 Complete the following sentences using the correct form of the verb in brackets. You will have to think about the sentence as a whole to decide whether to use the past tense or the present tense.
   a Yesterday I (be) in a bad mood.
   b When I (be) a baby, my father (disappear).
   c Whenever somebody pops a balloon I always (jump).
   d In the past cycling (be) not a fashionable sport.
   e My grandparents (be) freedom fighters during apartheid.
   f These days companies often (use) famous soccer players, such as Thierry Henry, in their advertisements.

We always change the tense of a verb by changing the way we write that verb. We do not put extra verbs in front of a verb to change its tense.

The simple and progressive aspects of regular verbs in the present tense

The English language allows you to indicate whether an action is still going on or whether it is completed. To do this you need to use the appropriate form of the verb, which would be the progressive form of the verb if the action is still going on, or the perfect form of the verb if the action is completed.

However, if you don't want to indicate whether an action is still going on or whether it is finished, you can simply use the simple aspect of the verb. So there are three aspects to choose from: the simple aspect, the progressive aspect and the perfect aspect.

The simple aspect

The simple aspect is the one we use without thinking about it. For example, 'I look' and 'he looks' are written in the present tense and the simple aspect. We have not changed the verbs to give them a different aspect.

The progressive aspect

If you want to show that an action is still going on you write the verb in the progressive aspect. A verb in the progressive aspect is made up of two words. The first word is the form of the verb 'be' that matches the subject and the tense. The second verb is made up of the base verb with 'ing' added on the end. For example, instead of writing 'I look' you can write 'I am looking'. Both forms are in the present tense, but 'I look' is in the simple aspect and 'I am looking' is in the progressive aspect.

'Progressing' means 'going on'.

A party tonight, with Matthew there! ... Ooh! I don't know if I feel pretty enough ... just wait while I look in the mirror ...

OK, now I am standing in the bathroom ... Yes, I *am looking* in the mirror for any new pimples ... but I think I look OK, so I guess I will come.

1 Use the appropriate form of the verb 'braid' in each of these speech bubbles. Use
either the simple present or the progressive present.

a

I _____ Dudu's hair right now!

b

I often _____ my friends' hair.

This table shows how to change regular verbs in the present tense from the simple aspect
to the progressive aspect.

The verb 'to look'			
		Present tense	
		Simple aspect	**Progressive aspect**
First person singular:	I	look	am looking
Second person singular:	you	look	are looking
Third person singular:	he/she/it	looks	is looking
First person plural:	we	look	are looking
Second person plural:	you	look	are looking
Third person plural:	they	look	are looking

What do you do?

I am studying to be an architect.

2 Change the following sentences from the present simple to the present progressive.
   a I look in the mirror.
   b You look out the window.
   c He looks at the girls.
   d We look everywhere for my key.
   e You always look behind you.
   f They look for their friends in the playground.

If you want to distinguish between the two words that make up a verb in the present
progressive, call the first word the 'progressive auxiliary verb' and the second word the
'participle showing the progressive aspect'. The first word is called an auxiliary verb
because it is a small but necessary part of a multiword verb. The second word is called
a 'participle' because it can only be part of a multiword verb; it could never stand as the
only verb in a sentence.

Although we use the progressive aspect for things that are happening while we speak,
we can also use it when talking about an ongoing activity that might not be going on
right now, as shown in the picture on the left.

The simple and progressive aspects of irregular verbs in the present tense

Irregular verbs do not always follow the normal rules of how to change into certain tenses and aspects. The irregular verbs shown here are 'be' and 'have'.

When you write a form of the verb 'be' in the present simple the verb is made of only one word. This verb must match the subject and the tense, as shown in the present simple column of the table below. As you can see, this verb does not follow the normal rules when in the present simple.

The verb 'to be'			
		Present tense	
		Simple aspect	**Progressive aspect**
First person singular:	I	am	am being
Second person singular:	you	are	are being
Third person singular:	he/she/it	is	is being
First person plural:	we	are	are being
Second person plural:	you	are	are being
Third person plural:	they	are	are being

When you write a form of the verb 'be' in the present progressive the first word is the form of 'be' that matches the subject and the tense. The second word is made up of the base form 'be' with 'ing' added on the end. The table above shows how to change the irregular verb 'be' from the present simple into the present progressive.

> Although the pattern of present-simple verbs is irregular, the way we change these irregular verbs from the present simple into the present progressive is the same as with regular verbs.

1   Change the following sentences from the present simple to the present progressive. Also add the adverb in brackets at the end of each sentence, to show that the statement you are making does not apply to every day.
   a   I am stupid. (now)
   b   You are sweet. (today)
   c   She is clumsy. (today)
   d   We are careful. (now)
   e   You are very thoughtful. (today)
   f   They are very formal. (now)

We do not often use the present progressive of the verb 'be', but when we do we are usually describing situations that we expect will change soon.

2   Add a sentence to each of your answers to 1 a–f above, explaining how things will soon change.

The table on the next page shows how to change the irregular verb 'have' from the present simple to the present progressive. Note that whenever you add 'ing' to a verb that ends with 'e' you must drop that 'e'.

The verb 'to have'		Present tense	
		Simple aspect	Progressive aspect
First person singular:	I	have	am having
Second person singular:	you	have	are having
Third person singular:	he/she/it	has	is having
First person plural:	we	have	are having
Second person plural:	you	have	are having
Third person plural:	they	have	are having

3 Change the following sentences from the present simple to the present progressive.
   a They have a swim after school.
   b I have a meeting.
   c She has a small lunch.

See page 177 for more information on how to use the present progressive to talk about the future.

We do not often use the present progressive of the verb 'have', because usually we either have something or we do not have it. However, when we are referring to an experience rather than an object we can use the present-progressive form of 'have'.

4 Here are some pairs of sentences where one is correct and one is incorrect. In each case choose which sentence is correct.
   a I have a headache.   I am having a headache.
   b I have a bad day.   I am having a bad day.
   c I have a bicycle.   I am having a bicycle.

Sometimes when we add 'ing' to a word we double the last consonant. For example, 'swim' becomes 'swimming'. This usually happens when the vowel in front of this consonant is a short sound.

5 Rewrite the following present-simple sentences into the present progressive.
   a I stop the car.
   b He sits on the bicycle's saddle.
   c They jet off to France for their holidays.
   d The mother labels all her son's school clothes.

6 The following sentences contain regular and irregular verbs in the present simple. Change these sentences into the present progressive.
   a You are grumpy today.
   b He rides a mountain bike on the dirt road.
   c I let my friend use my other car.
   d The tennis player hits the ball against the practice wall.
   e She admits to the crime.
   f I have guests tonight.
   g He creates beautiful statues out of metal and wood.
   h Dennis uses his brakes to stop the bicycle.
   i He is unusually stupid.
   j The film festival features *Tsotsi*, *Twist* and *Yesterday*, as well as many foreign films.

The simple and progressive aspects of regular verbs in the past tense

Sometimes we use the progressive aspect with a past-tense verb. This table shows how to change the regular verb 'look' from the past simple to the past progressive.

The verb 'to look'			
		Past tense	
		Simple aspect	Progressive aspect
First person singular:	I	looked	was looking
Second person singular:	you	looked	were looking
Third person singular:	he/she/it	looked	was looking
First person plural:	we	looked	were looking
Second person plural:	you	looked	were looking
Third person plural:	they	looked	were looking

1   Use a form of the regular verb 'listen' to complete the sentences in the speech bubbles below. Use either the past simple or the past progressive.

a

b

2 Change the following sentences from the past simple to the past progressive.
   a I looked out the window of the train.
   b You looked at him with an odd expression on your face.
   c He looked left and right.
   d We looked in the biscuit tin.
   e You looked at me in surprise.
   f They looked across the fields at the sunset.

We would normally use the past simple for sentences such as those in number 2 rather than the past progressive, unless we have a good reason to use the past progressive. When we tell a story we sometimes have a good reason to use the past progressive, because we say what we were doing (using the past progressive) and then say what happened while we were doing this (using the past simple). For example, 'While I was looking out the window a train went past in the opposite direction.' This tells the listener how the actions are linked in time.

3 Complete the following sentences with the appropriate past-progressive form of the verb in brackets.
   a While you (play) soccer, I walked around the field.
   b While they (watch) television, I made dinner.
   c While you (drag) your bag on the pavement, I saw the bottom come off.
   d While the hens (squabble) over those breadcrumbs, the duck ate the breadcrumbs.
   e While I (look) at the shirt in the shop window, you went in to find out the price.
   f While you (listen) to me, I explained how I thought he felt.
   g While she (explain) the answers on the board, I tickled my friend and made her giggle.
   h While we (dance) at the party, someone broke into our car.
   i While I (lie) in the sunshine, my brother poured a bucket of water over me.

The past progressive is often used in complex sentences with the past simple, but it can be used in many other ways as well.

The simple and progressive aspects of irregular verbs in the past tense

The irregular verbs follow the same pattern as the regular verbs when they change from the past simple to the past progressive.

This table shows how to change the irregular verb 'be' from the past simple to the past progressive.

The verb 'to be'			
		Past tense	
		Simple aspect	**Progressive aspect**
First person singular:	I	was	was being
Second person singular:	you	were	were being
Third person singular:	he/she/it	was	was being
First person plural:	we	were	were being
Second person plural:	you	were	were being
Third person plural:	they	were	were being

1 Change the following sentences from the past simple to the past progressive.
   a I was clumsy.
   b You were very appreciative.
   c She was shy.
   d We were cautious.
   e You were polite guests.
   f They were a good audience.

2 Complete the following sentences with the appropriate past-progressive form of the verb in brackets.
   a We (be) so naughty that our teacher kept us in after school.
   b They (be) such an appreciative audience that the performers sang two extra songs.

This table shows how to change the irregular verb 'have' from the past simple to the past progressive.

The verb 'to have'			
		Past tense	
		Simple aspect	Progressive aspect
First person singular:	I	had	was having
Second person singular:	you	had	were having
Third person singular:	he/she/it	had	was having
First person plural:	we	had	were having
Second person plural:	you	had	were having
Third person plural:	they	had	were having

3   Change the following sentences from the past simple to the past progressive.
   a   I had a small meal.
   b   You had a huge, four-course meal.
   c   She had a haircut.
   d   We had mutton stew.
   e   You had a good time together.
   f   They had guests for supper.
4   Complete the following sentences. Use the past-progressive form of the verb in brackets that matches the subject.
   a   While I (have) fun, I realised that my boyfriend was bored.
   b   While we (have) a swim at the dam, the grown-ups sat around at the house and chatted.
   c   While she (have) the baby, her husband never left her side.

We cannot use 'have' in the past progressive when it is showing possession of an object. For example, it is wrong to say 'I was having a handbag.' We should rather say 'I had a handbag.'

5   Correct the following sentences. Keep the tense the same but change the aspect.
   a   I was having a bicycle.
   b   We were having a small house in the countryside.
   c   He was having two tickets to the theatre.
   d   She was having a good sense of humour.

Proverbs and famous quotations

Proverbs

Proverbs are wise sayings that contain the wisdom of our ancestors but are not quotations from particular people. An example of a proverb that English has taken from Africa is 'It takes a village to raise a child.' This means that to learn everything they need to know, children must learn skills and correct behaviour from a whole community and not just from their mother and father.

1   Match the proverbs in column A with their meanings in column B.

Column A	Column B
a It's no use crying over spilt milk.	Women are continually looking after children and their homes, and these tasks need constant attention.
b Strike while the iron is hot.	Don't be too busy to enjoy life.
c Take time to smell the roses.	Do things when the opportunity is there and people are ready for action.
d A woman's work is never done.	Small/short people often have big personalities.
e Dynamite comes in small packages.	We cannot improve a situation by wishing that something had not happened.

Quotations

Sometimes the words that someone has said become famous. We then call these words famous quotations, and in time they may become proverbs.

2   Match the quotation is column A with the meanings in column B.

Column A	Column B
a 'Man is born free, but is everywhere in chains.' Jean-Jacques Rousseau	This means the ties we have to people and places are what are important in life.
b 'Workers of the world unite; you have nothing to lose but your chains.' Karl Marx	This means we must try hard to succeed in life.
c 'Freedom's just another word for nothing left to lose.' Mickey Gilley	If workers join together into trade unions they will have more power over their employers, and because they are presently being treated so badly they are not really risking anything.
d 'Get rich or die tryin'' 50 Cent	This means we should design the shapes of things based on what they will be used for.
e 'Form follows function.' Mies van der Rohe	This means that there are so many rules in modern society that people cannot do what they want to do.

Idioms

While a proverb is a wise saying, and therefore has to be a whole sentence, an idiom does not tell you how to live your life; it is simply a phrase that has a distinctive meaning. For example, the phrase 'to stand the test of time' means to continue to look good after many years. (It is not telling us we should look as good as we used to when we were young.)

1   Match the idioms in column A with their meanings in column B.

Column A	Column B
a to add colour	to be an answer that nobody knows, or an outcome that nobody can predict
b to be larger than life	to say something that other people feel is true and meaningful
c to steal the show	to act as if someone is a god/goddess
d to drag out a story	to make something more interesting
e to be wheeling and dealing	to be able to surprise people by doing something unexpected
f to put someone on a pedestal	to have a personality that attracts a lot of attention from other people
g to let slip information	to make an idea leave your mind
h to come back from the dead	to play against the best players, to race against the elite, etc.
i to shake off an idea	for government control and intimidation to be at its worst/harshest
j to have shock factor	to do everything you can to make something work
k to be anybody's guess	to be in a situation where it is hard not to make a mistake or say the wrong thing
l to strike a chord in people	to become totally involved in something
m to compete at the top end of a sport	to come alive again after being dead, or to recover after a serious illness
n to be walking through a minefield	to be making business deals all the time
o for oppression to be at its height	to have the same values and abilities as someone else
p to be king	to feel good/to feel perfectly OK
q to put your heart and soul into something	to be the most important person or thing in a particular area
r to strike gold	to be a better actor or actress than the main actor/actress
s to see something in the light of something else	to be squashed very closely together like fish in a tin
t to throw yourself into a task with your heart and soul	to choose not to do something
u to be cast from the same mould as someone else	to understand a statement by referring to a different statement which clarifies the meaning of the first statement
v to be packed like sardines	to find a way of making lots of money
w to bake someone's noodle	to give precious things or valuable knowledge to people who do not appreciate it
x to cast pearls before swine	to make a story last so long that it gets boring
y to turn your back on something	to confuse someone's brain
z to feel right as rain	to tell a secret without intending to

Noodles are a kind of food.

A human brain looks a bit like noodles.

The human brain is often metaphorically referred to as a 'noodle', because it is soft and has wiggly parts.

Stereotypes and clichés

A history of the printing process

When people invented printing they made little metal letters back to front. Then they stuck these letters onto pieces of wood. In this way they made stamps that could print particular letters. People then put ink on these stamps and made prints of them on pieces of paper. Once the letters were printed they were the right way round and easy to read.

Although making stamps took time, once someone had made them, printing was a quick way of producing a set of posters (or other texts where many copies were needed).

1 What word could be printed by the stamps in the picture?
2 How many times could you use these stamps to print this word?

When a person lined up some stamps of letters to make words, the line of stamps was called 'type'. The stamps were called 'movable type' because when the person wanted to print a different page he/she could move the stamps around to make different words. In this way a small set of movable type could be used to print a whole book.

3 What name was given to the lines of metal letters used to print pages of books?

Moveable type was expensive. When the letters on the stamps got worn down, the printers had to buy more. William Ged invented a cheaper way of printing. He made a page of movable type, and then he took a mould of this page. Then he cast this page in metal. So instead of printing with the expensive movable type and wearing it down, Ged printed with a solid metal sheet of type. This solid sheet of type was later called a 'stereotype'.

4 What two Greek words is the word 'stereotype' made of? What is the English meaning of each of these words?

Refer back to page 47 to check the meaning of the words.

The metaphorical meaning of the word 'stereotype'

Walter Lippmann, an American journalist, said that we make 'stereotypes' in our heads. He was using the word 'stereotype' in a metaphorical way to show that we develop fixed ideas about groups of people. He meant that we do not have completely original feelings every time we meet a person, instead we think about that person in the same way that we think about similar people. Lippmann did not say that stereotypical attitudes towards people were right or wrong, he just said that stereotypes were 'hard to shake'. Nowadays we often use the word 'stereotype' to mean a fixed idea we have in our heads of what certain people are like.

5   Does the word 'stereotype' have positive or negative connotations these days?

The metaphorical meaning of the word 'cliché'

'Cliché' is French word, which was originally an example of the sound device onomatopoeia. The French printers, hearing the noise of hot metal being made into a stereotype, called this noise a 'cliché' (pronounced 'clee-shay'), because that is the sound it made. Years later, the word 'cliché' was used as a synonym for the literal meaning of 'stereotype'.

Nowadays the word cliché is used only in a metaphorical way. We use the word 'cliché' to mean an old saying or idea that we are tired of.

6   Does the word 'cliché' have positive or negative connotations these days?

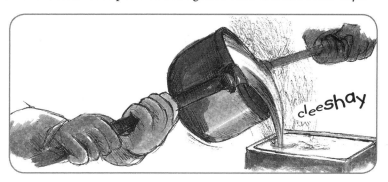

Many proverbs sound a lot like clichés, but when we think a saying is wise and worth repeating we do not call it a cliché. It is only when we think it was not worth repeating that we call it a cliché.

7   Divide the following sentences into the categories shown in the table below.
   ● Sugar is sweet and so are you.
   ● All black people dance well.
   ● They lived happily ever after.
   ● Don't judge a book by its cover.
   ● It takes a village to raise a child.
   ● German people think they are better than people of other nationalities.

Proverbs (wise sayings that most people respect)	Clichés (irritating sayings or ideas that people are tired of hearing)	Expressions of a stereotypical attitude to certain groups of people

Hyphens

Hyphens in words that are broken up between two lines

When you cannot fit a word onto one line, you can break it between two syllables and write a hyphen at the end of the first half of the word. Then put the second half of the word on the next line. (Words with more than two syllables have more than one place where you can put a hyphen.)

1   Imagine that the following words had to be broken in two so that they could fit into a column of text. Where would you put the hyphen?
    a   printing
    b   cliché
    c   stereotype

Hyphens in special phrases

Sometimes we use phrases that act as one word, so we hyphenate these phrases, as in the example below, to show the reader that we want the words to be read as if they were joined together.

adjective

Her attitude is very happy-go-lucky.

2   Place each of the hyphenated phrases in the box into one of the sentences below.

multi-platinum-sellers	Statue-of-Liberty-type
sixteen-year-old	laugh-out-loud

   a   Soon it will be my birthday and I will be a _____.
   b   I want to dress up as a goddess with one of those _____ crowns.
   c   She kept the same friends that she had from before her pop group became _____.
   d   I smiled at her joke, although it was not _____ funny.

Hyphens between prefixes and root words

Sometimes prefixes are joined to the rest of a word with a hyphen. This is usually done when the prefix has only recently been used with this root word, or if it does not fit nicely, making the word difficult to pronounce. However, some words have had prefixes for many years and these prefixes fit very nicely, yet these words are still hyphenated.

3   Put the hyphenated words in the box into the following table.

self-esteem	ex-husband	hyper-allergic
co-ordinator	re-assembled	multi-national

Words that have hyphens after their prefixes		
Words that have hyphens after their prefixes but the prefix has only recently been used with this root word	**Words that have hyphens after their prefixes but the prefix does not fit nicely**	**Words that have hyphens after their prefixes, when the prefix does fit nicely, and has for years, but the hyphen is still used out of habit**

Hyphens in compound words

A compound word is made out of two words that have been joined with a hyphen. We often join words in this way when we use two adjectives before a noun but we do not want them to separately describe the noun; we want them to work together to make a whole new adjective that describes the noun.

Look at the following examples.

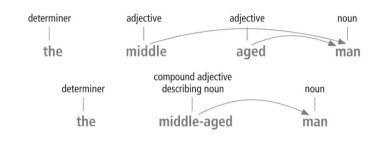

In the first sentence the two adjectives work separately, and they describe a man who is in the middle of a row of people and who is aged (very old). In the second sentence the adjectives work together as one compound adjective and they describe a man who is in the middle of his life (about 35 years old).

We also often make compound adjectives out of an adjective and a noun, and then use this compound adjective to describe another noun, as shown below.

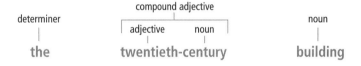

A compound word usually has a different meaning from the meaning that the two separate words would have, which is why it has been hyphenated.

The middle aged man

The middle-aged man

4 Put one hyphen into each of the following sentences in order to make a compound word.
   a In South Africa, drivers drive on the left hand side of the road.
   b Although they were both National Party leaders, F.W. de Klerk was a more forward thinking person than P.W. Botha.

Adverb-adjective combinations that come before the main verb in a sentence are often hyphenated, but these same combinations are usually not hyphenated when they come after the main verb, as shown in the examples below.

That tall man is well known.
That well-known man is tall.

5 Insert a hyphen into one of each of the following pairs of sentences.
   a This is a well written essay.
      This essay is well written.
   b Lambs that are full grown are called 'sheep'.
      Full grown lambs are called 'sheep'.

Activity D

The extract on page 77 is from the 'Theatre' section of the *Mail & Guardian* newspaper. It includes a list of what plays are showing at the moment and then there is a review of one of these plays. Read the extract and answer the questions below.

1   Why are the names of the venues printed in bold?
2   Is the ballet called *Giselle* recommended or not?
3   How many plays are discussed in the listing for the Sanlam Studio?
4   Rewrite the full names of the underlined abbreviations in the following listing:
    Theatre@The Pavilion, <u>V&A</u> Waterfront. Until November 25 is Mike McCullagh's
    That <u>80s</u> Show. <u>Tel</u>: 419 7661 regarding bookings.
5   a   The fifth venue on the list is showing a play called 'Modern Orthodox'. How do we
        know this will be a play about religion (among other themes)?
    b   Does the word 'orthodox' have positive or negative connotations?
6   The play that has been given a full review is called *You Strike a Woman, You Strike a Rock*.
    a   Why is this written in italics in the extract?
    b   Why is this written in bold in the review?
7   The words 'multi-award-winning' are hyphenated in this text because:
    a   they form a compound noun.
    b   they form a compound adjective.
    c   they form an adverb-adjective combination that comes before the main verb in the sentence.
8   This play is set in a time when:
    a   everybody was fairly free.
    b   apartheid was at its worst.
    c   apartheid existed, but it had become less oppressive.
9   What does the reviewer mean when she says the performances of the actresses are 'convincing'?
10 What does it mean that the 'play has lost some of its shock factor'?
11 We are told that at times the play 'drags'. Does this mean that:
    a   the play sometimes seems to go too slowly?
    b   the play sometimes seems to go too fast?
    c   the play pulls us into the past and makes us feel very involved?
12 a   In the metaphor 'we are bombarded by conscience-raising slogans' what is being compared to what?
    b   Why?
13 What does it mean when the reviewer writes that the play 'clearly struck a chord with the audience'?
14 Why is *Phambili ngomzabalazo* written in italics?
15 a   What is the tense of the sentence 'The struggle continues'?
    b   What is its aspect?
    c   Rewrite this sentence in the present progressive.
    d   Why do you think that the progressive aspect was not used in the original sentence?
16 What proverb from page 70 would be relevant to the lives of the three main characters in this play?
17 Based on what is reported in this review, how are men and women stereotyped in this play?

THEATRE

Lucy Jamieson

Arena Theatre, Artscape Theatre Centre, Foreshore. Currently running is Artscapes's spring season of new plays. Until November 4 is *Unforced Errors*, a comedy about domestic life in a small Australian town. Tel: 421 7695 regarding bookings.

★ **Opera House**, Artscape Theatre Centre, Foreshore. Closing on November 2, Tracy Li is *Giselle* in the popular classic staged by Cape Town City Ballet. Book at Computicket or Tel: 421 7695.

★ **Sanlam Studio**, Baxter Theatre. Until October 2 is *You Strike a Woman, You Strike a Rock*. On October 29 is *Four Women: End of the Floetics*, the last performance in this year's Playground Director's Choice Festival. Opening on November 1 is Pinter's classic *Betrayal*, directed by Lara Foot Newton. Tel: 685 7880 regarding bookings.

Theatre@The Pavilion, V&A Waterfront. Until November 25 is Mike McCullagh's *That 80s Show*. Tel: 419 7661 regarding bookings.

Theatre on the Bay, 1 Link Street, Camps Bay. Until November 11 is *Modern Orthodox*, a romantic comedy about faith, love and friendship, written by Daniel Goldfarb and directed by Allan Swerdlow. Tel: 438 3301 regarding bookings.

★ **Recommended**

The struggle continues

In 1976, 20 000 women marched on the Union Buildings in Pretoria to protest against the pass laws. To celebrate their courage, multi-award-winning director, Phyllis Klotz has joined with Sibikwa Players to restage **You Strike a Woman, You Strike a Rock**. *Sibikwa* is the Nguni word for 'we are spoken for', and this piece of apartheid protest theatre, workshopped in a township toilet during the 1980s, still speaks for millions of black working-class women in South Africa today.

It starts with three women selling chickens and oranges at a taxi rank, at a time when South Africa was under a state of emergency, oppression was at its height and violence was a daily occurrence. Connie Chiume, Poppy Tsira and Busi Zokufa (above) are completely convincing, their energetic and expressive performances add colour to the characters as they squabble over the quality of their goods and vie for customers. Their histories are recounted in simple vignettes that take us back first to the Transkei, where the women queue for cheques sent by their husbands working in the mines and, when the maintenance runs out, they climb aboard the bus bound for Cape Town. These vignettes are brought to life with songs, chants and syncopated rhythms that rouse the audience to join in.

To refer to the realities of oppression during the political turmoil of the 1980s was daring and risky. Today the play has lost some of its shock factor, but none of its relevance. After 12 years of freedom, the same women are at the same taxi rank, toiling to provide for their children – children still threatened by hunger, their fathers still absent or abusive. Then, the women took a stand against the injustice of apartheid; today the stand is against social injustice. Hope for the future lies in the resilience of these women, in their ability to keep their sense of humour, and their dignity in the face of hardship.

On the whole, the play is energetic and vibrant, but the plot is thin and it drags occasionally as we are bombarded by a string of conscience-raising slogans, but this clearly struck a chord with the audience, who chanted with the players. *Phambili ngomzabalazo*! The struggle continues. – *Lucy Jamieson*

At the Baxter Theatre until October 28.

Audience

We describe the people that watch a play as the 'audience' of that play. When analysing a text, we also use the word 'audience' to describe the people that read or view that text.

When people write or design a text they do not normally know exactly who is going to read it or view it. But writers and designers still have a good idea about the *type* of people that will read or view their text. Therefore they try to make their work appeal to these types of people. We call the people that the writers and designers imagine reading their text the 'intended audience' of the text.

The writers and designers need to consider the following aspects about their intended audience:
- age
- race
- gender
- sexuality
- nationality
- health and ability
- level of education
- place where they live (urban/rural)
- political leanings
- religion
- home languages and additional languages
- careers
- hobbies.

Here are some phrases that could be used to describe the intended audience of a text:
- black teenagers who are part of the ANCYL
- wealthy Americans who vote for the Republican Party
- South African mountain bikers
- white female accountants
- elderly Xhosa speakers
- disabled children living in rural settings.

1   By selecting one of each of the pairs of words in the brackets, describe the intended audiences of the texts in:
   a   Activity A (Americans/South Africans; children/adults; English speakers/Setswana speakers; people who listen to music/people who read poetry)
   b   Activity B (Americans/South Africans; children/adults; English speakers/Setswana speakers; people who listen to music/people who read poetry)
2   Now rewrite each of your answers to question 1 as single phrases that can be read easily, like the bulleted phrases above. (If necessary refer to page 16 for how to order adjectives.)
3   a   Do you think that the text in Activity C was written for a very specific audience?
   b   Why do you say this?
4   What can you say about the audience that the text in Activity D was written for?

Regular verbs in the present tense and the perfect aspect

> In this context, 'perfect' means 'completed' or 'finished'.

If you want to show that an action is completed you write it in the perfect aspect.

To change a regular verb into the present-perfect form you add the present-tense form of the verb 'have' that matches the subject in front of the base verb. Then you add 'ed' onto the end of the base verb. For example, instead of writing 'I look' you write 'I have looked'. Both forms are in the present tense, but 'I look' is in the simple aspect and 'I have looked' is in the perfect aspect.

This table shows how to change the regular verb 'look' from the present simple to the present perfect.

The verb 'to look'		Present tense	
		Simple aspect	Perfect aspect
First person singular:	I	look	have looked
Second person singular:	you	look	have looked
Third person singular:	he/she/it	looks	have looked
First person plural:	we	look	have looked
Second person plural:	you	look	have looked
Third person plural:	they	look	have looked

The rule to remember is: while forms of the verb 'be' are used to make the progressive aspect of other verbs, it is forms of the verb 'have' that are used to make the perfect aspect.

1　Change the following sentences from the present simple to the present perfect.
   a　I look up into the night sky.
   b　You look at the television.
   c　She looks at what is in the oven.
   d　We look for the car keys.
   e　You look under the table.
   f　They look out the door.
2　Complete the following sentences with the appropriate present-perfect form of the verb in brackets.
   a　I (look) at my friend's homework already.
   b　He (look) everywhere for you.

If you want to distinguish between the two words that make up a verb in the present perfect, call the first word the 'perfect auxiliary verb'. Then call the second word the 'participle showing the perfect aspect'. In the case of regular verbs this participle appears the same as a past-tense verb, but it does not in fact show tense; it shows the perfect aspect. The tense of the verb is shown by the auxiliary verb.

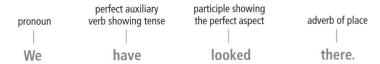

pronoun	perfect auxiliary verb showing tense	participle showing the perfect aspect	adverb of place
We	have	looked	there.

Irregular verbs in the present tense and the perfect aspect

When you change an irregular verb from the present simple to the present perfect you still begin with a form of the verb 'have' that matches the subject and the tense. This is the perfect auxiliary verb. But then, in the case of an irregular verb, the participle showing the perfect aspect is not made by just adding 'ed' to the base form of the verb. The participle has a special, irregular form.

These tables show how to change the irregular verbs 'be' and 'have' from the present simple to the present perfect.

The verb 'to be'			
		Present tense	
		Simple aspect	**Perfect aspect**
First person singular:	I	am	have been
Second person singular:	you	are	have been
Third person singular:	he/she/it	is	has been
First person plural:	we	are	have been
Second person plural:	you	are	have been
Third person plural:	they	are	have been

The verb 'to have'			
		Present tense	
		Simple aspect	**Perfect aspect**
First person singular:	I	have	have had
Second person singular:	you	have	have had
Third person singular:	he/she/it	has	has had
First person plural:	we	have	have had
Second person plural:	you	have	have had
Third person plural:	they	have	have had

1 Change the following present-simple sentences into the present perfect.
   a I am hungry.
   b She is lucky.
   c You have a big lunch.
   d He has a good time.
2 Rewrite the following past-simple sentences in the present perfect.
   a I was there.
   b I had a bad cold.

Note that while the verb 'have' uses the word 'had' for the past-simple verb and the participle showing the perfect aspect, the verb 'be' uses different words ('was' and 'been') for these two different purposes.

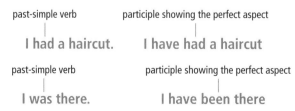

As in the case of 'have', many irregular verbs use the same word for the past-simple verb and for the participle showing the perfect aspect. For example, we can use 'won' in both these sentences.

I won the race.   *I have won the race.*

However, as in the case of 'be', some base verbs use a different word for the past-simple verb and for the participle showing the perfect aspect. For example, we use different forms of 'give' in the following sentences.

I gave him the money.   *I have given him the money.*

The table below shows how some verbs are formed when they become past-simple verbs and when they become participles showing the perfect aspect.

	Base form of verb	Past simple form of verb	Participle showing the perfect aspect
Regular verbs	look	looked	looked
	invite	invited	invited
	stop	stopped	stopped
	learn	learned	learned
	spill	spilled	spilled
Irregular verbs	learn	learnt	learnt
	spill	spilt	spilt
	be	was	been
	run	ran	run
	go	went	gone
	win	won	won
	fly	flew	flown
	throw	threw	thrown
	know	knew	known
	strike	struck	struck/stricken
	see	saw	seen
	wear	wore	worn
	tear	tore	torn
	find	found	found
	have	had	had
	meet	met	met
	lose	lost	lost
	spend	spent	spent
	keep	kept	kept
	sit	sat	sat
	put	put	put

The verbs 'learn' and 'spill' can be made into a regular or an irregular participle showing the perfect aspect.

3 Rewrite the following past-simple sentences into the present perfect.
  a I lost my jacket.
  b She threw the ball outside.
  c I spilled the bucket of water on the floor.

Purpose

A writer's purpose is his/her reason for writing. Here are some phrases that could be used to describe someone's purpose for writing:

- to entertain (as in the case of most cartoons, stories and play scripts)
- to satirise (to write about something important in a way that makes it sound stupid)
- to inform (as in the case of newspaper reports and informative brochures)
- to instruct (as in the case of recipes, safety instructions or instructions on how to play a game)
- to explain (as in the case of Natural Sciences text books or encyclopaedias)
- to persuade (as in the case of advertisements and propaganda)
- to thank (as in the case of letters of thanks)
- to complain (as in the case of letters of complaint)
- to request (as in the case of letters of request)
- to apply (as in the case of letters of application)
- to invite (as in the case of party invitations)
- to review (as in the case of theatre reviews and book reviews)
- to criticise (as in the case of newspaper columns)
- to protest (as in the case of placards in a protest march)
- to discuss (as in the case of some magazine articles)
- to analyse (as in the case of analytical essays and analytical reports).

1 What is the purpose of each of the following texts?

a

The Sun
The Sun is a huge ball of hot gas. It is made up of layers: a core, a surface and the surrounding atmospheric layers.

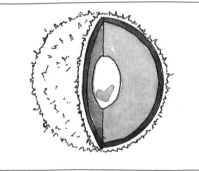

Children's encyclopaedia

b

He who dies with the most toys wins!

Bumper sticker

c

Unite against capitalist exploitation!

Placard

Regular verbs in the past tense and the perfect aspect

If we want to use a regular verb in the past perfect, we use two verbs: the perfect auxiliary verb and then the participle showing the perfect aspect. To make the perfect auxiliary verb we write the past-tense form of the verb 'have' that matches the subject, which is always 'had'. To make the participle showing the perfect aspect we add 'ed' onto the back of the base form of the verb.

This table shows how to change the regular verb 'look' from the past simple to the past perfect.

The verb 'to look'		Past tense	
		Simple aspect	Perfect aspect
First person singular:	I	looked	had looked
Second person singular:	you	looked	had looked
Third person singular:	he/she/it	looked	had looked
First person plural:	we	looked	had looked
Second person plural:	you	looked	had looked
Third person plural:	they	looked	had looked

1   Change the following sentences from the past simple to the past perfect.
   a   I looked over the fence.
   b   You looked at the brochures.
   c   She looked for her dog.
   d   We looked at the posters.
   e   You looked everywhere.
   f   They looked for a house to rent.

2   Complete the following sentences. Use the past perfect form of the verb in brackets that matches the subject.
   a   I (look) for my jersey everywhere, and then I realised I was wearing it.
   b   We (look) at all the dresses in the shop, but none of them was suitable for the wedding.

The past perfect is often used together with the past simple, as in sentences 2 a and b above. This technique allows the speaker to show which action happened further back in the past.

When we make the base form of a verb into the participle showing the perfect aspect, we sometimes double the last consonant. We do this when the vowel in the base word is a short sound.

Base form of a verb with a short vowel	Participle showing the perfect aspect, with a doubled last consonant
pat	patted
hop	hopped

3   Rewrite the regular verb 'knit' as a participle showing the perfect aspect.

Irregular verbs in the past tense and the perfect aspect

If you want to use an irregular verb in the past perfect you add the perfect auxiliary verb 'had' in front of the participle showing the perfect aspect.

This table shows how to change the irregular verb 'be' from the past simple to the past perfect.

The verb 'to be'		Past tense	
		Simple aspect	Perfect aspect
First person singular:	I	was	had been
Second person singular:	you	were	had been
Third person singular:	he/she/it	was	had been
First person plural:	we	were	had been
Second person plural:	you	were	had been
Third person plural:	they	were	had been

1 Change the following sentences from the past simple to the past perfect.
  a They were happy.
  b You were sad.
  c He was confident.

We often use the past perfect in sentences with two clauses. The past-perfect clause shows how things were in the distant past, and the present-simple clause shows how things were in the recent past (and probably how things still are in the present).

2 Rewrite the verbs in brackets into the past perfect.
  a I (be) very fit, before I spent three months in a hospital bed.
  b We (be) very materialistic, until we became Christians and realised there was more to life than worldly goods.

This table shows how to change the irregular verb 'have' from the past simple to the past perfect.

The verb 'to have'		Past tense	
		Simple aspect	Perfect aspect
First person singular:	I	had	had had
Second person singular:	you	had	had had
Third person singular:	he/she/it	had	had had
First person plural:	we	had	had had
Second person plural:	you	had	had had
Third person plural:	they	had	had had

We often use the verb 'had had' with the word 'enough' to show that the people do not want or need any more.

3   Rewrite the following past-simple sentences into the past perfect.
    a   I had enough supper.
    b   You had enough of me.
    c   She had enough of all the complaints.
    d   We had enough sweets.
    e   You had enough water.
    f   They had enough sunshine.

When we write irregular verbs in the past perfect we use 'had' and a participle based on the base verb to show the perfect aspect. Many of these irregular participles showing the perfect aspect are listed on page 81.

4   Rewrite the following past-simple sentences into the past perfect. Use the table on page 81 to help you.
    a   I struck a match.
    b   You met interesting people at university.
    c   We won the game!
    d   They saw the match on television.
    e   I put some money in the collection box.
    f   She tore her jeans on the fence.

5   Rewrite the following present-simple sentences into the past perfect. Use the table on page 81 to help you.
    a   I wear clothes with designer labels, such as Prada, Gucci and Chanel.
    b   He is a good father.
    c   They find ticks on their cows.
    d   You fly to Paris often.
    e   We run to the train station.
    f   Jessica and Tashiana sit on the bench.

6   Rewrite the following present-perfect sentences into the past perfect.
    a   I have spent all my money.
    b   You have had a serious illness.
    c   She has kept my secret.

Adverbs of manner, time, place and reason

Just as adjectives give you more information about nouns, most adverbs are used to give you more information about verbs. (The verb tells you what happened, and most adverbs give you extra information about how, when, where or why it happened.) However, adverbs can also modify other parts of speech, such as adjectives.

In the following sentence, the word 'looked' is a verb and the word 'admiringly' is an adverb that tells us how David performed this action.

David looked   admiringly at the beautiful woman.

Adverbs of manner
Here is a list of some adverbs of manner, which say *how* something is done.

beautifully	*extravagantly*	*perfectly*	*luckily*	*realistically*
correctly	*tenderly*	*progressively*	*well*	

Adverbs of manner are usually made by adding 'ly' to an adjective. For example, 'beautifully' is made by adding 'ly' to the adjective 'beautiful'. But there are exceptions. The adverb 'well' is spelt the same as the adjective 'well'.

1   Complete the following sentences using one of the above adverbs of manner.
   a   I thought I had lost my wallet, but then _____ I found it at the bottom of my bag.
   b   She sings _____ and can play the guitar as well.
   c   He always speaks very _____ to his wife.
   d   My aunt spends her money very _____, but at least that means she buys us great Christmas presents.
   e   I would like to be a doctor, but, if I am thinking _____, I know I will probably only get into a nursing course because my marks are not brilliant.
   f   My teacher decided that my essay was very _____ written.
   g   The cushions matched the couch _____ although we bought them at different shops.
   h   My health is getting _____ better now that I am eating healthy foods.
   i   My teacher always wants every word spelt _____, but I think style is more important than spelling.

Not all adjectives can be made into adverbs.

Adverbs of time

Here is a list of some adverbs of time, which say *when* something is done.

often	*sometimes*	*forever*	*weekly*
monthly	*yearly*	*now*	*then*

2   Complete the following sentences using the above adverbs of time.
   a   _____ I walk home from school, but other times I cycle.
   b   My mother goes shopping on a _____ basis, usually on Fridays.
   c   I get paid _____, normally on the last day of the month.
   d   I don't want to wait until after supper for my dessert; I want it _____!
   e   I _____ enter competitions, but I rarely win anything.
   f   When we got married I promised to love you _____.
   g   This publication comes out _____, but other magazines are published more frequently.
   h   I locked the house, and _____ I realised that I had left my keys inside.

While prepositions that refer to time have to come before a noun or pronoun, adverbs of time do not.

Adverbs of place

Here is a list of some adverbs of place, which say *where* something is done.

inside	*outside*	*here*	*there*

3   Complete each of the following sentences using one of the above adverbs of place.
   a   The sun is shining _____ so I am going for a walk today.
   b   My sisters prefer to stay _____ and read books.
   c   They lie _____ on that couch all day.
   d   It is not surprising that I am the thinnest child around _____.

While prepositions that refer to place have to come before a noun or pronoun, adverbs of place do not.

Adverbs of reason

Here is a list of some adverbs of reason, which are concerned with *why* something is done. Adverbs of reason look a lot like conjunctions, but they do not need to join two clauses. You can put them at the beginning of a sentence with one clause.

Conjunctions are discussed on pages 142–144 and clauses are discussed on page 119.

therefore	*however*	*nevertheless*

4   Complete the following paragraphs using one of the above adverbs of reason.
   a   He is kind and funny. _____ his daughters like to be in his company.
   b   He is not a responsible father. _____ his daughters love him very much.
   c   He is very busy. _____ he makes time to help his children with their homework.

In most cases 'however' and 'nevertheless' can be used interchangeably.

Adverbs and adverbial phrases that show degree or intensity

Adverbs of degree

Some adverbs of manner and time can be used to express degree, just as the adjectives discussed on page 17 are used to express degree. These adverbs can be in the absolute, comparative or superlative degree. The comparative degree is used when two people or two things are being compared. The superlative degree is used when more than two people or things are being compared.

These irregular adverbs of degree are common and you have probably seen them before.

Irregular adverbs in their absolute form	Irregular adverbs in their comparative form	Irregular adverbs in their superlative form
badly	worse	worst
well	better	best

Most adverbs need to be made into adverbial phrases when they are changed into their comparative or superlative form. According to the regular pattern, we use the adverbs 'more' or 'less' plus the absolute form of the core adverb to create the comparative form, as shown in the following adverbial phrase of degree.

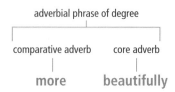

We use the adverbs 'most' or 'least' plus the absolute form of the core adverb to create the superlative form.

Regular adverbs in their absolute form	Regular adverbial phrases in their comparative form	Regular adverbial phrases in their superlative form
beautifully	more beautifully less beautifully	most beautifully least beautifully
extravagantly	more extravagantly less extravagantly	most extravagantly least extravagantly
tenderly	more tenderly less tenderly	most tenderly least tenderly

The comparative forms of the regular adverbs of degree are used far more often than the superlative forms.

Some adverbs, such as 'perfectly', cannot be made into a comparative or superlative form, because things are either done perfectly or they are not.

1   Complete the following sentences by changing the adjectives in brackets into the appropriate adverb or adverbial phrase.
   a   She spends money (extravagantly) than her sister.
   b   He cooks (well) than his brother.
   c   Of all the members of the choir, it is Hugh who sings (beautifully).

We often insert the word 'the' in front of the superlative form of an adverb. The answer to 1 c could also be written as:

Of all the members of the choir, it is Hugh who sings the most beautifully.

Adverbs of intensity

An adverb can intensify an adverb that is modifying a verb without making a comparison to something else.

The above adverb 'quickly' can be intensified if we add 'very' in front of it.

Adverbs of degree make direct comparisons. Adverbs of intensity do not. These adverbs do not compare the way Jeff ran to the way anyone else ran, but they do give us a feeling of how fast he ran.

Often it is not polite to make direct comparisons. Then it is better to use adverbs of intensity than adverbs of degree. Here are some adverbs that can be used as adverbs of intensity without making a direct comparison.

- very – this adverb shows that an action happens intensely.
- really – this adverb shows that an action happens intensely.
- fairly – this adverb shows that an action happens with medium intensity.
- quite – this adverb shows that an action happens with medium intensity.

2   How tenderly is the cat being stroked in each of these pictures?

a
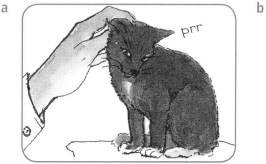

b
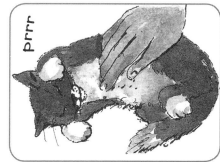

He stroked the cat _____ tenderly.   He stroked the cat _____ tenderly.

When we do something in excess, we use the adverb 'too' with an adverb in the absolute degree, as in the following sentence.

I ran too fast, so I slipped and hurt myself.

When we do something just a little bit, we use the adverb 'slightly'. We usually use this adverb in combination with an adjective in the comparative degree.

I walked slightly faster than usual, because I was late for the train.

3   Insert 'too' or 'slightly' in each of the following sentences.
   a   He is _____ clumsy for his own good.
   b   She is _____ taller than her mother.

An adverb of negation – 'not'

An adverb of negation is added into a sentence to give the sentence the opposite meaning. The most important adverb of negation is 'not'. If the verb is made up of more than one word, we put 'not' between the first and second words that make up the multiword verb.

If the verb is just one word, and it is a form of the verb 'be', we put the adverb 'not' after this verb. (However, if the verb is just one verb, and it is not a form of the verb 'be', we use a special construction that is discussed on page 165.)

1　Insert 'not' into the following sentences to make them mean the opposite of what they previously meant.
   a　You are coming with me.
   b　He is a capitalist.
   c　We are negotiating a deal.

When we use 'not' and 'ever', we contract them into one word: 'never'. This word is a negative adverb of time. We often use 'ever' in questions, and then we use 'never' in the answers to these questions, as shown below.

Will I ever be thin?
No, you will never be thin.

2　By following the pattern shown above, answer the following questions in the negative.
   a　Will you ever love me?
   b　Will I ever succeed?

We usually contract 'not one thing' into one word: 'nothing'.
We usually contract 'not one', into one word: 'none'.
We usually contract 'not one person' into the word 'no-one'.

3　Rewrite the following sentences using contractions that combine 'not' with one or more words.
   a　I have got not one thing in my lunchbox because I forgot my sandwiches in the fridge.
   b　Not one of my essays got a good mark.
   c　Not one person knows the answer to that question.
   d　Of all the villagers, not one was left alive.
   e　I told your secret to not one person.
   f　Since I put on weight not one thing in my wardrobe fits me.

Register

We call the level of formality of language that we use the 'register'.

We normally use formal language when we are speaking to people we do not know very well, when we are speaking to important people, or when we are speaking to the public. The use of formal language normally shows that we respect the person to whom we are talking. We do not use contractions in formal English.

1   Which of the following sentences is slightly formal and which is very formal?
    a   Good evening, ladies and gentlemen. I have the honour of officiating during tonight's debate.
    b   Good evening. I will be chairing tonight's debate.

However, sometimes people use formal language to put emotional distance between themselves and others, because when we speak formally to someone this shows we are not on intimate terms with that person. If your friend starts talking to you in a formal way, this could mean that he/she is cross with you.

2   Which of the following sentences, said by one friend to another, shows that all is not well in this friendship?
    a   Thanks for your opinion.
    b   Thank you for giving me the benefit of your advice.

People speak in informal English to their friends and family. Often they use informal synonyms for more standard English terms. For example, the word 'trendy' is an informal word for 'fashionable'.

Slang

When friends of the same age use very informal words that only their peer group can understand we call their language 'slang'. Slang has an important purpose; it creates a bond between the people who use it. However, slang excludes other people. For example, the British youth use the word 'riveting' to mean 'really interesting', but if you do not know British slang then you would not understand what was meant by this term.

3   The following two sentences mean the same thing. Which of them is written in formal English and which is written in youth slang?
    a   They're scrubs, and some are junkies, and I don't hang out with the likes of them.
    b   They are worthless young men, and some are drug addicts, and I do not socialise with such people.

Some slang words have become so fashionable that they are widely used by the writers of magazine articles who are trying to sound trendy.

	Slang	Very informal	Slightly informal	Formal
Adjective	bling	flash	showy	ostentatious
Noun (can be used as subject or object)	bling	splurge	spending spree	conspicuous consumption
Verb	bling	sparkling, glittering, shining		

4   What parts of speech can the word 'bling' be used as?

Activity E

Read the following magazine article and then answer the questions that follow.

Fit for a bling

Cycling is the fastest-growing sport in South Africa, and bikes and equipment have become status symbols. By Oliver Roberts

Thanks largely to Lance Armstrong, a Texan who recovered from life-threatening cancer, won the sport's most famous race – the Tour de France – seven times in a row and then got engaged to the rock star Sheryl Crow, cycling has emerged as one of the most popular physical pursuits in the world and is the fastest-growing sport in South Africa.

For keen cyclists, the chosen mode of exercise is not something they slip into for a few hours four times a week; it's an entire existence involving keeping fit, eating right and, more significantly, splurging cash on accessories in the name of fashionable form, followed by function.

Cycling helmets, shoes, gloves, shirts and shorts are just a few of the important items in a cycling kit.

The cost of the kit you *should* be seen wearing and riding seems extravagantly expensive to the hairy outsider, but to the super-smooth, cycling narcissist, image is vital. In this muesli-for-breakfast world, names like Trek, Cervélo, Giro, Assos Clonago and Bianchi promote the same envy as Gucci, Prada, Hugo Boss and Yves Saint Laurent do for dedicated followers of fashion.

'This kind of status anxiety in cycling is found all over the world, but I think it's particularly strong in South Africa,' says Andrew McLean, a former professional cyclist who now co-presents the magazine show SuperCycling on SuperSport. 'The ongoing success of the cellphone market here is a perfect example of how we feel the need to be constantly updating. We're a nation of flash cars, materialism and gadgets; cycling fits in perfectly with that mindset.'

Because of one man, the aforementioned Lance Armstrong, several companies are enjoying their highest profits in years – Trek with its bikes, Giro with its helmets and Nike with its shoes and clothing. Giro promotes its top of the range helmet with the line 'Lance Wears It', Nike has a range of regalia marked with the insignia '10/2' (the date Armstrong was diagnosed with cancer) and the American is signed to Trek for life to promote its bikes. He is every marketer's dream come true – back from the dead to dominate probably the most demanding sports event in the world.

Cyling equipment is branded with the logo of the company that made it. Here the Nike 'swoosh' logo, which looks like a tick, is on these cycling shoes.

Cycling is also starting to have an effect on how people are conducting business. With all this focus on image, and the potential to express your financial status through the cost of your equipment, cycling has become the next moneymaking playground for those who have grown tired of golf.

A recent article in *The New York Times* documented the growing number of 50-year-old plus 'capitalists' who, while accumulating hundreds of kilometres a week on their custom-built bikes, use that time to network and negotiate. One subject, Randy Komisar of California, spoke of how he often arrives on a Monday morning greeted by stories of how five other top executives had spent the weekend on their bikes, quite literally wheeling and dealing.

'Cycling is the new golf,' says Sean Badenhorst, South African editor of *Bicycling* magazine.

In South Africa, Cycle Lab has large cycling clubs at both its branches and McLean says a business culture is certainly developing among some of its members. 'After a long cycle you'll see some guys meeting up and talking business over a coffee or an energy drink.'

'Cycling is the new golf,' says Sean Badenhorst, South African editor of *Bicycling* magazine. 'It's certainly a less frustrating way to spend three hours. While I don't think cycling will realistically replace golf as the next business networking

tool, it's giving the more fitness-conscious business people an alternative way to launch a business relationship.'

Just as a tailored suit and a pair of Italian shoes give off the right impression in the traditional business world, for the style-conscious cyclist, getting ready is more complicated than you might think. There is a certain *savoir-faire* attached to everything, from the length of your socks (long is currently in vogue) to whether or not it's acceptable to have a tool bag hanging beneath your R850 Sella San Marco saddle.

It should be noted though, that this kind of sensitivity belongs almost entirely to road cyclists. Mountain bikers are generally far less trendy and more relaxed. They enjoy getting themselves and their kit as dirty as possible and don't always shave their legs. In this world, mounties are the *über*sexuals.

But how is cycling, traditionally a white-dominated, European sport, being received by the black community? 'Interest is growing,' Badenhorst remarks. 'The good news is that a number of talented black cyclists here are now racing successfully at the top end of the sport.'

However, as McLean observes, it's going to take time to shake off certain perceptions of a bike that are the result of South Africa's past. 'Some black people still consider the bicycle to be the poor man's transport, but that's certainly changing.'

Cycling, in its rawest form, free of worldly envy and lust, is still a beautifully simple activity that acts as a great stress reliever, keeps you healthy and swells your self-esteem.

1 Why do many business people play golf with other business people?

2 According to the writer, what sport is now also being used as an opportunity to make business contacts?

3 The writer says that cycling is the 'fastest-growing sport in South Africa'. What is cycling being compared to in this phrase?

4 We are told that to non-cyclists, cycling equipment seems 'extravagantly expensive'. How does the adverb 'extravagantly' add meaning to the adjective 'expensive'?

5 What famous quotation is subtly referred to in paragraph 2?

6 We are told that Andrew McLean 'co-presents the magazine show *SuperCycling*'.
   a Do you think he presents this show by himself? Why do you say this?
   b Do you think this show deals with many different cycling topics in each programme or just one? Why do you say this?

7 Why does the writer say that Lance Armstrong is 'back from the dead'?

8 The word 'subject' has many meanings. In paragraph 7, is the word 'subject':
   a a grammatical term?
   b a word that means 'someone who is ruled over by a king'?
   c a synonym for 'topic'?
   d a word that means 'person being studied'?

9 a Explain the idiom 'wheeling and dealing'.
   b What does the writer mean when he says that executives that go cycling together are 'quite literally wheeling and dealing'?

10 The word 'capitalists' is in quotes to show that it was used in a different article, and because the writer of this article may not be comfortable with this term. What synonym with more positive connotations could the writer have used instead of using the word 'capitalists'?

11 What does it mean to race 'at the top end of the sport'?

12 Do the cyclists showing an attitude of *savoir faire*:
   a act like they know exactly how to present themselves?
   b act like they are going to a carnival?
   c act fairly to everybody they do business with?

13 Rewrite the following sentence in the past perfect.
   Interest is growing.

14 According to the writer of this article, are male mountain bikers or male road cyclists more sexy?

15 Do you think the purpose of this article is:
   a to invite and request?
   b to protest and complain?
   c to discuss and entertain?

16 a What slang word has the writer used in the title of his article?
   b Has he used this word to seem fashionable or to exclude readers?
   c If 'fit for a cycle' means 'ready to go for a cycle', what does 'fit for a bling' mean?

Style

A writer's style is the way that he/she writes. Here are some adjectives that could be used to describe someone's style of writing:

- descriptive – if the text is fill of adjectives and little details
- action-packed – if there is lots of physical action in the text
- dialogue-rich – if there is lots of direct speech in the text
- humorous – if the text is meant to make you laugh
- serious – if it is trying to deal with an important topic in an appropriate way
- reflective – if the writer is being very thoughtful and not argumentative
- discursive – if the writer is discussing a topic from more than one point of view
- polemical – if the writer is arguing for a specific point of view
- concise – if the writer gets to a point quickly
- long-winded – if the writer takes a long time to make a point
- anecdotal – if the writer tells lots of little stories as he/she writes
- cynical – if the writer does not seem to believe in anything but challenges and questions what people say
- satirical – if the writer is trying to show that something is ridiculous by writing ironically about it
- ridiculous – if you laugh at a text because it is silly, but it wasn't meant to be funny.

1   Use the most appropriate term from the list above to describe the style of each of the following extracts.

   a

   > Some people used to say that Dad had so many children that he couldn't keep track of them. Dad himself used to tell a story about one time when Mother went off and left him in charge at home. When Mother returned, she asked him if everything had run smoothly.
   >   'Didn't have any trouble except with that one over there,' he replied.
   >   'That's not one of ours, dear,' she said. 'He belongs next door.'

   b

   > I turn away from staring out the window. Outside the oval airplane window, a night sky jets soundlessly by. Inside is the sound of engines, of the tiny seat fans as they stir the stale air. Most of the overhead seat lights are off. Tiny airline blankets are tucked around the shoulders of some dozing passengers. Others read newspapers and magazines, smoke, or talk softly.

   c

   > The first to emerge was a young and highly indignant green mamba, reputedly the most deadly snake in Africa. I tried to pin him down with a fork but he wriggled free and fell off the table onto the floor. It was only then that I realised that although the others had had fled to the veranda and left the disaster to me, the D.C. had stayed on. The green mamba, in that irritating way that snakes have, with the whole of the room to choose from, wriggled straight towards the D.C., who remained rooted to the spot, his face going a rather interesting shade of blue.

2   For each of the extracts above, say whether the narrator (main storyteller) is using the past tense or the present tense.

Emotive language

Emotive language is language that is designed to make the listener or reader feel certain emotions. Here is a list of emotions that a person might want his/her intended audience to feel.

love   hate   hope   anger   respect   sorrow   bravery   desire

However, the person who uses emotive language does not usually mention these emotions; instead the person uses language that will inspire these emotions, often by using words with strong connotations. If the person wants to encourage positive feelings he/she uses words with positive connotations; if the person wants to encourage negative feelings he/she uses words with negative connotations.

1   Read the following extract from the children's story *The Witches* by Roald Dahl, where a very important witch is talking to a gathering of English witches about killing children. (The witch talks with a German accent, so the writer has repeated some letters and used 'v's instead of 'w's to show what her voice would actually sound like.)

'Children are rrree-volting!' screamed The Grand High Witch. 'Vee vill vipe them all avay! Vee vill scrrrub them off the face of the earth! Vee vill flush them down the drain!'

'Yes, yes!' chanted the audience. 'Wipe them away! Scrub them off the earth! Flush them down the drain!'

'Children are foul and filthy!' thundered The Grand High Witch.

'They are! They are!' chorused the English witches. 'They are foul and filthy!'

'Children are dirty and stinky!' screamed The Grand High Witch.

'Dirty and stinky!' cried the audience, getting more and more worked up.

'Children are smelling of dogs' drrroppings!' screeched The Grand High Witch.

'Pooooooo!' cried the audience. 'Pooooooo! Pooooooo! Pooooooo!'

'They are vurse than dog's droppings!' screeched The Grand High Witch. 'Dogs' droppings is smelling like violets and primroses compared with children!'

'Violets and primroses!' chanted the audience.

2   The Grand High Witch is an emotive speaker. What emotion is the Grand High Witch encouraging in her audience?

3   The Grand High Witch uses many words with negative connotations when she talks about children. Her words, which are often spelt incorrectly to indicate her strange pronunciation, are then repeated correctly by the audience. List all the words with negative connotations that the audience repeats.

4   Do you think the High Witch is stereotyping children or seeing them as a group of individuals?

5   Because the Grand High Witch's home language is German, she does not speak English correctly. She uses the wrong aspect of the verb 'smell'. Rewrite the following sentence using the simple aspect instead of the progressive aspect.
Dogs' droppings is smelling like violets and primroses compared with children!

Statements, commands and questions

Most English sentences are statements. A statement is a sentence that gives a piece of information. Sentences can also be questions (asking someone to do something) or they can be commands (telling someone to do something).

1 Are the sentences below statements, commands or questions?
   a What is your name?
   b My name is James Lebron.
   c What sport do you play?
   d I play basketball.
   e Can you jump very high?
   f Jump!
   g Pass it to me!
   h Thank the referee.

Sentences that are commands do not have nouns before the verbs. In fact, there is an invisible 'You' sitting in front of these statements. For example, 'Jump!' actually means 'You jump!' It is a rule of English that only 'you' (singular or plural) can be left out from the start of a sentence in this way.

2 Rewrite the following commands by inserting 'you' in the correct place.
   a Do it again!
   b Just pass the ball!
   c Aim for the hoop.
   d Try to score now!

The word 'order' is a synonym for 'command'. Both of these words have negative connotations because people do not like being told what to do. The word 'instruction' is similar in meaning but has neutral connotations.

3 Which of the following sentences can be called a command or order, and which can be called an instruction?
   a Do your homework now!
   b Water the seedlings after you have transplanted them.

Instructions do not usually have an exclamation mark at the end, while commands and orders often do.

Values and attitudes

People have different ideas about what is most important in life. We call these ideas their 'values'.

1 When choosing a career it is important to decide what values are most important to you. Put the following values into order, from the one that is most important to you to the one that is least important to you.
   - wealth
   - easiness
   - power
   - mobility
   - service to the community
   - free time to spend with friends and family
   - job security
   - stimulation
   - status
   - novelty
   - independence

2 What values/s are important to the following teenagers?

a

I want to be in charge and I want people to respect me. I want enough money to buy whatever car I like.

Vusi

b

I love my community. I want to help the people in my community stay healthy. I also want to have a steady job so I don't have to worry about running out of money.

Lerato

c

I want to travel. I don't like jobs that are too challenging.

Yvette

d

I want to do a job that is interesting, where you are dealing with new information all the time. I can't stand doing the same easy thing over and over again. I get so bored!

e

I do not want to take orders from anyone. Like Yvette, I like to travel.

James

Jenny

3 Of the jobs listed below, what one do you think would be most appropriate for the teenagers shown on the previous page?
a air hostess
b business person
c nurse
d driver of own transport truck
e producer of television documentaries

Values are ideas that we have deep inside us, so deep that often we don't even know they are there. But attitudes are the feelings we have towards certain things, and are based on our values. It is easier to feel what our attitudes are because they seem closer to the surface of our personalities, and we often talk about them. When you analyse someone's attitude towards something, first say if it is positive or negative, then add more details.

4 a What is Lerato's attitude to her community?
b What is Jenny's attitude to boredom?

Our attitudes towards something can change quickly, but our values usually change very slowly over time. For example, imagine that Yasmin was thinking about becoming an air hostess but then realised that she was scared of heights. Her attitude towards that career would have changed, but not her values.

5 What other jobs could Yvette do that involve travel but do not involve flying?

However, people's values do sometimes change over time. For example, imagine that Yvette worked on a cruise liner, and then later got married and had a baby.

6 What value might then become more important to her than mobility?

The terms 'point of view' and 'perspective' have a similar meaning to the word 'attitude'. But if you are asked about someone's point of view or perspective you should give much more detail.

7 a What values do the road cyclists described in Activity E have?
b What attitudes would these cyclists have towards cheap, low-quality equipment?

People have very different attitudes towards America. Some people think it is the 'Land of the Free', others dislike it because they feel it bullies less powerful countries into doing what it wants. Other people think that Americans have become too materialistic and lost sight of what is important in life.

8 What is your attitude towards America?

Propaganda using persuasive and manipulative language

Persuasive language is language used by people who are trying to make you do what they want you to do. Advertisements often use persuasive language.

Political advertisements are called 'propaganda'. Governments, or their political opponents, often try to influence people's attitudes, particularly before a war or an election. To do this they use propaganda.

The following posters are examples of propaganda that the British government used during the First World War, which was called 'The Great War' at that time. They use some basic persuasive techniques that you need to be able to identify.

1 Look at the first poster. It is trying to persuade young men to sign up for the army.
   a How has the artist used the expressions on the faces of the soldiers to create good connotations about the army?
   b How has the artist drawn the men's bodies to create good connotations about being in the army?
   c Does the poster have statements or commands on it? Why?
   d Why does it use the noun 'boys' instead of 'men'?
   e Why does it use the adverb 'today'?

When someone is trying to be too persuasive or secretly persuasive we say that that person is 'manipulative'.

> The word 'persuasive' has neutral connotations, but the word 'manipulative' has negative connotations.

2 Look at the second poster. It is trying to manipulate young men to join the army.
   a Is the scene showing a possible situation in the young man's past, his present, or his future?
   b What do you think a father would like to be able to say to his children when asked this question?
   c How does this poster make young men feel afraid?
   d Why do we call this poster 'manipulative' rather than 'persuasive'?
   e The word 'you' is printed in bold capital letters. How does this add impact to the message of the poster?

3 Look at the following two propaganda posters on this page. Which one uses a positive image to attract young men and which one uses a negative image to scare young men?

4 Explain how language and a picture are used in the bottom left propaganda poster to persuade young men to join the army.

5 Women often try to stop their boyfriends, husbands and sons joining the army and going to war because they are scared their men will be killed. How does the bottom right poster stereotype British women in order to manipulate them?

Alternatives to stereotyping

Women's magazines usually contain advertisements that show slim young women. This is true even in Africa, where plump women have traditionally been perceived as happy and healthy. This is because the fashion industry is dominated by Europe and America, and in these countries the stereotype of a beautiful woman is a thin woman.

The famous doll called Barbie epitomises America's idea of a beautiful woman.

An alternative way of doing something is way of doing something that is different to the normal way.

These days some South African magazines try to represent some real women as an alternative to always showing pictures of unusually thin women. For example, on the opposite page is an advertisement that appeared in *True Love* magazine.

1   What products are being advertised in this advertisement?
2   How is the model's body different to most models?
3   How is the model's facial expression different to most models?

On a different page readers are told that:
Hip Hop's first lady, Relo Tsotetsi, is the face of Donna-Claire's new range, Love it! The collection, designed for a voluptuous woman, is created to suit current fashion trends that reflect a modern and fun-loving woman.

4   What celebrity has been paid to model these products? What band is she part of?

The following names are famous brands in the fashion industry: Dolce & Gabana, Prada, Gucci, Chanel, Hilton Weiner, Jenny Button and Daniel Hechter. Many people who buy these products buy them so they can feel special and sophisticated. Donna-Claire is also a brand name, and 'Love it!' is a particular range of clothes produced by this brand.

5   In what way is the name 'Love it!' an alternative to the sophisticated-sounding names usually chosen by the fashion industry?

love*it*
SIZES 16–24
by Donna-Claire

Strappy top R190
Tiered skirt R250

V-neck top R210
Cropped pants R250

Love it as worn by Relo from Skwatta Kamp is exclusive to Donna-Claire and available in selected stores. Contact us on 0860 104764.

Adverbs of limitation

There are a number of adverbs that modify a sentence by excluding other possibilities. The most important of these is 'only', which is shown used in a short dialogue below.

Mother (*angrily*): Where have you been walking?
Daughter: I walked only up the hill.

In this example, the adverb 'only' shows that the daughter went to one place: the top of the hill. The daughter has used it to emphasise that she did not go anywhere else.

When the adverb 'only' is put in a different place in a sentence it has a different effect, as shown by the dialogue below.

Father (*suspiciously*): You are meant to be training for your cycling race. Why were you walking and pushing your bike up the hill? Tell me the truth now. I don't want excuses.
Son: I only walked up the hill. I cycled all the rest of the way home.

In this second dialogue the son is using 'only' to emphasise that he cycled almost all the journey.

1 Insert 'only' into the following sentences.
   a I don't do much exercise; I walk.
   b I don't buy cheap clothes; I buy brand names that I trust. However, I buy vegetables from the stalls at the station, so I save money that way.

The adverbs 'just', 'simply' and 'merely' are used in a similar way to 'only'. However, when we use these words as synonyms for 'only' we must remember that we can use them only in front of verbs, and that the adverb 'just' is used only in informal English.

2 Insert the adverb in brackets into these sentences.
   a I walked along to the shops. (just)
   b I let down the hem to make this skirt longer. (simply)
   c I asked whether you wanted some coffee. (merely)
   d I wanted to help. (only)

3 Nike, a company that makes sports equipment uses a particular slogan. This slogan appears with the Nike logo in picture A, and it appears on a banner alongside a running track in picture B.
   a What is Nike's slogan?
   b What message is this slogan communicating about people and exercise?
   c How is the phrase 'Just do it!' different from the phrase 'Do it!'

B

A

American English versus British English

Although English is spoken in many places around the world, it is spoken slightly differently from place to place.

American English started out as British English, but after centuries of being separated from the British by the Atlantic Ocean, Americans developed their language in a different way. British English also changed in its own way over time, so now there are many differences in vocabulary between these two varieties of English. For example, Americans call people who are African in terms of their racial origin 'negros', while British people call them 'black people'.

1   In the table alongside, match the British English nouns on the left with the American English synonyms on the right.

British English nouns	American English nouns
autumn	sidewalk
pharmacy	fall
pavement	drugstore

Americans also have some of their own idioms. Many of these use the words 'cent', 'dime' or 'dollar', which are words for different amounts of money in America.

2   Match the American idioms in the left-hand column to the explanations in the right-hand column.

American idiom	Explanation
to give your five cents worth	to tell a secret
to talk a dime a dozen	to feel very good
to feel like a million dollars	to talk very fast
to spill the beans	to say what you think

American spelling is sometimes different to British spelling, as indicated in the table alongside. (South African spelling follows the rules of British English.)

British spelling	American spelling
aeroplane	airplane
favourite	favorite
metre	meter
modelled	modeled

> When putting a verb into the past tense, or creating a regular participle to show the perfect aspect, Americans do not double the last consonant.

3   Is the following advertisement an American advertisement or a British advertisement? How do you know?

A match

A match

Homonyms and homophones

Homonyms

There are some words in English that are spelt the same way as one another, and are even pronounced in the same way, but which mean completely different things. We call such pairs of words homonyms. For example, the word 'match' could be a noun meaning a game played by two opponents, or it could be a noun meaning the little stick with the flammable tip that you strike against rough paper when you want to light a fire. The fact that these words are spelt the same and sound the same is just a coincidence.

1   Match the words in column B with their meanings in column A and C.

Column A	Column B		Column C
object for creating wind	a	just	expensive
fungi found on the surface of food or other objects	b	beat	young cow/bull
win against	c	fan	group of people who get together for a particular purpose
apartment	d	dear	recently
stop living	e	light	abbreviation for 'fanatic'
only	f	mould	shape you pour liquid into, before it sets into something hard
thick wooden stick	g	club	level
party after a funeral	h	die	rhythm/syllable
kind, sort	i	flat	person who is ruled over by a king or queen
not dark	j	wake	record the number of things
topic	k	calf	object with numbers on, for throwing in games of chance
title of a certain kind of nobleman, male equivalent of a 'countess'	l	scale	not heavy
muscle on the lower part of the leg	m	type	stop sleeping
beloved	n	count	object you weigh things on
climb	o	subject	metal letters

2   Complete each of these sentences with one of the words from column B.
   a   Please don't walk on the kitchen floor; I've _____ washed it and it is still wet.
   b   He lives in a _____ with a view over the city.
   c   There is something wrong with that _____; every time I throw it I get a 'one'.

3   a   The cartoon on the right is meant to be funny. What word, which has two meanings, is the key to understanding this cartoon?
   b   What two meanings does this word have in this cartoon?

Homophones

There are some words in English that are pronounced in the same way, but are
spelt differently and mean completely different things. We call such pairs of words
homophones. For example, the noun 'eye' means the thing in your head that you see
with, but the word 'I' is a way of referring to yourself. The fact that these words sound the
same is just a coincidence.

4   Match the words in column A with their descriptions in column B.

Column A	Column B
a dear	back part of foot
b soul	something you see, or your ability to see
c heart	spirit
d peek	leather that is not smooth
e lore	part of your body that pumps your blood
f heel	game where you hit a little white ball into a far-away hole
g sight	part of a plant that is underground
h suede	not old
i golf	a verb meaning to make something higher
j new	knowledge, collected wisdom on a particular topic
k root	secret look at something
l raise	beloved

5   Match the words in column A with their descriptions in column B.

Column A	Column B
a deer	flat bottom part of a shoe
b sole	top of a mountain
c hart	a verb, the past tense of 'know', meaning to understand and remember something
d peak	rule
e law	way to get from somewhere to somewhere else
f heal	male deer
g site	beams
h swayed	model of car made for a famous German brand
i Golf	place (either physical or on the internet)
j knew	a verb, the past tense of 'sway', meaning to move gently from side to side
k route	antelope
l rays	a verb meaning to make a sick person healthy

6   Complete each of these sentences with the appropriate word from the tables in 4 and 5.
   a   When the wind blew, the trees _____ in the wind.
   b   The mountain _____ was covered in clouds.
   c   He did everything to save his marriage; he threw himself into it _____ and
       _____.
   d   I was researching where to buy running shoes with spikes for extra grip, and I
       found the information on the club's web_____.

Jargon and technical language

Technical language is language that is used in specific fields of work. When other people hear a specialist using the advanced words that he/she uses in the workplace, these listeners are usually either impressed or irritated. They could be impressed because the person speaking sounds so intelligent and educated, or they could be irritated because it is impolite to use complicated words in front of people that do not understand them. Technical language that is too complicated is called 'jargon'. The term 'jargon' has negative connotations.

1   Look at the advertisement below. What phrase is written in technical language?
2   Do you think this phrase is an example of unnecessary jargon or do you think it is technical language that has been used for a good reason?

Activity F

The following article appeared in the British magazine *Touch*, which is written for urban British youth. Read the magazine article then answer the questions on page 110.

When sports giant Nike offered the trainer-junkies at *Touch* the trip of a lifetime to the company's US headquarters, how could we refuse? Especially when we get an exclusive preview of their amazing new Lebron James III basketball shoe ...

They would have you believe that it's all about the track. They'd have you believe that should you take a peek into the heart of Nike you'll see that the company comes complete with a set of running spikes. But here, if you go inside Nike, you get to know a different truth. And the truth is this: no matter how much they praise the lore of the track, inside the world of Nike, basketball is king.

To actually get inside Nike you fly to Seattle. Situated a five-hour drive below Seattle lies the state of Oregon. Its capital, Portland, is outdoorsy and quaint, in a glad-I'm-only-here-for-a-day kinda way. But 20 minutes outside Portland, in Beaverton, sits the HQ for the world's biggest sporting company.

'BASKETBALL IS THE COMPANY'S HEARTBEAT. IT'S WHERE NIKE STRUCK GOLD WITH URBAN CULTURE.'

Their Swoosh logo is up there with the Coca Cola Wave and McDonald's Golden Arches as one of the world's most recognisable corporate brand symbols. And their wealth is ... well, let's just say the accountants are happy.

The enormous Nike complex houses several high-tech buildings named after Nike's favourite sons and daughters. There's the Michael Jordan building, for example, the Lance Armstrong, the Ronaldo. Within their walls lie an Olympic-size swimming pool, basketball courts, running track, library, art gallery and research laboratories.

Right now, I'm sitting in the Tiger Woods building. Laid out before me is a dazzling array of Nike footwear: the Uptempo circa '06, the Air Max in various guises and the king of them all, the Air Jordan, still looking lovely after all these years.

As Kris Akerman, Nike's Global Basketball Director, speaks, there is one pair of kicks that I can't take my eyes off. In the midst of all this super-advanced Air soles, carbon fibre, heel TPU, sneaker jargon I'm transfixed by the startling sight of the Nike Bruin, one of Nike's first basketball shoes. Conceived in 1974, it remains one of Nike's best-looking shoes. It's a classic suede number that's high on style and easily stands the test of time.

Nike may profess to a love of running, and they may dabble in other sports – tennis, football, golf – but basketball is where it's at. It's the company's heartbeat. Their best ad campaigns and sneaker designs, the most press garnered, their biggest-selling shoes, all derive from basketball. It's where Nike struck gold with urban culture.

The cynic in me wants to know whether Nike really cares about the sport and those who play it. A healthy debate ensues, and the outcome: Nike loves basketball.

And nowhere is that more on show than on the face of Ken Link, the man who's designed the sexy Lebron James III sneaker. This self-proclaimed mad scientist could talk all day about sneakers. In minute detail he'll explain the process of designing and building a sneaker for an elite athlete. It's riveting stuff, seriously. What really gets me juiced is when he spills the secrets of Nike's success – something he does without even knowing. Ken talks about watching Lebron in action, how Lebron elevates, how he gets around the court in seconds. Talking a dime a dozen about Lebron's power and pace, Ken lets slip that his ultimate aim is to provide the athlete with a shoe that'll help him 'control his body and improve his game by a few millimeters, a couple of inches here or there. Because at that elite level, that's the difference between a block and a basket. It's the difference between being another player or an MVP [most valuable player]. It's the difference between winning and losing.'

'MY ULTIMATE AIM IS TO DESIGN A SHOE THAT'LL HELP THE ATHLETE TO IMPROVE HIS GAME BY A COUPLE OF INCHES HERE OR THERE.' – KEN LINK, NIKE FOOTWEAR DESIGNER

Yeah, the aesthetics are cool. The big love afforded by the streets is nice n' all. And Nike admits they really do enjoy watching the balance sheets scale new heights; heck, this is a business after all. But beyond that, pushing the boundaries of sports technology is where it's at for Nike. The sports stars who wear their apparel have to transcend their sport or at least die trying, otherwise there's no point to it. And that leaves a mark on me like on branded cattle. The mark says 'Just do it'. I just did. And now I'm a believer.

1 a In the title of the article, does the '+' symbol stand for 'plus' or 'and'?
   b We would normally use the words 'heart' and 'soul' together. Why does this title use the spelling 'sole' instead of the spelling 'soul'?

2 In the introductory paragraph, why is the word '*Touch*' in italics?

3 Does the writer use emotive language in the introductory paragraph? Quote some words to support your answer.

4 The writer says that the people who work at his magazine are 'trainer-junkies'?
   a In this context, what is a trainer?
   b What is a standard English synonym for the slang term 'junkie'?
   c The term 'trainer-junkie' is a metaphor. In this metaphor, what is being compared to what and why?

5 Based on the introductory paragraph, what values do you think are important to the writer of this article?

6 Nike used to concentrate on producing athletics equipment. What sport has now become more important to this company?

7 a In paragraph 2, the writer says that Portland is 'outdoorsy and quaint'. Both these adjectives have positive connotations. But the writer has mixed emotions about Portland. How does he communicate these mixed emotions?
   b Does this show that he comes from a rural context or an urban context?
   c Why does the writer hyphenate 'I'm-glad-I'm-only here-for-a-day'?

8 In paragraph 6, the writer uses the slang term 'kicks'. Based on how this word is used in its context, as well as thinking about its root meaning, what do you think this slang term means?

9 a What does it mean when the writer says that the make of shoe called the Nike Bruin stands 'the test of time'?
   b Is the Nike Bruin made out plastic or leather? How do you know?

10 In paragraph 6 the writer uses the term 'jargon' instead of the term 'technical language'. Why?

11 What do the following abbreviations stand for?
    a HQ (paragraph 2)
    b high-tech (paragraph 4)
    c ad (paragraph 7)

12 What abbreviation, used later in the article, is the writer unsure whether the readers will know?

13 a Rewrite the following sentence from paragraph 8 in the past tense:
       The cynic in me wants to know whether Nike really cares about the sport and those who play it.
    b Why is most of the article written in the present tense when it is clear that the writer's trip to the USA is over?

14 The writer tells us that Nike invited representatives of *Touch* magazine to visit the company. However, he tries not to give a one-sided view of the company in his article. Would his style best be described as 'discursive', 'polemical' or 'satirical'?

15 a In paragraph 9, the writer says that Ken Link is 'talking a dime a dozen'. Why does the British writer use this American idiom?
    b Is the word 'millimeters' spelt in the British way or the American way in this article? Why?

16 a What goddess is the company 'Nike' named after?

b Why is this name appropriate, viewed in the light of the aims stated by the company's scientist, Ken Link?

17 In paragraph 9, do most of the words have positive connotations or negative connotations?

18 In paragraph 9 the writer says that listening to the scientist talk about designing and building a sneaker is 'riveting stuff'. How do we know he is not being ironic?

19 In the final paragraph, does the writer:

a stereotype the company Nike as a business that is only interested in making money?

b stereotype the company Nike as an industry that is only interested in helping sportspeople play better?

c not stereotype the company, and instead represent the company Nike as being interested in both profits and helping sportspeople play better?

20 In the final paragraph the writer says that 'The sports stars who wear their apparel have to transcend their sport or at least die trying'. In this sentence the writer is choosing his words so as to refer to a quotation of a famous American singer. Who is this singer and what is the quotation that the writer is making a reference to?

21 The writer quotes the Nike slogan 'Just do it' in the final paragraph.

a Is this slogan a statement, a question or a command?

b What attitude towards exercise is embodied by this slogan?

c How does encouraging this attitude help Nike to sell their products?

22 In the final paragraph the writer quotes the Nike slogan 'Just do it'. Then he writes, 'I just did.'

a In the Nike slogan, does the adverb 'just' mean 'only' or 'recently'?

b In the sentence that follows this slogan, does the adverb 'just' mean 'only' or 'recently'?

c In the second sentence 'I just did', what helps us to understand that 'just' means 'recently'?

23 The term 'believer' is normally used in a religious context. Why has the writer chosen to use it here?

Exercise 61

Polysemes

When we *drain* water out of some cooked noodles the water goes down the *drain*.

There are some words in English that are pronounced in the same way as one another, and spelt in the same way as one another, but, unlike homonyms, their different meanings are clearly related to one another. We call such pairs of words polysemes. Polysemes have similar meanings because they came from the same root word but then developed different meanings over time.

The noun 'smoke' and the verb 'smoke' are a pair of polysemes. The noun 'smoke' refers to the cloud that is given off when something burns. The verb 'smoke' refers to the action of giving off this cloud, which could result from a fire or a person with a cigarette. Clearly these two words come from the same root as they have related meanings. Because they are also spelt the same and sound the same they are called polysemes. Similarly the noun 'drain' and the verb 'drain' have similar meanings. The noun 'drain' refers to the system of pipes that carry water away. The verb 'drain' refers to the action of removing water from something by letting it run out of pipes, holes and so on.

A pair of polysemes are not always different parts of speech. For example, 'look' can mean 'try to see' or 'look' can mean 'appear'. In both of these situations the word is a verb but the meanings of these verbs differ. Similarly the adjective 'noble' can mean 'born into a high position in society' or it can mean 'moral, selfless and virtuous'. These words are linked because people used to believe that high-born people acted in a moral and virtuous way.

1 Match the words in column B with their meanings in column A and C.

Column A	Column B	Column C
front of head where the eyes, nose and mouth are	a trainer	piece of paper giving a person permission to enter somewhere
hit	b icon	well-made
goal	c pass	push
kind, well-intentioned	d face	symbol of an era
go past something	e press	point something at something else
media that use the printed word	f aim	person who trains someone else in a sport or a skill
outgoing and ready to take risks	g strike	using thick lines
hollow cylinder	h good	group of lions
picture of religious figure, painted on wood (common in Greek orthodox and Russian orthodox churches)	i tube	stopping work temporarily in protest against employers
self-respect and honour	j bold	train system that uses underground tunnels
sports shoe	k pride	to look in a specific direction, or to be confronted with a specific problem

2 Write down the meanings of the words in italics. Use the context of these words to help to decide on their meanings.

   a The *strike* lasted three days, and then the employer decided to give the workers a small raise, as long as they returned to work immediately.

   b He is a *good* man and regularly attends mosque.

   c Ned is very interested in the design of a *trainer*; he is conscious of small differences in style.

Separating the base verb from auxiliary verbs and participle suffixes

When we read a multiword verb it can be difficult to spot the base verb. The base verb in a multiword verb indicates the core action or state of being.

The term 'base verb' is a grammatical term that refers to how a word functions in a sentence. The term 'core verb' refers to the meaning of the word.

Look at the following sentences.

I am looking at you.

The verb in the above sentence is a multiword verb that is made up of two words: 'am' and 'looking'. The participle 'looking' contains the base verb and the core meaning of the verb, which is 'look'. It also shows that the verb is in the progressive aspect. The verb 'am' is an auxiliary verb that shows that the verb is in the present tense.

I have looked at you often.

The verb in the above sentence is a multiword verb that is made up of two words: 'have' and 'looked'. The participle 'looked' contains the base verb and the core meaning of the verb, which is 'look'. It also shows that the verb is in the perfect aspect. The verb 'have' is an auxiliary verb that shows that the verb is in the present tense.

You should practise finding the base verb (showing the core meaning of the verb) in amongst the auxiliary verbs and the participle suffixes such as 'ed' and 'ing'.

1   What is the base verb in each of the following sentences?
   a   He is looking at the crocodiles in the river.
   b   We were striking for better pay.
   c   He has walked a long way.
   d   He had torn the paper into two pieces.
   e   We have kept his secret.
   f   She has had a headache for three days.
   g   We have been to the station already.

2   Fill the missing words into the following explanation.
   We call the verbs that come before any participles or before the verb containing the base verb 'auxiliary verbs'. An auxiliary _____ (a) gives tense to a multiword verb when the verbs that follow do not. Therefore auxiliary verbs are finite verbs that come in front of non-finite verbs. The verbs 'am', 'is', 'are', 'was' and '_____' (b) can be auxiliary verbs, but only when used in front of a participle showing the progressive aspect. When they are not being used as progressive auxiliaries they are just normal finite verbs that stand alone. The verbs 'have', 'has' and 'had' can be auxiliary verbs, but only when used in front of a participle showing the _____ (c) aspect. When these verbs are not being used as perfect auxiliaries they are just normal finite verbs that stand alone.

There are other auxiliary verbs that influence the meaning of the sentence. These are discussed on pages 159–169, and pages 212–215.

Regular verbs in the present tense and the perfect-progressive aspect

People sometimes use perfect-progressive verbs, although these are not common. These are verbs that have two aspects: the perfect aspect and the progressive aspect. When these aspects are used together they give the impression that we expect something to change although it has been going on for a while.

When we change a regular verb into the present perfect progressive we use the present-tense form of the verb 'have' that matches the subject, then we add the word 'been', then we add the base form of the of the core verb and put 'ing' on the end.

This table shows how to change the regular verb 'look' from the present simple to the present perfect progressive.

The verb 'to look'			
		Present tense	
		Simple aspect	Perfect-progressive aspect
First person singular:	I	look	have been looking
Second person singular:	you	look	have been looking
Third person singular:	he/she/it	looks	has been looking
First person plural:	we	look	have been looking
Second person plural:	you	look	have been looking
Third person plural:	they	look	have been looking

1 Change the following sentences from the present simple to the present perfect progressive.
   a I look everywhere for my father.
   b You look at that young man very often.
   c James looks at the car's engine.
   d We look for the needle on the floor.
   e You look deeply into each other's eyes.
   f They look out the window.

2 Answer the questions below using the same pattern as in this example.

   a Do you often look for your mother in the shebeen? (Yes, recently I …)
   b Does Ms Tekateka look at your homework every day? (Yes, recently Ms Tekateka …)
   c Do they look in their postbox every morning? (Yes, recently they …)

Irregular verbs in the present tense and the perfect-progressive aspect

When we change an irregular verb into the present perfect progressive we use the same pattern as with regular verbs. We insert a present-tense form of the verb 'have' that matches the subject, then we add the word 'been', then we add the base form of the core verb and put 'ing' on the end. We often use this construction when we talk about something that has been going on for a while but which we expect to change.

This table shows how to change the irregular verb 'be' from the present simple to the present perfect progressive.

The verb 'to be'			
		Present tense	
		Simple aspect	Perfect-progressive aspect
First person singular:	I	am	have been being
Second person singular:	you	are	have been being
Third person singular:	he/she/it	is	has been being
First person plural:	we	are	have been being
Second person plural:	you	are	have been being
Third person plural:	they	are	have been being

1   For each of these pairs of sentences change the first sentence from the present simple to the present perfect progressive.
   a   Ewetse is violent this evening. (But he will be embarrassed in the morning.)
   b   We are unfair to him. (But now we will be nice to him.)
   c   He is a brat. (But he will change when he becomes older.)

This table shows how to change the irregular verb 'have' from the present simple to the present perfect progressive.

The verb 'to have'			
		Present tense	
		Simple aspect	Perfect-progressive aspect
First person singular:	I	have	have been having
Second person singular:	you	have	have been having
Third person singular:	he/she/it	has	has been having
First person plural:	we	have	have been having
Second person plural:	you	have	have been having
Third person plural:	they	have	have been having

2   For each of the pairs of sentences below change the first sentence from the present simple to the present perfect progressive.
   a   I have a good time at school. (This is because I have met many new friends recently.)
   b   Geoffrey has a haircut every month. (So that he can look professional for his new job.)
   c   They have breakfast before 6 o' clock. (So that they can catch the early train.)

Regular verbs in the past tense and the perfect-progressive aspect

When we change a regular verb into the past perfect progressive we use the past-tense form of the verb 'have' that matches the subject, which is always 'had'. Then we add the word 'been', and then we add the base form of the core verb and put 'ing' on the end. We often use these verbs when we talk about something that had been going on for a while before it stopped, or before some other thing happened.

This table shows how to change the regular verb 'look' from the past simple to the past perfect progressive.

The verb 'to look'			
		Present tense	
		Simple aspect	**Perfect-progressive aspect**
First person singular:	I	looked	had been looking
Second person singular:	you	looked	had been looking
Third person singular:	he/she/it	looked	had been looking
First person plural:	we	looked	had been looking
Second person plural:	you	looked	had been looking
Third person plural:	they	looked	had been lookig

1 Change the following sentences from the past simple to the past perfect progressive.
   a I looked in my suitcase.
   b She looked in the mirror.
   c We looked for you everywhere.

2 For each of these pairs of sentences change the first sentence from the past simple to the past perfect progressive.
   a I looked for your name on the list of results. (Then I realised you had not written the examination.)
   b You looked for his face at the party. (Then you remembered he was in Johannesburg.)
   c She looked in her cupboard for the dress. (Then she remembered she had outgrown it.)
   d We looked for mussels on the rocks. (Then we remembered there had been a red tide recently and they would not be edible.)
   e They look up at the stars. (Then they found the Southern Cross and worked out which direction was home.)

Irregular verbs in the past tense and the perfect-progressive aspect

The irregular verbs follow the same pattern as the regular verbs when they change from the past simple to the past perfect progressive. We use 'had', then 'been', and then we add the base form of the core verb and put 'ing' on the end.

This table shows how to change the irregular verb 'be' from the past simple to the past perfect progressive.

The verb 'to be'			
		Present tense	
		Simple aspect	Perfect-progressive aspect
First person singular:	I	was	had been being
Second person singular:	you	were	had been being
Third person singular:	he/she/it	was	had been being
First person plural:	we	were	had been being
Second person plural:	you	were	had been being
Third person plural:	they	were	had been being

1   Change the verbs in brackets from the past simple to the past perfect progressive.
   a   Before my mother arrived, we (were) lazy.
   b   Before I realised his father was HIV-positive, I (was) very flippant about people with AIDS.

This table shows how to change the irregular verb 'have' from the past simple to the past perfect progressive.

The verb 'to be'			
		Present tense	
		Simple aspect	Perfect-progressive aspect
First person singular:	I	had	had been having
Second person singular:	you	had	had been having
Third person singular:	he/she/it	had	had been having
First person plural:	we	had	had been having
Second person plural:	you	had	had been having
Third person plural:	they	had	had been having

2   Change the verbs in brackets from the past simple to the past perfect progressive.
   a   Before the doctor arrived, he (had) convulsions.
   b   Before the teacher walked into the classroom, my friend (had) her sandwiches as a morning snack.
   c   Before they started to argue, they (had) a romantic walk through the veld.

Finite verbs and real sentences

The word 'finite' means limited. Finite verbs are limited in terms of the subjects they can be matched up with, and in terms of tense. Non-finite verbs are verbs that can be used together with any subject or in either tense.

If a verb is finite in terms of tense, then it will also be finite in terms of the subjects it can be matched up with. So, to find out if a verb is finite, all we really need to do is ask 'Does it belong in a particular tense?'

1 Do the following verbs belong in a particular tense? If your answer is yes, which tense do they belong in: past or present?
   a trains
   b looking
   c torn
2 Which of the verbs in 1 a–c are finite verbs?

Labelling verbs is not useful unless it helps us to use English better. So, how does knowing whether a verb is finite or non-finite help us to speak and write better? It helps us decide which group of words is a sentence, and which is not a sentence. This allows us to structure and punctuate sentences properly.

A sentence:
- begins with a capital letter
- contains a finite verb
- has a subject (unless the verb implies a second-person subject)
- contains other words, if necessary, so that the sentence makes sense
- ends with a full stop (or other punctuation mark that may be used to end a sentence, as discussed on page 152).

3 For each of the following groups of words, say whether it is a full sentence or not. Think about the words and the punctuation. If it is not a sentence, explain why not.
   a Dancing.
   b I looked for you yesterday.
   c Flying to London.
   d Exploded.
   e I am inviting you to the party.
   f Justin flew to New York
   g Smoke your cigarettes.
   h No smoking.
   i Died and gone to heaven.
   j she is coming.
   k Come with us.

When a group of words does not have a finite verb we call it a 'phrase'.

4 Rewrite the phrases from question 3 as sentences.

In certain special cases some professional writers use full stops after phrases, but you should avoid doing this until the rest of your text is flawless. Otherwise it will seem like a mistake and not a special effect.

Sentences, clauses and phrases

A simple sentence has only one finite verb. Some sentences have more than one finite verb.

1   Which of the following sentences are simple sentences?
    a   Many people around the world do not like the materialistic values of American and British people.
    b   Most Londoners have a Christian background, but some Londoners have a Muslim background.
    c   Some young British Muslims are very angry because Britain helped America go to war against Iraq, which is a predominantly Muslim country.
    d   'Al-Qaʾeda' is the name of an international Muslim terrorist group.
    e   A few members of Al-Qaʾeda have strapped bombs to their own bodies and then they have blown up trains or busses, as well as themselves.
    f   Bombers who blow themselves up are called 'suicide bombers'.

When a sentence has more than one finite verb, this means that it can be divided into more than one clause, as in the example below.

first clause	conjunction	second clause
Most Londoners have a Christian background,	but	some Londoners have a Muslim background.

A clause is a group of words that could stand as a sentence if they were separated from other words by a capital letter and a full stop. When two clauses are joined together in one sentence they are usually joined by a conjunction. A conjunction is normally considered part of the clause that it introduces. (However, if that clause were to stand alone as a sentence, that conjunction would need to be removed.)

2   Identify the clauses in the following sentences.
    a   Most Muslims were shocked by the London bombings and they disagreed with the actions of the bombers.
    b   Some Christians think that all Muslims are evil although most are good and peaceful people.
    c   Christians do not believe in suicide because it shows a lack of faith in power of God to make things better.

A phrase is a word or group of words that does not have a finite verb.

3   Identify the phrases in the following sentences.
    a   After the bombing, the tube trains stopped running.
    b   Many Londoners were trapped underground, fearing death.
    c   Squashed under my shoe, the ice cream no longer looked enticing.

Putting paragraphs in order

When you write a text you should divide your information into paragraphs. Paragraphs are made up of one or more sentences about a particular point. You should always arrange your paragraphs in a logical order.

1   The following article was written for the British newspaper *The Telegraph*. The paragraphs have been jumbled up here. Decide in what order these paragraphs would have appeared in the original article, and then write down the letters of each paragraph or group of paragraphs to show this order.

Al-Qa'eda brings terror to the heart of London

a   The co-ordinated attacks were being compared to the train bombings in Madrid last year which killed 190 people. There were fears that the bus explosion, which left 13 people dead in Tavistock Square, was also the work of a suicide bomber.

b   The Tube was shut down and bus services in the centre of the city halted, causing widespread travel disruption. Mainline stations were also closed for much of the day. In the immediate aftermath of the attacks, Jack Straw, the Foreign Secretary, said the explosions 'bore all the hallmarks' of al-Qa'eda.

c   The attacks were the worst terrorist attack on British soil since the bombing of Flight 103 over Lockerbie in 1989, which killed 270 people. The Queen, 'deeply shocked', sent a message to victims and relatives and Tony Blair urged defiance of the bombers who were trying to 'cow' the nation.

d   Three terrorist bombs ripped through London Underground trains during the morning rush-hour on Thursday, July 7

and a fourth destroyed a double-decker bus, killing at least 52 people and wounding more than 700 others.

e   MI5 and Scotland Yard's anti-terrorist branch have consistently said that an attack on London, or anywhere else in the country, was inevitable and that the only question was when it would happen.

Newspaper articles often use very short paragraphs because they set these paragraphs in thin columns. However, most other texts would use longer paragraphs than those used in newspaper articles.

Ordering sentences within paragraphs

Paragraphs are made up of one or more sentences that deal with one main idea. Paragraphs usually have between one and five sentences, although a paragraph may be longer if it is still dealing with one main idea.

Good paragraphs usually have a topic sentence that summarises the main idea of that paragraph. The rest of the sentences give information that supports this main idea. The topic sentence does not have to be the first sentence in a paragraph, but it often is.

Paragraphs that are made up of only one sentence either do not contain supporting information, or have added supporting information into the topic sentence by using a sub-clause or additional phrase.

1   Reorganise the sentences in the following paragraphs, which come from some of the texts already used in this book but have been jumbled up.

   a   (Ironically, it was Cleveland who, as Governor of the State of New York, had earlier vetoed a bill by the New York legislature to contribute $50 000 to the building of the base.)
       On October 28, 1886, the Statue of Liberty was dedicated by President Grover Cleveland in front of thousands of spectators.

   b   William Ged invented a cheaper way of printing.
       Moveable type was expensive.
       So instead of printing with the expensive movable type and wearing it down, Ged printed with a solid metal sheet of type.
       This solid sheet of type was later called a 'stereotype'.
       He made a page of movable type, and then he took a mould of this page.
       Then he cast this page in metal.
       When the letters on the stamps got worn down, the printers had to buy more.

   c   Hope for the future lies in the resilience of these women, in their ability to keep their sense of humour, and their dignity in the face of hardship.
       To refer to the realities of oppression during the political turmoil of the 1980s was daring and risky.
       After 12 years of freedom, the same women are at the same taxi rank, toiling to provide for their children – children still threatened by hunger, their fathers still absent or abusive.
       Today the play has lost some of its shock factor, but none of its relevance.
       Then, the women took a stand against the injustice of apartheid; today the stand is against social injustice.

2   Identify the topic sentences in your answers to 1 a–c.

Activity G

The article on page 123 was published by *The Telegraph* on the same day as the article on page 120. It deals with the same topic, but from a different angle.

Read the article and answer the questions that follow.

1 In paragraph 1, is the word 'train' a verb meaning 'teach' or a noun meaning 'line of carriages linked together and pulled along tracks by a locomotive'?
2 Give a synonym for the word 'blast', as it is used in paragraph 1.
3 What is the base verb in the following clause?
a blast tore through one of the carriages
4 In paragraph 2, the writers used the past perfect progressive tense in the multiword verb 'had been standing'. Why was it more appropriate to use the past perfect progressive in this context than, for example, the past perfect 'had stood' or the past progressive 'were standing'?
5 In paragraph 2, do the following words act as a sentence, a clause or a phrase?
crushed shoulder to shoulder
6 Referring to a common English idiom, Angelino Power said that the passengers in his carriage were 'like sardines'. In what way were the passengers like sardines?
7 How many clauses are there in the following sentence?
He was catapulted out of his seat as the bomb exploded.
8 In paragraph 5 Fiona Trueman is quoted as saying that "There was a huge whoosh of smoke then glass went flying through the train."
    a What part of this sentence is an example of onomatopoeia?
    b We normally see and smell smoke. Through what other sense did Fiona Trueman experience the smoke from the bomb blast, indicated by her use of this onomatopoeia?
9 Rewrite the following sentence and underline the finite verbs.
Eventually, staff reached the carriage and led survivors through the train and on to the tracks to King's Cross.
10 Rachel McFadyen also said the following sentences, and they formed the next paragraph, which was removed from the article. Put these sentences in the correct order, and add quotation marks on either side.
They hadn't even heard what had happened.
I said to my parents 'I've just got off the train; I've escaped the bomb.'
I immediately phoned my partner then my parents, who live in Norfolk, to tell them I was OK.
11 The purpose of both the article on page 120 and this article is to inform the reader. However, the style of these articles and what they choose to focus on is very different. Explain what is different.
12 The title of the article is a quotation from a survivor of the Picadilly Line bomb blast. It is unusual to use a quotation as a heading. By comparing the content of this article with the content of the more typical article on page 120, suggest why the writers used a quotation as the title.

'We were like sardines in there, just waiting to die'

By Sally Pook, Catriona Davies and Duncan Gardham

King's Cross

The Piccadilly Line train was only minutes out of King's Cross Station when, without warning, a blast tore through one of the carriages.

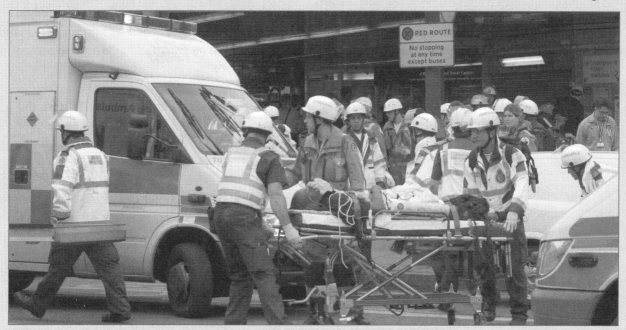

Emergency services ferry the injured away from King's Cross.

It was 8.56am. Many passengers on the crowded train heading for Russell Square had been standing, crushed shoulder to shoulder.

Injured and shaking survivors spoke of bodies slumped on seats, commuters who had lost limbs, glass tearing through skin and choking smoke. Many were unable to breathe. All thought they were going to die.

'We were like sardines in there, just waiting to die,' said Angelino Power, 43, a barrister on his way to a court hearing. He was catapulted out of his seat as the bomb exploded.

Fiona Trueman, 26, a television marketing executive, was on her way to Chelsea for a training course. Still covered in shards of glass, she described endless screaming coming from the carriage in front and the fear that she would die. 'I knew it was a bomb because of the force of the blast,' she said. 'There was a huge whoosh of smoke then glass went flying through the train. We all went flying, even though the train was packed.'

Eventually, staff reached the carriage and led survivors through the train and on to the tracks to King's Cross. Many of the injured from the blast were taken to the Royal London Hospital, in Whitechapel, east London: businessmen with bloodied faces still carrying their briefcases, marketing executives covered in soot, trying to contact relatives on their mobile telephones.

Rachel McFadyen, 34, of Highbury, north London, said, 'We started filing off the train through the driver's carriage and we made our way cautiously along the tunnel. It took about 15 minutes to get to Russell Square.'

Bias and impartiality

In some situations it is expected that we look after our family and friends more than we would look after strangers. For example, we give our family and friends birthday presents but we do not give birthday presents to strangers.

However, in most professional contexts we should not be influenced by whether somebody is a family member or a friend. For example, if you were a judge and you had to decide if someone was guilty of murder, you should not be soft on that person if that person is a family member or a friend. A judge must be fair, and a judge's decision should not be influenced by personal feelings. Similarly, if you were a journalist, you should not write nice things about people just because they are family members or friends, and if you worked for a large company you should not employ someone just because that person is a family member or a friend.

When someone is meant to behave the same to all people, whether or not they are from the same family, village, country, race or religion etc., then we say that person must be 'impartial' or 'objective'. If a person is meant to be impartial but is not, we say that person is 'biased' or 'prejudiced'.

1   Which of the following statements shows a biased attitude and which shows and impartial attitude?
    a   Black people and white people are equal, and both may apply for this job.
    b   I prefer to employ white people.

We can be biased or prejudiced towards people we like, or we can be biased or prejudiced against people we do not like.

2   Which of the following newspaper headlines is biased towards a certain group of people and which is biased against a certain group of people.
    a   I am not friends with any Christian fundamentalists as they do not like to have any fun.
    b   I prefer to employ Muslims as they are punctual, respectful and efficient.

We do not say that someone is prejudiced against someone else if there is a good reason not to like that other person. If we have a good reason to dislike someone then we say that we dislike that person 'with good reason'.

3   a   Can you spot any sign of prejudice in the following website news article from *The Telegraph* online?
    b   Journalists have to be careful about what they write and how they write it or they could end up in court. How has the journalist made Dhiren Barot seem evil without saying he is evil?
    c   Discuss whether the use of the term 'Muslim fanatic' stereotypes all Muslims as being fanatics.

The British Muslim fanatic who plotted to kill thousands

By Duncan Gardham

A British al-Qa'eda fanatic plotted to murder thousands of innocent people, a court heard yesterday.

The detailed plans of Muslim convert Dhiren Barot revealed his goal of striking at major buildings and railway stations with gas bombs in cars, detonating a radioactive bomb and blowing up a train under the River Thames in London.

'Imagine the chaos that would be caused if a powerful explosion were to rip through here and actually rupture the river itself,' he wrote. 'That would cause pandemonium, what with the explosions, flooding, drowning, etc. that would occur.'

The same document told of plans to fill limousines with gas canisters and drive them into car parks beneath important buildings where they would be blown up.

As he planned his attacks in Britain, Barot bought a copy of *The Hazardous Chemical Handbook* and used a forged pass to do research at Brunel University in west London.

Barot has pleaded guilty to conspiracy to murder and faces life in jail. He is expected to be sentenced today.

The River Thames

Breaking up a sentence into its functional phrases

Parts of speech

We can divide up a sentence according to parts of speech, or we can divide up a sentence according to functional phrases. Both are useful ways of looking at words and how they fit together, but they are different ways of dividing up a sentence. Try to think of them as different systems that sometimes overlap.

We have already discussed parts of speech. When we divide up a sentence according to parts of speech we use the following terms: noun, determiner, pronoun, adjective, verb, adverb, preposition, conjunction.

When we divide up a sentence according to its functional phrases we use the following terms: subject, verb, direct object, indirect object, complement, adverbial phrase, conjunction. We do not use the words 'noun', 'determiner', 'pronoun' or 'adjective', because these parts of speech are contained within the subject, verb, direct object, indirect object or complement. We do not use the words adverb or preposition because these parts of speech are contained in the adverbial phrase.

Functional phrases

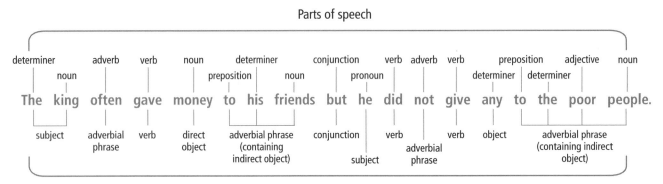

We must choose to use the system that is more useful in a particular situation. When we are thinking about whether to use the determiner 'a' or 'the' in front of a noun, then we must think in terms of the system called parts of speech (because only the system called parts of speech identifies determiners). When we are thinking about whether to use the pronoun 'I' or 'me' then we must think in terms of the system called functional phrases (because the functional labels will show whether the pronoun is the subject of the verb or the object).

1   a   Divide the following sentence up according to parts of speech.
        The queen ruled a small powerful country.
   b   Now divide the same sentence up according to functional phrases.

2   Write the following sentences out using correct English. Say whether you used parts of speech or functional phrases to help you work out how to rewrite these sentences.
   a   The king decided he would meet (she/her) the next day.
   b   Do you think it is good for a country to be ruled by (a/the) king?

Subjects

Most of the time, the subject is the word or group of words that comes before the verb. For example, in this sentence 'Queen Elizabeth II' is the subject.

But in the following sentence 'Queen Elizabeth II and the British government' is the subject.

Sometimes there are other words that come before the verb that are not part of the subject (for example, adverbial phrases).

1   Identify the subjects of the verbs in italics.
    a   England gradually *became* very powerful.
    b   It *colonised* its neighbouring countries first.
    c   Wales, Scotland and Ireland *were incorporated* into the United Kingdom, which was controlled by whoever ruled England.
    d   During the seventeenth, eighteenth and nineteenth centuries, the United Kingdom *colonised* places all over the world.
    e   The people who lived in these places *became* the subjects of the English king or queen, depending on who was on the English throne.
    f   In the twentieth century, the United Kingdom *relinquished* control over many of these places, such as the Bechuanaland Protectorate.
    g   This area then *became* an independent country called 'Botswana'.
    h   The people of Botswana now *elect* their president democratically.

Sometimes we use a parallel subject to insert extra information into a sentence. This parallel subject shares the same verb as the first subject. The parallel subject is always within a pair of commas, as shown below.

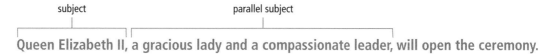

2   What is the parallel subject in each of these sentences?
    a   Manuel, the father of Keneilwe, wanted to know if we could look after her on Saturday evening.
    b   Thabo Mbeki, the second president of a democratic South Africa, focused on maintaining a strong economy.

Verbs can be made up of one word or more than one word. There can be different groups of verbs in one sentence.

3 Identify the verbs of the subjects in italics.
   a *South Africa* is a democratic country.
   b In the north, *South Africa* borders Namibia, Botswana, Zimbabwe and Mozambique.
   c *Many Africans from these countries* have come to South Africa.
   d While many Zimbabweans come to work in South Africa, *few South Africans* go to work in Zimbabwe.

A singular subject must be followed by a singular verb. A plural subject must be followed by a plural verb. Collective nouns, such as 'the group', seem to be plural but, in terms of grammar, they are singular.

4 Rewrite these sentences so that the verbs reflect the fact that their subjects are singular.
   a The library (be) over there.
   b The flock of sheep (be) grazing in the field.
   c The pride of lions (look) at the herd of cattle.

It often feels right to use plural verbs with singular nouns that refer to groups of people. However, we must use singular verbs if, in grammatical terms, the subject is singular.

5 Rewrite the following present tense sentences, deciding whether the verbs should be singular or plural.
   a The Botswanan government (decide) how much money to spend on education.
   b The governments of African countries sometimes (meet) to plan Africa's future.

Although it is right to use a singular verb in front of a singular subject such as 'government', it never sounds completely right, even though it is grammatically correct. Therefore it is better to avoid writing sentences where singular subjects that refer to groups of people take singular verbs, as in the following sentence.

The Botswanan government decides how much money to spend on education.

This sentence could be rewritten as follows.

The Botswanan education budget is decided on by the Botswanan government.

We will discuss how to turn sentences around in this way on pages 212–217, when we discuss using the passive voice.

Direct objects and transitive verbs

The most common pattern in English sentences is subject-verb-object.

There are two kinds of objects: direct objects and indirect objects. Direct objects are discussed here. Indirect objects are discussed on page 132.

The direct object is the thing that is influenced by the verb. It comes after the verb.

direct object

Jamila ate   the cookie.

Not all sentences have direct objects. For example, the sentence 'Jamila walked.' has no direct object.

1   Identify the direct objects in the following sentences.
    a   He drove a Polo Playa.   c   Daniel hit Michael.
    b   A drought struck southern Botswana.   d   Sera planted some carrots.

Verbs that have direct objects are called transitive verbs.

> Transitive verbs transfer an action from the subject to the direct object.

2   Underline the transitive verbs in each sentence.
    a   Themba hit the cricket ball.   c   Matome is making biscuits.
    b   We enjoy ice cream and chocolate sauce.   d   I have a fast car.

Some verbs are always transitive verbs, and they cannot be used without a direct object. Here are some examples of verbs that are always transitive (must have a direct object).

have   *make*   *hit*   *enjoy*

> Sometimes people make the mistake of using a verb that can only be a transitive verb, and not giving it a direct object.

3   Complete the sentences below by adding a direct object from the box. Use each direct object once only.

| my own television | delicious pap |
| my attacker | romantic comedies |

    a   I make …   c   I enjoy …
    b   I hit …   d   I have …

An intransitive verb does not have a direct object.

4   Complete the sentences below by adding an intransitive verb from the box. Use each direct object once only.

| laughed   smiled   cried   frowned |

    a   When she heard the joke Khanyi _____.
    b   When I said she was pretty Jessica _____.
    c   When Aaron heard the bad news he _____.
    d   When Martha got angry she _____.

While some verbs are always transitive verbs and others are always intransitive, some verbs can be either. Then, when you use them in a particular situation, you have to decide whether they need an object, and, if so, what object is appropriate.

Complements and adverbial phrases

When we divide a sentence into its functional parts, such as subjects, verbs, direct objects and conjunctions, we can also label some parts as complements or adverbial phrases. Complements are words or groups of words that are needed to complete a sentence. Adverbial phrases are not needed, but they add meaning to the sentence.

Complements

Sometimes, instead of an object, a verb is followed by a complement. A complement is a word or group of words that is needed to complete a sentence but which is not an object. Many verbs need complements in the same way that transitive verbs need direct objects.

For example, in the sentence below, the adjective 'sad' is a complement, and the sentence would not make sense if this word was missing.

subject	verb	complement
He	was	sad.

1   The following sentences need complements. Add one of the adjectives from the box into each of the sentences in order to complete these sentences.

oppressive   happy   convincing   ridiculous

   a   I am _____.
   b   That unprepared play was _____.
   c   During daytime in the Sahara the heat is _____.
   d   The police found his story _____.

Complements are not always adjectives. Other parts of speech can form all or a part of the complement, if they are needed after the verb for the sentence to make sense.

2   Identify the complements in the following sentences.
   a   The swimmers were wet.
   b   Today is such a sunny day!
   c   She wants to be a good dancer.
   d   That is my dog.

Adverbial phrases

Adverbial phrases are words or groups of words that act as adverbs. They can be introduced by an adverb or a preposition. The verb does not need them in order to make sense, but they do add meaning to the sentence, as shown in the example below.

adverbial phrase of time

She wants to be a good dancer in one week's time.

adverbial phrase of place

That is my dog on the pavement.

adverbial phrase of manner

I am travelling by foot.

adverbial phrase of reason

He is studying for his History examination.

adverbial phrase of degree

He is studying harder than his sister.

adverbial phrase of intensity

His sister is studying fairly hard.

3 Identify the adverbial phrases in the sentences below and say what types of adverbial phrase they are.
   a I am driving to Gauteng.
   b He is travelling by bicycle.
   c We will be leaving in the morning.
   d He visited my grandmother in the village of Riebeek-Kasteel.
   e He eats more quickly than me.
   f They run very fast.
   g Priscilla is studying for her Mathematics examination.
   h I gave the cup to my sister.

4 Put the phrases in brackets in the correct order so that you make a sentence. Add a capital letter at the beginning of the sentence and a full stop at the end.
   a (using feet, yards and miles) (in some countries) (people) (measure) (distances)
   b (distances) (people in other countries) (measure) (in terms of centimetres, metres and kilometres)

5 Label your answers to question 4 a–b as functional phrases.

Indirect objects

The indirect object refers to something that is indirectly affected by the action described by the verb. Look at the following sentence.

subject	verb	object	adverbial phrase of place
I	gave	the cup	to my sister.

This sentence can be changed so that instead of having an adverbial phrase it has an indirect object.

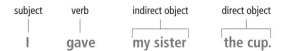

subject	verb	indirect object	direct object
I	gave	my sister	the cup.

Indirect objects come before direct objects and they are not introduced by prepositions.

1 Change the following sentences around so that they have an indirect object before the direct object. Remove the preposition.
   a The boy gave the bucket to his father.
   b Thandi told the news to her aunt.
   c They took the present to him.

2 Complete the following sentences by adding an indirect object from the box. Use each phrase from the box once only.

the striker   her friends   her hungry family

   a She wrote the invitations to _____ .
   b Mrs Khama made a big meal for _____ .
   c I passed the ball to _____ .

3 Change the indirect objects in the following sentences into pronouns.
   a I kicked my sister the ball.
   b She baked her father a cake.

> When we use a pronoun as an indirect object we must remember to use the correct form, as discussed on page 35.

When a noun or pronoun is part of an adverbial phrase we do not call it an indirect object. However, when a preposition and a pronoun are used in an adverbial phrase we use the same form of the pronoun as we would for the indirect object.

4 In each of the following sentences, change the noun in the adverbial phrase into an appropriate pronoun.
   a I kicked the ball to my sister.
   b She baked a cake for her father.

Using infinitives

When we are talking about verbs we often write the verb like this: 'to look'. This is like calling the verb by its full name. We do not often use the verb's full name, because when we use the verb in our speech and writing we change its tense and aspect.

We call this full form of the verb that has 'to' in front of the base verb the 'infinitive' form. As the prefix 'in' (meaning 'not') shows, this kind of verb is not a finite verb. Therefore if you want to use an infinitive in a sentence, you still need to use a finite verb as well in order to make this sentence a real sentence.

Look at the following sentences, which have been labelled according to their parts of speech.

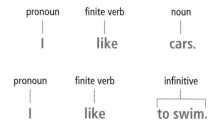

If you think about how it is used in the second sentence, the infinitive acts more like a noun than a finite verb.

1   Identify the infinitives in these sentences.
    a   I like to store my favourite songs on my MP3 player.
    b   I enjoy swimming but I don't like to put my head under water.
    c   To be an actress is all I really want.
2   Insert the present simple of the first verb in brackets and the infinitive of the second word in brackets into the sentences below.
    a   Cecilia (want) (go) to the zoo.
    b   We (prefer) (go) swimming.

Remember that the word 'to' can be part of the infinitive or it can be a preposition.

3   Insert the present progressive of the first verb in brackets and the infinitive of the second word in brackets into the sentences below.
    a   Peter (go) (go) to university.
    b   Simon (hope) (become) a carpenter.
4   Insert the present perfect of the first verb in brackets and the infinitive of the second word in brackets into the sentences below.
    a   Zoleka (wait) (open) the Christmas presents for a long time now, but the rest of the family is still sleeping.
    b   The aspiring guitarist (want) (play) with a band for a long time.
5   Not all verbs can be used in front of an infinitive verb. List those that can, based on the exercises on this page.

Using infinitives with finite verbs showing mental states

Most of the verbs that can be used as finite verbs in front of an infinitive verb show the mental state of the subject, as shown in the example below.

	verb in the present simple	infinitive	
He	wants	to go	to the party.

A mental state refers to what a person is thinking and feeling in their brain.

The verb 'have' belongs to this group only when it means 'must', and not when it means 'possess'.

However, not all verbs showing mental attitudes can be used in this way. The following words are many of those that can be used before the infinitive in this kind of pattern.

want	desire	wish	love	intend
have	hope	aspire	try	plan
ought	need	expect	fear	hate

1 Some of the words above are synonyms. Find synonyms for the following words among the words listed in the box.
   a desire
   b aspire

2 Write the correct forms of the verbs in brackets. You must make the verb in the first pair of brackets into a present simple verb that matches the subject, and you must make the verb in the second pair of brackets into an infinitive, as in the following example.

   He (want) (go) to the party.
   He wants to go to the party.

   a Monako (intend) (be) a lawyer when she grows up.
   b I (hate) (leave) my family behind when I go to the mines to work.
   c We (wish) (incorporate) more youthful designs into our advertising campaign.
   d Maya (love) (eat) but she does not gorge on food.
   e A man (ought) (trust) his wife, and she (ought) (give) him good reason to do so.
   f I (plan) (study) architecture after school.
   g Our school (hope) (build) a new set of classrooms.
   h Jeff (aspire) (have) a penthouse and a sports car.
   i I will (try) (arrive) on the early train.
   j You (have) (know) the truth about who your father is!
   k They (want) (meet) the shortlisted candidates.
   l He (need) (work) hard to get ahead in this industry.
   m He (expect) (earn) a good salary as an accountant.
   n The children (fear) (enter) the haunted house.
   o Many young people (desire) (travel) around the world.

Gerunds

Sometimes we can use the 'ing' participle, which is normally used to show progression, to act as a noun in a sentence. When we do this we do not call it a participle, but a gerund.

Look at the following sentences.

A gerund is not a finite verb. Therefore if you want to use a gerund in a sentence, you still need to use a finite verb as well in order to make this sentence a real sentence.

1   Read the following pairs of sentences and, for each one, decide which one is a sentence written in the present progressive and which one is a sentence written in the present simple that contains a gerund.
    a   i I enjoy swimming in the school pool.
        ii I am swimming in the school pool.
    b   i If you are running a lot this can hurt your knees.
        ii Running can be bad for your knees.
    c   i We like performing plays.
        ii We are performing a play in the school hall.

Not all verbs can be used in front of a gerund. The following verbs are some of those that can be.

like   *enjoy*   *go*

2   For each of the following groups of words, put the words in order to make a sensible sentence. Add a capital letter and a full stop.
    a   cycling he goes in types weather all of
    b   sauce we ice-cream enjoy and chocolate eating
    c   to like going coast on holiday they the

Using gerunds with finite verbs showing mental states

While certain verbs showing mental states can be used with infinitives (see page 134), other verbs showing mental states can be used with gerunds, as shown in the example below.

	present simple verb	gerund	
I	anticipate	paying	a high price.

But not all verbs can be used in this way. The following words are some of those that can be used with gerunds in this kind of pattern.

adore	*love*	*hate*	*detest*	*intend*
try	*anticipate*	*fear*	*prefer*	

1   Write the correct forms of the verbs in brackets. You must make the verb in the first pair of brackets into a present simple verb that matches the subject, and you must make the verb in the second pair of brackets into a gerund, as in the example below.

    He (anticipate) (score) at least one goal.
    He anticipates scoring at least one goal.

    a   I (adore) (have) a hot bath on a cold day.
    b   We (love) (eat) tomato sauce on everything.
    c   She (hate) (see) people feeling sad.
    d   He (detest) (talk) to strangers.
    e   They (intend) (settle) in Kimberley.
    f   Sonwabile (try) (save) money by switching off unnecessary lights.
    g   The government (anticipate) (collect) billions of rand in taxes this year.
    h   Many people (fear) (go) to the dentist.
    i   I (prefer) (watch) comedies to horror films.

2   Correct the following sentences by replacing the finite verb with a synonym that can be used in the existing pattern, or by changing the pattern to one that the existing finite verb can be used in.
    a   I anticipate to arrive soon.
    b   I expect leaving today.
    c   I want succeeding.

3   What verbs can be used in front of infinitives and gerunds? (Base your answer on what you have learnt on pages 133–136.)

Activity H

Read the extract from Unity Dow's novel *Juggling Truths*. Then answer the questions that follow.

Mrs Moloi, our Standard Three teacher, wanted to know what each of us wanted to be when we grew up. It was a question that had been asked many times before. Every teacher asked it and the responses hardly ever changed. Half the girls said they wanted to be teachers and most of the other half said they wanted to be nurses. Maureen wanted to be an air stewardess. This was because one of our books had a beautiful white girl, with long flowing hair, serving drinks to men in an airplane. And Mary wanted to be a bank-teller. There was a van that came into the village every month with big letters saying 'Mobile Bank' and the woman who gave out the salaries to the teachers called herself a bank-teller. I didn't think I wanted to do that kind of job. Bank-telling seemed rather boring and, in any case, there didn't seem to be lots of job openings in bank-telling. I didn't find the uniform particularly impressive either and the repaired collar suggested that the job was not well paying. Some of the boys wanted to be school principals. There was clearly going to be a problem because they couldn't all be school principals, otherwise who would do the teaching? A couple of them wanted to be pilots. This was also on account of the book with the beautiful stewardess. It also had a picture of a handsome young man at the controls of an airplane. It was my turn and the class was waiting for a reply.

'Monei, are you with us? What do you want to be when you grow up?' I had stood up as was the custom when answering a question or making any contribution in class, but I had not said anything. There was impatience in Mrs Moloi's voice, but then I was one of her star pupils so she was not threatening to cane me. Yet.

'The Queen,' I blurted out. The class burst into laughter and Mrs Moloi frowned, then she laughed as well. I wanted to swallow back the answer but it was too late. 'You want to be the Queen? As in the Queen of England?' Mrs Moloi finally asked. She was trying to puzzle some sense out of the answer. She slipped her thick bottom lip into her mouth, as she always did when she was waiting for a response to an important question. I hung my head embarrassed but did not answer.

Mrs Moloi let her pink wet lip slip out of her mouth and regarded me thoughtfully, but still with some amusement, and declared, 'Well, you are not going to be the Queen of England, so can you come up with a more realistic ambition?' The class erupted again.

I wanted to explain but instead tears of humiliation sprang to my eyes. What I meant was that I wanted to make decisions like whether or not pupils should learn inches or centimetres. If I were the Queen, I would have allowed pupils all over the British Bechuanaland Protectorate to continue to use inches. Especially since some of them had just figured out that there are three feet in a yard and there are one thousand seven hundred and sixty yards in a mile. It did not seem right that the Queen would just decide that distance should be measured in centimetres, metres and kilometres just as I had come to grips with inches, feet and yards. But there was no time to explain. There were still ripples of laughter and I had to think of an answer quickly!

First I had thought I wanted to be a doctor but I knew that, as a girl, I could be a nurse only, not a doctor. I had seen only two doctors in my life and they had both been men and white. And I knew at least four girls called Nurse and three boys called Doctor. Nurse was a girl's name and Doctor was a boy's name. But the Queen was a woman so I though I had a chance there. Of course, there was talk of our country being independent from the Queen of England and a president going to take over. I could not say I wanted to be president though because only men became presidents. And not just any men, but men who had been chiefs before or were at least related to one. That was why I wanted to be a queen. It had all seemed to make sense as I worked it out in my mind. But within the four walls of my classroom, my classmates and my teacher were not seeing things my way. Clearly I had said something ridiculous.

'When I grow up, I want to be a teacher,' I whispered, still burning under the humiliation brought on by my quick answer.

'Good girl,' Mrs Moloi praised me on my revised professional plans. 'You will make an excellent teacher.'

I wanted to tell her that I did not want to be a teacher because I had no intention of hitting young children. I could not imagine standing over small children waving a threatening cane, but I could not see how one could become a teacher without doing exactly that. Every time I declared that I wanted to be a teacher I spent the rest of the day worried that I would actually end up one.

1   The first sentence of this extract has a parallel subject. Write down this parallel subject.

2   Identify two infinitives in the first sentence of the extract.

3   What part of the following sentence is a complement?
    Some of the boys wanted to be school principals.

4   Which word in paragraph 1 is a gerund?

5   In paragraph 2 Monei tells us that she is a star pupil, so her teacher has patience with her on this rare occasion that she has said something silly.
    a   If she had been a disruptive pupil, what would the teacher have done?
    b   Is this an example of prejudice or not? Explain your answer.

6   a   Identify the two direct objects in the following sentence.
        This was because one of our books had a beautiful white girl, with long flowing hair, serving drinks to men in an airplane.
    b   Is the verb 'had' always a transitive verb, or can it be an intransitive verb?

7   Monei is influenced by the cultural stereotypes she finds in the world around her. When choosing a career, is she predominantly influenced by:
    a   racial stereotypes?
    b   gender stereotypes?
    c   religious stereotypes?

8   a   The Queen of England allowed the units of measurement to be changed throughout the British Commonwealth, including in the Bechuanaland Protectorate. Does this show her to be prejudiced against the people in this area?
    b   Why?

9   Write out the following sentence and label it according to its functional phrases.
    The class erupted again.

10 Monei reluctantly says, 'When I grow up, I want to be a teacher.'
    a   Would it also be correct for her to say 'When I grow up, I want being a teacher.'
    b   Why?

11 a   In paragraph 5, find three words that are spelt the same way in British English, but differently in American English.
    b   In paragraph 1, find a word that is spelt the same way in American English, but differently in British English.

Using participles as adjectives

When we write in the progressive aspect or the perfect aspect we use a participle, as in the examples below.

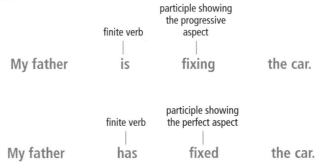

Sometimes we can also use these participles as adjectives in a sentence, but not always. In the example below, the participle usually used to show that a verb is in the perfect aspect is now being used as an adjective to describe the noun 'car'.

However, we may not use the participle 'fixing' in the same way.

	Participles, usually used to show the progressive aspect, that can be used as adjectives	
Regular verbs	whining	aching
Irregular verbs	striking	ringing

1   Complete the following sentences with one of the participles from the above table.
   a   His _____ head is a sign that he drank too much beer last night.
   b   The _____ child has been raised badly by her parents.
   c   I do not feel the need to answer that _____ telephone.
   d   The _____ workers hoped for better working conditions and higher pay.

	Participles, usually used to show the perfect aspect, that that can be used as adjectives		
Regular verbs	invited	uninvited	charted	uncharted
Irregular verbs	known	stricken	spilt	known

2   Complete the following sentences with one of the participles from the above table. Use each participle from the table only once.
   a   The _____ honey attracted flies.
   b   Sheep were dying in the drought-_____ area.
   c   The captain will only take the ship into _____ waters.
   d   I have prepared food for the _____ guests but not the _____ guests.
   e   The explorers were nervous when they left the k_____ world and entered _____ territories.

3   Complete the following proverb by inserting a participle that acts as an adjective.
   It's no use crying over _____ milk.

Various punctuation marks that may be used to mark the end of a sentence

Full stops

The end of a sentence is usually used marked with a full stop, as shown in this sentence.

The player is fast.

However, not all sentences end with a full stop. We can also use an exclamation mark, a question mark or ellipsis marks to show that a sentence has ended.

Exclamations marks

We use an exclamation mark (!) when we want to emphasise a point. When we use an exclamation mark we must not add a full stop afterwards.

We do not use exclamations in formal texts. We can use them in informal texts, but mostly they are used in direct speech. When someone is talking loudly we use an exclamation mark, and it can also be used after statements expressing anger, pain or surprise, as shown here.

That is a fantastic goal!

Question marks

We use a question mark (?) at the end of a question. When we use a question mark we must not add a full stop afterwards, as shown in this example.

What is the time?

Ellipsis marks

An ellipsis is three dots (…). Instead of ending a sentence with one dot (a full stop) we can end it with three dots (an ellipsis). These three dots signal that the sentence has not been finished properly and that something has been left unsaid, as in the example below.

I heard that you broke up with your boyfriend a while ago …

An ellipsis can be used to create a feeling of suspense.

The ball arced above the goalie's hands towards the corner of the goals …

1 Insert a different punctuation mark at the end of each of the following sentences. Do not use a full stop for any of them.
   a What is your name
   b Stop right there, you thief
   c I see you aren't eating the rest of your chocolate pudding

Compound sentences and co-ordinating conjunctions

Sentences that have more than one clause are called either compound sentences or complex sentences. Compound sentences have two clauses of equal importance. This is because the conjunctions that join these clauses do not make it seem that one is more important than the other, as shown in the following examples.

He went swimming and she went cycling.
He must have gone to the shops or he must have gone to the bank.

A compound sentence is joined by a semi-colon or one of the following co-ordinating conjunctions:

and   *or*   *but*   *yet*

All other kinds of sentences with more than one clause are called complex sentences, and these are discussed on pages 144–148.

When 'yet' is used as a conjunction it has a similar meaning to 'but'. However, the word 'yet' is more old-fashioned than the word 'but' and sounds more dramatic because it is not used so often.

1   Insert one of each of the co-ordinating conjunctions into each of the following compound sentences.
    a   I ate all the overcooked vegetables on my plate _____ then I felt sick afterwards.
    b   I can take you to your boyfriend's house _____ I can give you a lift to your parents.
    c   I was very sure that he loved me, _____ I wondered if he could ever be faithful to one woman.
    d   We danced _____ we sang.

We can use commas between clauses, just before the conjunction, but we do not have to.

Sometimes we shorten compound sentences that use 'and' or 'or' as the co-ordinating conjunction. This is because, if the clauses share information, we do not need to repeat the information, as shown in the following sentences.

Zara hugged Daniel, and Refilwe walked away from Daniel.
Zara hugged Daniel, and Refilwe walked away.

He must choose to become a businessman or to he must choose to become a minister of the church.
He must choose to become a businessman or a minister of the church.

We still think of the shortened sentences as compound sentences, although separating the clauses is no longer easy, as part of one clause is now invisible. We say this invisible part is 'implied' by the way the rest of the sentence is constructed.

2   In the following shortened compound sentences there are two clauses, but part of one is implied/invisible. Rewrite the sentences in full so it is easy to identify each clause. Do not use pronouns but repeat the subject in full when necessary.
    a   I was travelling up the escalator and I saw my mother travelling down.
    b   He is angry or drunk.

Co-ordinating conjunctions are sometimes used with traditional phrases that emphasise the fact that they are co-ordinating two things.
    Look at the following phrases.

He has either come home early or he never went to work.
She neither does the housework nor has a job.

The word 'either' helps 'or' do its co-ordinating job.
The word 'neither' (meaning 'not either') helps 'nor' (meaning 'not or') do its co-ordinating job.

3   Use 'either … or' or 'neither … nor' in the gaps in the following sentences.
    a   Justin is a financial disaster. He has _____ the ability to earn money _____ the ability to save it.
    b   Samkele is always busy. She is _____ out with her friends _____ she is working as a waitress at The Africa Café.

A semi-colon (;) can be used to join two clauses instead of a conjunction. However, the clauses must mean the same thing or be so clearly linked that a conjunction is not needed to explain their relationship (for example, they are in direct contrast to each other, or they are a cause and its effect, or a command and an explanation for this command).
    Look at how the semi-colon is positioned in the following sentence.

You can't go to both the weddings; you must choose which one to attend.

4   Now rewrite the following sentences and insert a semi-colon between the clauses.
    a   Being dumped by your partner hurts dumping your partner hurts in a different way.
    b   She lit the fuse the bomb exploded.

We use semi-colons very rarely, as a special effect. Do not use them because you cannot think of the correct conjunction, because that is bad style.

Complex sentences and subordinating conjunctions

Complex sentences are sentences with two or more clauses, where one clause is more important than the others. The less important clause or clauses are introduced by subordinating conjunctions. Subordinating conjunctions show that the clause that follows them contains supporting information. Most conjunctions are subordinating conjunctions.

These are some common subordinating conjunctions.

because	*unless*	*although*	*if*	*when*
while before	*after*	*so*	*until*	

You might recognise some of these words and think they are adverbs. If they introduce a phrase they are called adverbs, but if they introduce a clause they are called conjunctions.

Look at how the following sentence can be divided up according to its clauses.

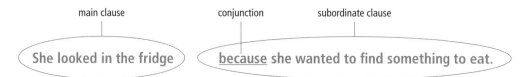

1 Copy out the following sentences. Then circle the clauses and underline the subordinating conjunctions.
  a I would like to become a professional soccer player because I want to earn money doing something I enjoy.
  b I will not have a chance of becoming a professional soccer player unless I train regularly.
  c I do score a few goals sometimes although I am a natural midfielder.
  d I would like to play in the PSL if I had the opportunity.
  e I try hardest when my team is losing.
  f I get scared we will lose the match so I put extra effort into scoring a goal.

Subordinating conjunctions are always at the front of subordinate clauses, but sometimes these subordinate clauses come before the main clause of a sentence.

2 Copy out the following sentences. Then circle the clauses and underline the subordinating conjunctions.
  a While I was playing last Saturday, I knew the talent scouts were watching me.
  b Until I get offered a contract by a club, I have to think about other careers.
  c I was dreaming about playing for Manchester United before I realised I have to succeed in South Africa first.
  d After I make a name for myself here, I want to play for Manchester United.

3 Add an appropriate conjunction in each of these sentences.
  a My mother wants me to go to a technikon _____ she thinks there is no financial security in the world of professional soccer.
  b _____ my father knows she is right, he also understands I have to follow my dream.

Complex sentences using a relative determiner

The subordinate clause in a complex sentence is not always introduced by a subordinating conjunction. Instead, we can use a relative determiner that shows there is a link between the main clause and the subordinate clause. Relative determiners are a kind of determiner we have not yet discussed. Revise determiners by looking at pages 34 and 38. Then look at the following examples.

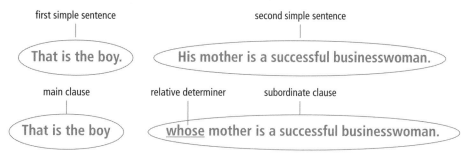

When we join the two sentences we change the determiner from a possessive determiner to the relative determiner 'whose'. The relative determiner shows there is a relationship between the word 'boy' in the main clause and the word 'mother' in the subordinate clause. The relative determiner 'whose' can be used only to talk about people.

1   Combine the following sentences into one sentence. Put the relative determiner 'whose' in the place of the possessive determiner. Insert a comma before 'whose' if you feel the second sentence is adding extra information, but not if you feel it is helping to distinguish who you are talking about.
    a   That is the coach. His training methods are unusual.
    b   This is my friend. Her favourite sport is also soccer.
    c   Those are my classmates. Their favourite team is Orlando Pirates.
    d   These are my teammates. Their dream is to win the Polar Ice Cup.

Relative determiners must come at beginning of their clause. Sometimes when we form a subordinate clause after a relative determiner, we have to change the word order so that the relative determiner comes first. We do this when the original determiner was not at the beginning of the sentence.

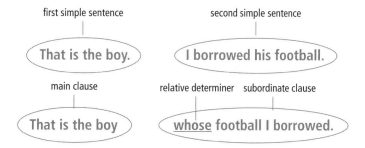

2   Combine the following sentences into one sentence. Put the relative determiner 'whose' in the place of the possessive determiner. Then change the word order following the pattern in the example above.
    a   That is the player. I like his style.
    b   This is the goalie. I admire his skill.

Complex sentences using relative pronouns

The subordinate clause of a complex sentence can also be introduced by a relative pronoun.

Relative pronouns referring to people

When we are referring to a person in the main clause, and the relative pronoun that is being used to do this is the subject of the subordinate clause, then we use the relative pronoun 'who'. Look at the following examples.

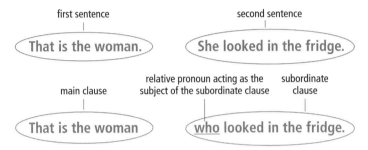

1 Rewrite the following pairs of simple sentences as complex sentences joined by the relative pronoun 'who'.
   a That is the man. He works in the Western Deep Level Mines.
   b That is the girl. She makes her own dresses and skirts.

If we are referring to a person in the main clause, and the relative pronoun that is being used to do this is an object of the subordinate clause, then we use the relative pronoun 'whom'. Look at the following examples.

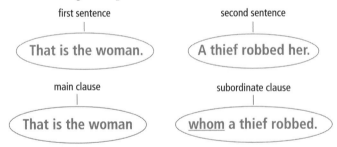

2 Rewrite the following pairs of simple sentences as complex sentences joined by the relative pronoun 'whom'.
   a That is the player. I admire him.   b That is the girl. I like her.

Of course, it is easier to change sentences that are already in the second stage of this process.

In the above examples, 'whom' is taking the place of the direct object. If we want 'whom' to take the place of an indirect object then the process is more complicated. We first need to change the sentence with the indirect object into a sentence with an adverbial phrase introduced by a preposition. Then we join the sentences with the preposition we have added and the relative pronoun 'whom'. Look at the following examples.

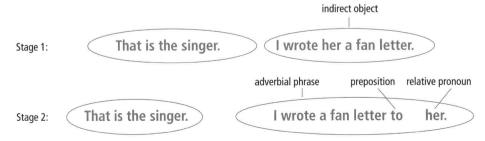

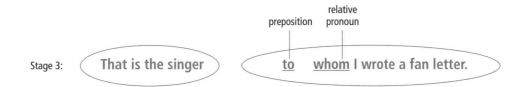

Stage 3: That is the singer | to whom I wrote a fan letter.

preposition *relative pronoun*

This pattern is used in formal English, but is often not used in informal English.

3 Rewrite the following pairs of simple sentences as complex sentences joined by the relative pronoun 'whom'.
   a That is the doctor. I am very grateful to her.
   b That is my grandmother. I painted some pictures for her.

Relative pronouns referring to things

When we are referring to a thing in the main clause, we use the relative pronoun 'that' or 'which'. These relative pronouns can replace 'it', 'this', 'that', 'these' or 'those'. We use 'that' when the subordinate clause gives necessary information, as in Jabu's statement below.

Mzi: You have lots of balls. Is one better than the others?
Jabu: *(This is the ball. It stays firm.)* This is the ball that stays firm.

4 Rewrite the following simple sentences in italics as complex sentences joined by the relative pronoun 'that'.
   a Cindi: I can mend the dress that is torn, if you want.
      Thandeka: *This is the dress. It is torn.*
   b Nkosana: Didn't you lose one of your balls?
      Elvis: *That is the ball. It was lost.*

We use 'which' when we are adding extra information, as shown in these sentences.

Dictionaries give you the denotative meaning of a word. This is its literal meaning.
Dictionaries give you the denotative meaning of a word, which is its literal meaning.

5 Rewrite the following pairs of sentences as complex sentences joined by the relative pronoun 'which'. Change the word order in the subordinate clause if necessary.
   a This text is from an encyclopaedia called *Wikipedia*. This is on the Internet and is free for everyone to use.
   b Here is a list of some adverbs of place. These say where something is done.

The above sentences use 'which' to replace a direct object. If, when we join two sentences, we use 'which' to replace a noun or pronoun in an adverbial phrase, we must then also use the preposition from the adverbial phrase to join the two sentences.

When we put a preposition in front of 'which' we do not use a comma.

This is the table. We eat supper at it.
This is the table at which we eat supper.

6 Join the following pairs of sentences using a relative pronoun.
   a This is the box. I put all the balls in it.
   b These are the books. I learned about nuclear physics from them.

Complex sentences with embedded clauses or embedded phrases

Embedded clauses

On page 144 you learned about subordinate clauses that are introduced by conjunctions, and you learned that these can come before the main clause or after the main clause. However, when we use a relative determiner or a relative pronoun to introduce a subordinate clause, we can also place this subordinate clause in the middle of the main clause. When we do this we call the subordinate clause an 'embedded clause' because it is embedded in the main clause.

Look at the following example of a sentence with an embedded subordinate clause that is introduced by the relative determiner 'whose'.

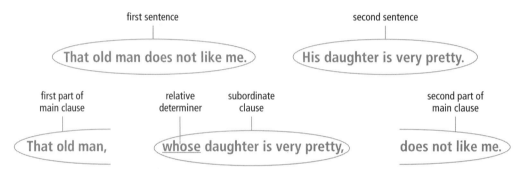

1　Join the following simple sentences by making one into an embedded subordinate clause that is introduced by the relative determiner 'whose'. Put a comma before and after the embedded subordinate clause.

   a　That loan shark has a bad reputation. His loan rates are very unreasonable.

   b　My friend does not know what to do. His debt is getting bigger.

   c　My teammates have asked the banks for car loans. Their cars were expensive.

Look at the following example of a sentence with an embedded subordinate clause that is introduced by the relative pronoun 'who'.

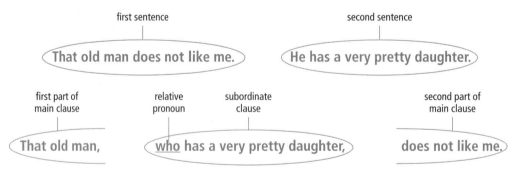

2　Join the following simple sentences by making one into an embedded subordinate clause that is introduced by the relative pronoun 'who'. Put a comma before and after the embedded subordinate clause.

   a　My friend now has a bank loan at a reasonable lending rate. He repaid the loan shark.

   b　I am struggling to open a bank account. I hate filling in forms.

   c　My friend is helping me go through the process. My friend is very helpful.

3 Join the following simple sentences by making the second one into an embedded subordinate clause that is introduced by the relative pronoun 'that'. Do not put a comma before and after the embedded subordinate clause.

  a The bank has a good reputation. The bank is on the corner of Kerk Street and Hani Street.

  b The autobank is on the right. The autobank is working.

  c The form was three pages long. I filled it in.

4 Join the following simple sentences by making the second one into an embedded subordinate clause that is introduced by the relative pronoun 'which'. Put a comma before and after the embedded subordinate clause.

  a This shampoo makes my hair glossy. This shampoo is my favourite.

  b These CDs belong to my sister. These CDs are very romantic.

  c This shirt is torn. I caught it on barbed wire.

5 Which relative determiner or relative pronoun should be used in each of the following sentences?

  a The MP3 player, _____ looks very cool, is basically a modern walkman.

  b The radio _____ has a green handle is not as expensive as the others.

  c Those people, _____ are walking towards the train, are gangsters.

  d The police, to _____ I am very grateful, found my stolen car.

Embedded phrases

Phrases are groups of words without a finite verb. Embedded phrases are phrases within a pair of commas that we place in the middle of clauses, as shown below.

6 Choose a phrase from the box to go into each of the following sentences.

> ideal for people on public transport
> looking for investment opportunities
> realising she was on the wrong train
> suffering from bad eyesight for years

  a Zimasile, _____, finally saved up to afford glasses.

  b This MP3 player, _____, can store hundreds of songs.

  c Jeremiah, _____, investigated setting up a pay phone.

  d Rayda, _____, stepped back onto the platform.

Sentences with three clauses

We can write sentences with more than two clauses. If a sentence has three clauses we will need two words that link these clauses, which could be conjunctions, relative pronouns or relative determiners.

Look at the following examples, which have three clauses joined by two conjunctions. In the first example the main clause comes first, while in the second example the main clause comes between the first and second subordinate clauses.

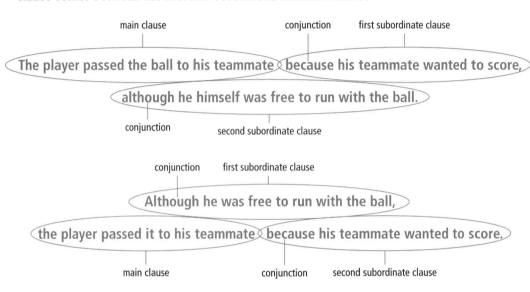

1 Underline the main clause in the following sentences and circle the subordinating conjunctions.

   a The goalie jumped left as the striker took the free kick, although it was too soon to know where way the striker would aim.

   b While he was jumping, the goalie realised he had guessed incorrectly, but it was too late to change direction.

   c Because the striker had kicked the ball rather high, the shot seemed unlikely to be a goal, unless the ball bumped the goal post on its way into the goal box.

The example and sentences 1 a–c all have one main clause and two subordinate clauses because in each case two subordinating conjunctions are used. However, some sentences have one subordinating conjunction and one co-ordinating conjunction, and some have two co-ordinating conjunctions. Sentences that have only co-ordinating conjunctions have more than one main clause. Sentences that have a subordinating conjunction and a co-ordinating conjunction might have one main clause or two, depending on where these conjunctions are placed.

2 In the following sentences, circle the subordinating conjunctions, and put a square around the co-ordinating conjunctions. Underline the main clause or clauses.

   a The ball bumped the goal post and it went into the goal box, and the striker was very pleased with himself.

   b The striker pulled his shirt over his head with happiness and ran round the soccer pitch, but then he bumped into one of his teammates.

   c His teammate gave him a hug because he was also happy, or perhaps he just wanted to seem appreciative in front of the crowds.

Some sentences with three clauses use two relative pronouns, one in front of each of the subordinate clauses. In these cases the main clause usually comes at the start of the sentence, as shown in the example below.

3 Underline the main clause in the following sentences and put a triangle around the relative pronouns.
  a This is the shirt that I was looking for, which I need to wear for the match.
  b An unusual type of abbreviation that is often used in the motor industry is '4x4', which stands for 'four-by-four'.
  c This is the group of funny-looking letters, which belong to the huge International Phonetic Alphabet which has a symbol for each sound in every language.

Some sentences with three clauses use one relative pronoun and one conjunction, as shown in the example below.

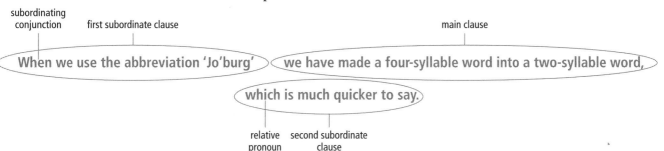

4 Underline the main clause or clauses in the following sentences. Put a circle around the subordinating conjunctions, a square around the co-ordinating conjunctions and a triangle around the relative pronouns.
  a I like ice cream, although frozen yoghurt is also nice, and it is healthier.
  b When the midfielders fell back to help the goalie, the opposition team tried harder to score a goal, but this never happened.
  c We can talk about 'a ceremony organised to respectfully bury a dead person' or we can use the word 'funeral', which means the same thing.

When sentences have three clauses, one of the subordinate clauses can be an embedded clause.

5 In the following sentence, underline the main clause once and underline the embedded subordinate clause twice. Do not underline the other subordinate clause.
  We, who are all older than him, call him 'Junior', although perhaps it is time to stop.

Using punctuation marks to show where sentences, clauses and phrases begin and end

Examples of punctuation marks are full stops, commas and capital letters. We can use punctuation marks for many different purposes when we write, but perhaps the most important use for them is to show where sentences begin and end.

We use a capital letter to show where a sentence begins. (Of course, capital letters are also used for the first letters of proper nouns, the first words and the important words in headings, and in abbreviations.)

We usually use a full stop to show where a sentence ends.

To separate a phrase or clause from the rest of a sentence we usually use a comma or a pair of commas. However, we do not need to mark out every clause and every phrase with commas. To help you decide when to use commas, think about whether the reader should pause at a clause boundary or a phrase boundary. If you think the reader should pause there, you should probably insert a comma. Look at the examples below.

After he ate the piece of bread, he started coughing.

He can eat small bits of food, like grains of rice, but do not let him have bigger bits at this age.

We may not separate sentences with commas. We have to use a full stop or a punctuation mark that contains a full stop.

1   Rewrite the following text and insert capital letters, commas and full stops where appropriate.

> Exclamations marks, question marks and ellipsis marks contain a full stop and can therefore also show where a sentence ends.

> comma separating two clauses

> two commas separating a phrase that is in the middle of a long sentence

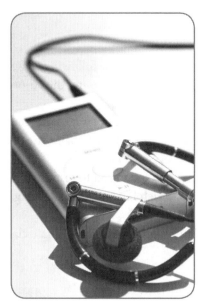

dynamite
bang & olufsen's latest device is a pocket-friendly mp3 player that stores hours of music and it's so simple and intuitive to use that you can operate it without taking it out of your your pocket it is stylishly constructed in aluminium and rubber and the earphones are comfortable and can be used with any bang & olufsen audio system the earphones come with their own specially designed leather carrying case and an extension cord don't let its size fool you because the sound quality is second to none in the portable mp3 arena

We must not put a single comma between a subject and its verb because this breaks the smooth flow of a sentence. Therefore, if we embed a clause or phrase between a subject and its verb, we must use two commas, one on either side of the embedded words. This results in the reader pausing twice. Then, in the reader's mind, the main clause flows around the embedded phrase like a stream flows around a rock.

Look at the following examples.

The French goalie, who was the eldest member of the team, wore the captain's armband when the captain was carried off the field after an injury.

> **an embedded clause giving extra information about the subject**

Soccer, the 'Beautiful Game', requires great skill and stamina.

> **an embedded phrase giving extra information about the subject**

Violent behaviour on the field, such as headbutting an opponent, is never allowed by the referee.

> **an embedded phrase giving an example**

2 Insert no commas, one comma or two commas into the following sentences, depending on what is appropriate.
   a France lost the 2006 World Cup to Italy.
   b After Zidane had been sent off the field France was playing with only ten men.
   c Italy which had all its strikers to choose from scored the most goals during the penalty shootout.

A dash marks a longer pause than a comma, and can also be used to separate a clause or a phrase from the rest of the sentence. A pair of dashes can also be used to separate part of a sentence from the words that surround it. Dashes are used instead of commas on those special occasions when we want a longer pause, in order to create a more dramatic effect. Look at the following example.

Zidane lost his temper during the 2006 World Cup final – and his headbut shocked the world.

> **dash separating two clauses**

Zidane – very embarrassed by his behaviour – explained that the Italian player had insulted his mother.

> **a pair of dashes used to separate an embedded phrase from the rest of the sentence**

3 Insert one or more dashes into the following sentence.
   I expected public opinion to be against Zidane but most people were very sympathetic to his situation.

Comparison and contrast

Comparison
When we make a comparison we are identifying the aspects of two things that are similar. We can also make a comparison between something that actually happens and our accurate expectations about what would happen, or we can compare a story to other similar stories.

1   The words and phrases in the box below can all be used when we compare things. Insert one of the words or phrases in the box into each of the following sentences.

alike	same	in common	share	not much difference	little contrast
like	as	similar	in a similar way		from the same mould
as could be expected		as predicted		predictable	imitates
usual	stereotypical	clichéd		done before	resembles

a   Zee is a lot _____ his father.

b   Just _____ his father wanted to be a professional footballer, so does Zee.

c   Zee's father is always reminding him to keep his eyes on the ball, but Zee is actually very focused, and his style of play _____ his father's.

d   Festus is Zee's brother and he is cast _____ as Zee and his father.

f   There is _____ in age between Zee and Festus.

g   Zee has a girlfriend called Julia, and they _____ an interest in photography.

h   _____, Julia takes many photographs of Zee playing soccer.

i   She likes Zee to wear light colours when she photographs him playing; if he wears dark colours there is _____ between his clothing and his skin.

j   On Valentine's Day, Zee sent Julia a teddy with 'I love you' written on its T-shirt, which is quite a _____ thing to do.

k   Julia does not mind if this has been _____; she is pleased with her teddy.

l   Julia enjoys reading romantic novels, even if they have _____ characters.

m   'The heroines in your novels all seem the _____,' commented Zee.

n   'Don't you get tired of reading stories that are so _____?' asked Zee.

o   'No,' smiled Julia, 'I enjoy guessing correctly about what will happen. Now in this novel, I think the man that seems so unfriendly in the beginning is going to fall in love with the heroine, because they have so much _____.'

p   The story did continue _____, and ended with the heroine marrying the man who had seemed so unfriendly in the beginning.

q   They say that art imitates life, but sometimes life also _____ art.

r   _____ to the gruff heroes of Julia's novels, Zee, who had not always seemed a romantic person, started to talk about marriage.

s   When the big day came, Julia wore a white dress, as is _____ for brides.

t   Festus was Zee's best man, and they looked quite _____ in their dark suits and white shirts.

u   Even the way that Festus looked at the bride was _____ to the way that Zee looked at her …

Contrast

When we contrast two things we are looking at how they are different. We can also contrast something that happens to our inaccurate expectations about what would happen, or we can contrast an original story to other clichéd stories we have heard.

2 The words and phrases in the box below can all be used when we contrast things. Insert one of the words or phrases in the box into each of the sentences below.

not	alternatively	or	more	than	less	previously
preferring	differ	however	no comparison possible			
although	but	even if	in contrast to		unexpectedly	
other	different	unlike	unusual			

a When she was young, Julia liked the idea of marriage _____ she was scared she would not be able to be faithful to one man.

b She was _____ beautiful than most young woman.

c When she walked through a crowd men's eyes followed her, _____ those men had girlfriends or wives with them.

d Julia did not have a steady boyfriend for many years, _____ to date a new man every few weeks.

e _____ her best friend, Linah, managed to find a nice young man, named Zee.

f Zee was sport-mad, _____ he was also good to Linah.

g He was taciturn to her best friend, Julia, though, and Linah did not understand why he seemed so _____ when Julia was around.

h She told him, 'When Julia is here you seem so _____ your usual self.'

i 'I didn't know I had done anything _____,' replied Zee.

j 'It's not what you do,' explained Linah, 'it's what you do _____ do that is strange. You don't smile. You don't make jokes. You don't even meet her eyes.'

k 'Well,' muttered Zee, 'perhaps I don't find her very respectable. _____ you, Julia seems to have very loose morals.'

l 'Well, our opinions of Julia do _____,' retorted Linah. 'She is a good friend and you could try to be a little _____ judgmental.'

m Zee shrugged and joked, '_____, you could get a new best friend.'

n 'That will never happen!' exclaimed Linah. 'She will always be my best friend, whether you like it _____ not.'

o Linah tried to arrange situations where Zee and Julia did not have to be in each other's company. They did a lot of things with their _____ friends.

p One day Linah _____ saw Zee and Julia sitting on a park bench together.

q As Linah came up behind them she heard Julia say, in a softer voice _____ usual, 'But I thought you were in love with Linah.'

r 'Julia, oh, Julia,' Zee murmured, 'when I think about how I feel about you, there is _____. I have been trying to hide my feelings from myself for too long, but now … now I have my eyes on the ball.'

s As they kissed, Linah gasped and stumbled away from her boyfriend and the person she had _____ thought was her best friend.

Activity I

1 Read the following article and insert appropriate conjunctions, relative pronouns or relative determiners into the spaces. Do not use any word twice.

2 Within which paragraphs is Chippa's behaviour contrasted with that of other soccer players?

3 Within which paragraph are two similar types of supportive behaviour compared?

Moroka Swallows' star turns his back on bling – well almost – and reveals a steely determination.

HE'D hit the jackpot at the beginning of the season _____ (a) a big-bucks club signed him up and promptly doubled his salary, paving the way for him to book the latest Beemer, buy a plush pad and stock his wardrobe with designer threads. That's what many young men do when they make their mark in the PSL, right?

But Tsweu 'Chippa' Mokoro isn't like most guys. He is only 24 but the Moroka Swallows sensation is determined to build a business empire with the money he earns playing the game – and not fritter it away on fast cars, hard partying and beautiful women. He's too aware the life of a soccer hero is fleeting _____ (b) is adamant he won't be left high and dry when he hangs up his boots for good. Already the tough midfielder is honing his entrepreneurial skills by investing in two Vodacom pay phones in his hometown of Sasolburg.

He's starting small, he admits – _____ (c) this is only the beginning. He has many ideas to secure a comfortable future when his playing days are over. The car he drives is another example of how level-headed Chippa is. He's shunned the fancy BMWs, Mercs, Chrysler PT Cruisers and soccer players' favourite, the Golf V GTI, and drives a modest yet sporty blue VW Polo Playa because 'it's far more affordable than those expensive fuel guzzlers'. Still, to show he's no nerd he pimped it up by adding tinted windows, mags and a flashy boot spoiler – but that's about as extravagant as he gets, he says.

'Believe me, I've seen a lot of former great players living at the mercy of good Samaritans when they quit the game,' he says earnestly. 'But I won't let that happen to me. I will not die penniless like those _____ (d) live for the moment and don't plan for the future.'

We catch up with Chippa at his two-bedroom flat in a high-rise building in Germiston just around the corner from the Swallows' grounds. When he moved here on loan from SuperSportUnited, his main consideration was being able to walk to the training grounds – another example of how serious he is about saving money.

Casually dressed in Puma sneakers, shorts and a T-shirt, he hits a button on the remote to turn off the TV and waves us to a comfortable sofa in the lounge.

'I'm renting this flat so I can save money to buy a house in the suburbs,' he explains. 'It will have to be big because I want my father, who is living with one of my brothers in Sasolburg, to move in with me. I also want to be able to rent it out _____ (e) I one day decide to play overseas.'

His dad, a retired factory worker, is his biggest fan and watches every match his boy plays on television. Afterwards he gives him feedback – just like his mother did before she died of a heart attack in 1998.

Chippa has vivid memories of that terrible day. He arrived home from school thinking about his training session at Wits University's under-17 side later in the day to find a group of people outside his home.

'I can still picture the scene,' he recalls. 'A huge crowd of friends, neighbours and relatives were gathered but no one would tell me what was going on. Later relatives said they couldn't bring themselves to tell me _____ (f) they thought it would break my heart.'

Eyes on the future

Chippa Mokoro seems to have it all worked out already – his game, his love life, a future career.

It did – but Chippa was determined not to use the tragedy as an excuse to avoid training. Still numb with shock the next day he set off the next day for the grounds. 'My mother wouldn't have condoned me missing practice,' he says.

As fate would have it another woman soon entered his life to help heal his aching heart. Playing for SuperSport in Pretoria he met Yvonne, a pretty call centre agent at First National Bank, when she visited friends with _____ (g) he was staying. 'She was the most beautiful woman I'd ever seen and I knew I couldn't let the chance pass,' he says. 'I asked her out and we've been together ever since. We're setting a date for our wedding next year.'

A pink and white teddy bear with an 'I love you' card from Yvonne sits in his dressing room, _____ (h) reveals a tender side to the macho player.

An added bonus is that Yvonne gets on well with Chippa's three-year-old daughter Neo from a previous relationship.

Neo, _____ (i) mother still lives in Sasolburg, naturally stays in that town as well. However, Chippa makes sure that he makes time to see his daughter. 'Neo makes me feel very mature and responsible,' he says.

_____ (j) he went for trials with Wits' junior teams, Chippa first turned out for junior teams in Sasolburg. Then he became part of a junior team at Wits. But commuting from Sasolburg to Johannesburg was expensive and he had to leave school early on training days. One day on the train to Wits he saw an advertisement in a newspaper for the new Barney Molokwane Football Academy in Johannesburg. It offered promising boys an education while developing their football talent. With backing from his coach at Wits he was accepted and spent two years there as a boarder. It was tough leaving family and friends but he knew it was a way to fast-track his soccer career – and get a decent education.

Chippa prospered, but just before his Matric year Free State Stars talent scouts offered him and four other students an opportunity to train with the club.

'It was unbelievably tough,' he recalls. 'We had to run up mountains. The

food _____ (k) they served was terrible – tough, overcooked meat and pap. The others couldn't handle it and after one extremely hot day they dropped out. But I was determined to hang in there no matter what it took.' It's just as well he did. At the end of the camp he was signed by Stars and the four drop-outs must have kicked themselves when they saw Chippa on TV in a game for the club.

They returned to Stars hoping the manager would have a change of heart but they had no luck. 'I took pity on them though and gave them money for transport back to the academy in Jozi,' big-hearted Chippa says. 'They were broke and I was earning a salary.'

Two years later he was again headhunted, this time by SuperSport United – one of the toughest and most successful clubs in the league. Unfortunately he was plagued by injuries, _____ (l) his misfortune turned out to be a lucky break when he was loaned to Swallows to bring much-needed stability to the team's midfield.

When he found the net five times in his first season, Swallows bought out his remaining contract with SuperSport.

Chippa is so enthusiastic about his new club that he walks from his flat to the training grounds an hour early to work on his free kicks and corner shots.

It's the kind of commitment that should see him go a long way in the PSL and perhaps even on to earn a fortune at an overseas club. Then, of course, he'll be more ready than ever to set up that business empire ...

Using 'let' in commands, suggestions, requests and invitations

The word 'let' means 'allow' or 'permit'. These three verbs are synonyms.
We can use the word 'let' in commands, as shown in this example.

FATHER: (*giving a command*) Let the dog off his lead now.

We can use the word 'let' in suggestions, as shown in this example.

MOTHER'S FRIEND: (*making a suggestion*) Let your son go to visit his friend.

When speaking, the tone that people use when they say 'let ...' indicates whether the
sentence is a command or a suggestion. When we are reading and we find a sentence
beginning with 'let', we can normally tell from the context whether the sentence is a
command or a suggestion.

1   Are the following sentences commands or suggestions?
  a   FATHER: Let me help you with those heavy bags.
  b   FRIEND: Let him kiss you, but don't let him do anything else.
  c   TEACHER: Let your partner mark your work.
  d   GOD: Let there be light.

We can use the word 'let' in requests. Requests should have the word 'please' in them,
otherwise they sound like commands. In the following sentence, if the word 'please' were
not included this would be a command, which would be rude coming from a son to his
father.

SON: (*making a request*) Let me go to the party, Dad, please!

We can use the word 'let' in invitations that include ourselves, as shown below.

MOTHER: (*inviting her daughter to join her*) Sweetie, let us walk together to the shops.

2   Are the following sentences requests or invitations?
  a   FRIEND: Please let me have a bite of your sandwich.
  b   MINISTER: Let us give thanks to the Lord.
  c   FRIEND: Let us make a date for Friday then, for dinner at my place.
  d   SONS: Dad, let us go fishing by ourselves, please.

Sometimes people use 'let' in a sentence that sounds like a suggestion, but in fact it is a
command, as in the example below. This could be considered persuasive language.

POLITICIAN: Let us vote for a leader who will provide jobs, health care and education.

Showing physical ability using the auxiliary verb 'can'

On page 113 we discussed the auxiliary verbs that are used in front of participles (for example, 'are' and 'have'). These auxiliary verbs give tense to multiword verbs and allow participles to change the aspect of a sentence. Many other auxiliary verbs affect the meaning of a sentence in a bigger way.

For example, we use the auxiliary verb 'can' to show that the subject of the sentence is physically able to do whatever the rest of the sentence is describing. The following examples show how a sentence in the present simple changes when the auxiliary verb 'can' is placed in front of the core verb.

The second sentence does not mean that the baby girl is actually drinking from a bottle; it means only that the baby girl can drink from a bottle when she is thirsty.

When we use the auxiliary verb 'can' we do not put it in front of the present-tense verb that would normally go with that subject. The auxiliary verb 'can' is always followed by the base form of the core verb that shows the action/state of being.

1 Change the following present simple sentences by adding the word 'can'.
   a The boy rides a bicycle.
   b The woman types a letter on the computer.
   c I swim.
   d The child eats with a knife and fork.

It is important to note that the base verb that follows 'can' does not show tense. This job has been taken over by the auxiliary verb 'can', which indicates the present tense.

> The verb 'can' does have a past tense form, which is discussed on page 179.

2 The following sentences combine 'can' incorrectly with the present progressive or the present perfect. Correct these sentences by changing the verbs after the auxiliary verb into the base form of the core verb.
   a The man can is using a computer.
   b The young man can is driving a car.
   c I can have made my own clothes.

When we use 'can' before the adverb 'not', we write these words together as one word 'cannot'. This is an unusual thing to do, and other verbs are not joined to the adverb 'not' in this way.

3 Insert 'not' into the following sentences.
   a I can walk.
   b We can vote.

Showing social permission using the auxiliary verb 'may'

'May' also has another meaning, as discussed on page 161.

We usually put the auxiliary verb 'may' in front of other verbs to show that people think that it is acceptable for the subject to do whatever the verbs describe.

The following sentences show how a sentence changes when the auxiliary verb 'may' is inserted into a present-simple sentence.

The second sentence does not mean that Thembi is actually wearing a short skirt. She could be wearing jeans. However, it shows that her parents let her wear short skirts if she wants to.

When we insert 'may' into a present-simple sentence, we do not use the present-tense form of the verb that would normally go with that subject. The auxiliary verb 'may' is always followed by the base form of that verb.

It is important to note that when 'wears' changes to 'wear', in the second sentence, it is no longer a finite verb and therefore does not indicate tense. As well as changing the meaning of the sentence, the auxiliary verb 'may' now indicates that the sentence is in the present tense.

1   Change the following present simple sentences by adding the word 'may.'
    Change the finite verb in these sentences into a base verb that follows the auxiliary verb.
    a   My friend looks at my diary.
    b   Khutso goes to the party.
    c   Zwelinzima has another plate of food.

When we say that someone may not do something, we place 'not' between the auxiliary verb and the base verb, as shown in this example.

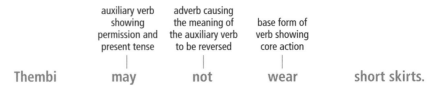

2   Rewrite your answers to question 1, inserting 'not' so they mean the opposite of what they did mean.

Showing possibility using the auxiliary verb 'may'

We can use 'may' with a different meaning from that discussed on page 160. Often we use 'may' to show the possibility of something happening, while emphasising that this is not certain to happen.

The sentences below show how a sentence in the present progressive changes when the auxiliary verb 'may' is inserted. The progressive participle remains unchanged. However, a participle showing progression must be introduced by a form of the verb 'be', yet this form can no longer be a finite form such as 'is', as the auxiliary verb has taken over the job of showing the tense of the sentence. Therefore we use the base form 'be' to stand in front of the participle.

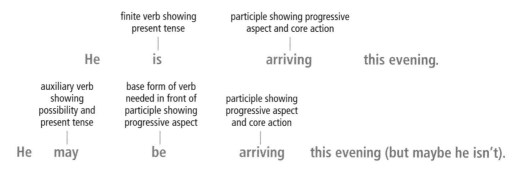

1 Add the auxiliary verb 'may' in the following present-progressive sentences to show that the action is possible but not definite.
   a I am going to Welkom this week.
   b We are driving to town tomorrow.

The sentences below show how a sentence in the present perfect changes when the auxiliary verb 'may' is inserted.

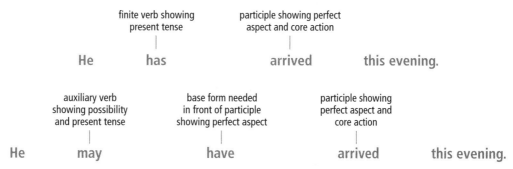

'May' is the first verb in the multiword verb, then the base form 'have', and then the participle showing the perfect aspect.

2 Add the auxiliary verb 'may' in the following present-perfect sentences.
   a They have gone to church.
   b He has torn his jeans.

Showing necessity using the auxiliary verb 'must'

'Must' has another meaning, as discussed on page 163.

The word 'must' is an auxiliary verb that is usually used to show that some action is necessary. We can use the auxiliary verb 'must' to show either physical necessity or our need to fulfill social expectations.

The sentences below show how a sentence in the present simple changes when the auxiliary verb 'must' is inserted.

The last example sentence does not mean that Zwelinzima is actually marrying Patricia; it only means that he is supposed to marry her according to society's rules.

When we insert 'must' into a present-simple sentence, it is always followed by the base form of the verb.

1   Change the following present simple sentences into present simple sentences that include the auxiliary verb 'must'.
    a   We are polite to our grandparents.
    b   The boy clicks on the arrow to get to the next section of the website.
    c   The minister christens the child.
    d   You use the key to unlock the door.

When we insert 'must' into a present-progressive sentence, it is followed by the base form 'be' and then the participle showing the progressive aspect. This construction is usually only used as a polite way of leaving a social situation. It implies that you do not want to leave, but you are needed somewhere else.

2   Change the following present progressive sentences into present-progressive sentences that are introduced by the auxiliary verb 'must'.
    a   I am going home now.
    b   We are leaving now.

Declaring an explanation using the auxiliary verb 'must'

We can also use the auxiliary verb 'must' to declare an explanation for something.

The following sentences show how a sentence in the present perfect changes when the auxiliary verb 'must' is placed in front of the present tense verb.

Irregular participles showing the perfect aspect, such as 'gone', which is used here, are discussed on page 83.

The second sentence does not mean that Janet has gone home; it is only a suggestion that gives a possible reason for why she is not here.

1   Change the following present-perfect sentences in brackets to include the auxiliary verb 'must'.
    a   There is no ice cream in the freezer. (Timothy has eaten it.)
    b   The front door was open when I came home. (S'bu has left it open.)
    c   Our lights and our electrical appliances do not work. (The electricity is off.)
2   Change the following present perfect-progressive sentences in to include the auxiliary verb 'must'.
    a   Her eyes are red. (She has been crying.)
    b   No one saw them cross the border. (They have been travelling at night.)
    c   My mother is angry because I was late. (She has been wondering where I was.)
3   Answer the following questions using the words in brackets. You will need to put the words in brackets into the correct order.
    a   Who is in the bathroom? (my must it be father)
    b   Where did he find those strange clothes? (found he have at the second-hand them shop must)
    c   What was that big development we just drove past? (must been a new it shopping mall have)
    d   Why was your mother cross with your father? (last must had they an have argument night)

Using 'do' to show action or to give emphasis to a sentence

Sometimes we use forms of 'do' as ordinary finite verbs, and sometimes we use forms of 'do' as auxiliary verbs.

Using 'do' as an ordinary finite verb
We often use a form of 'do' as the only verb in a sentence. In this case it is the finite verb and it shows an action. We must use the form of 'do' that matches the subject.

The verb 'to do' in the present tense		
First person singular:	I	do
Second person singular:	you	do
Third person singular:	he/she/it	does
First person plural:	we	do
Second person plural:	you	do
Third person plural:	they	do

1   Rewrite the following present tense sentences using the form of 'do' that matches the subject.
   a   I (do) more than one job.
   b   She (do) the washing up every evening.
   c   He (do) little exercise.

The verb 'do' is a vague verb, therefore when 'do' is the only verb in a sentence or clause the direct object usually gives extra information about the core action.

Using 'do' as an auxiliary verb to show emphasis
We can add a form of the verb 'do' into a sentence to show emphasis. When we do this we must choose the form of the verb 'do' that matches the subject. This form of the verb 'do' then becomes the auxiliary verb, which is a finite verb. It is then followed by the base form of the verb that would have followed the subject in the present simple sentence, as shown in the second sentence below.

FATHER: *(talking about his son) Are you sure he needs new shoes?*
MOTHER: *Yes, he does need new shoes.*

In the above conversation, the father is not sure that his son needs new shoes. The mother is sure that her son does, and she tries to emphasise this in order to convince his father. To give emphasis to her sentence she adds 'do' into it. This is then followed by the base form of the core verb 'need'.

2   To show emphasis, rewrite the following sentences inserting 'do' or 'does'. Write the verb that follows the auxiliary verb in its base form. Only change the verbs in italics.
   a   She *knows* a lot about cooking, but she uses too many herbs.
   b   I *love* her, but sometimes I need to be alone.

We do not use 'do' in front of finite forms of the verb 'be' when these are in statements. However, we can use it in front of the base form 'be' when this is part of an emphatic invitation, such as 'Do come to the party!'.

Using 'do' and 'not' to make a negative statement

When we use the adverb 'not' in a statement we usually use it with an auxiliary verb. When you read page 160 you practised using the auxiliary verb 'may' with 'not'. You should remember from that page that 'not' is inserted between the auxiliary verb and the base form of the core verb.

However, sometimes we want to make a statement negative but there is only one verb, as in the example below.

This is a problem because we need to insert the adverb 'not' between two verbs. Therefore we add the appropriate form of 'do' into the sentence in front of 'not'. Grammatically, the 'do' or 'does' functions as an auxiliary verb, but it does not change the meaning of the sentence. Only the adverb 'not' changes the meaning of the sentence. This construction allows us to use the standard pattern for a negative sentence even when there was no auxiliary verb in the positive form of the sentence.

In the above example, the subject is followed by the form of the verb 'do' that matches this subject. This verb becomes the finite verb. It is then followed by the adverb 'not' and the base form of the core verb. (In this construction the form of the verb 'do' is called a 'dummy auxiliary verb' because, in the same way as a shop dummy is not a real person that can walk and talk, the dummy auxiliary verb is not a real auxiliary verb that changes the meaning of the sentence. It just acts like an auxiliary verb in grammatical terms.)

1   Rewrite the following positive statements as negative statements.
    a   She learns Zulu at school.
    b   The waitress spills the cocktails often.
    c   I wear jeans.

However, we may not use this pattern with sentences using forms of the verb 'be'. Instead we place the adverb 'not' after the finite verb that is a form of the verb 'be'. If there are other verbs, these follow the 'not', as shown below.

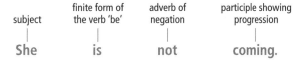

2   Rewrite the following positive statements as negative statements.
    a   Niren and Moses are going to Gauteng.
    b   The boy at the back of the classroom is Simon.

A shop dummy allows clothes to be displayed as if a real person was wearing them.

Reviewing the auxiliary verbs that have been discussed up to this point

The auxiliary verbs that we have discussed so far in this book can be used for a number of different reasons, which are summarised in this table.

Types of auxiliary verb	Reasons for using this type of auxiliary verb	Examples of auxiliary verbs that can be used in this way
progressive auxiliary verbs	to show the progressive aspect	am, is, are, was, were
perfect auxiliary verbs	to show the perfect aspect	have, has, had
modal auxiliary verbs	to change the meaning of the sentence	can, may, must, do, does
dummy auxiliary verbs	to stand in front of 'not' so that a negative sentence can be made following the usual pattern	do, does

This list is not a complete list of reasons for using auxiliary verbs. It only shows those verbs that have been discussed in this book up to this point. The modal auxiliaries 'will' and 'shall' are not included here, nor are past tense modal auxiliaries or passive auxiliaries.

The term 'auxiliary' means 'helper', and can also be used to describe someone who helped someone else commit a crime.

1   Insert a progressive auxiliary verb into each of the following sentences.
  a   Simone _____ going to the cinema tomorrow.
  b   Yesterday she _____ looking for her pencil case.
  c   I _____ studying for my examinations.
  d   Yesterday we _____ waiting for the bus, but it never came.
  e   We _____ not expecting the bus to come today.

2   a   Which of the progressive auxiliaries show that a sentence is in the present tense?
     b   Which of the progressive auxiliaries show that a sentence is in the past tense?

3 Insert a perfect auxiliary verb into each of the following sentences.
   a I _____ eaten enough food already today.
   b Yesterday my brother _____ not eaten anything until supper.
   c My father _____ left for work already this morning.
4 a Which of the perfect auxiliaries show that a sentence is in the present tense?
   b Which of the perfect auxiliaries show that a sentence is in the past tense?

The verbs 'am', 'is', 'are', 'was', 'were', 'have', 'has', and 'had' are not always auxiliary verbs. Sometimes they are normal verbs that do not come in front of participles.

5 Which of these sentences do not contain a progressive auxiliary or a perfect auxiliary?
   a I am hungry.
   b She is looking in the fridge.
   c Michael and Robin are dancing.
   d The teacher was cross.
   e The workers were striking.
   f We have a dream: to own our own home.
   g He has a big appetite.
   h They had gone to the shops already.
6 Insert an appropriate modal auxiliary verb into each of the following sentences. Use a different modal auxiliary in each sentence.
   a I _____ attend school although I do not want to.
   b I still _____ love you!
   c He still _____ love you.
   d We _____ not smoke on the train.
   e I _____ open that using a tin-opener.
7 Insert a dummy auxiliary verb into each of the following sentences.
   a We _____ not want to go.
   b She _____ not like to read.

We can use an auxiliary verb in front of a participle, in front of a verb in its base form, or in front of the adverb 'not'.

8 By thinking about the rule stated above, decide which of the following underlined verbs are auxiliary verbs. Some of these underlined verbs are auxiliary verbs we have not yet discussed in this book; others are not auxiliary verbs.
   a I shall be angry.
   b She ought to go to school
   c He will go to the cinema.
   d She needs to go the bathroom.
9 In response to question 5 you probably decided that two words were auxiliary verbs because their sentences followed the auxiliary verb-base verb pattern. Now look at the table on page 166 and decide which type of auxiliary verb you would categorise these new auxiliaries as.

Talking about the future using the auxiliary verbs 'will' and 'shall'

We can use certain modal auxiliary verbs to show that we are predicting the future. To do this we usually use the auxiliary verb 'will', as shown in the example below.

subject	auxiliary verb	base verb showing core action	
Nokthula	will	look	in the fridge (when she comes home from school).

Nokthula will look in the fridge. I wonder if there is some fruit left for her.

As with all other auxiliary verbs, this auxiliary verb is a finite verb that shows whether the sentence is in the present or the past tense. The verb 'will' shows that the sentence is in the present tense. In the example above, Nokthula's mother is speaking in the present.

'Will' is a modal auxiliary verb that changes the meaning of the sentence in a special way. Traditionally, the special way that 'will' changes a sentence is that it predicts the future actions of the subject of the sentence, even if the subject does not intend doing this action yet. In the example above, Nokthula is probably not thinking about the fridge at all.

When we use 'will' in the present simple we do not put a present-tense verb after it. It must be followed by the base form of a verb.

1 Rewrite the present tense sentences in brackets as present-tense sentences that use the auxiliary verb 'will' to predict the subject's actions in the future.
   a She is in love with John now. (However she becomes irritated by John after the wedding.)
   b Mrs Mujuru does not like to travel. (However, she comes to her brother's funeral.)
   c Samuel is bad at Mathematics. (But he passes this year's examination.)
   d You are laughing now. (But tomorrow you are crying.)
   e You want to see the rainbow later. (However it is gone.)
   f Richard loves his new car. (But it is stolen in one month.)

Traditionally we use a different auxiliary verb, 'shall', when the subject is in the first person (when it is 'I' or 'we'). In these cases the subject is predicting his/her own future.

As with 'will', when we use 'shall' in the present simple we do not put a present-tense verb after it. It must be followed by the base form of a verb.

2   Rewrite the present-tense sentences in brackets as sentences that use the auxiliary verb 'shall' to predict the subject's actions in the future.
   a   My boyfriend wants to get married. (I marry him.)
   b   We were given an invitation to Richard's party. (We go.)
   c   He is coming to beat me up. (However soon I am gone.)
   d   We always go to Cape St Francis for our holidays. (This year we are travelling by car.)

Many people no longer use 'shall'; they use 'will' with all subjects. Other people only use the old-fashioned form 'shall' when they want to emphasise what they are saying. Some translations of the Bible also use 'shall' for emphasis.

When we use 'shall' or 'will' in front of 'I' or 'we', we are not always predicting what will happen in the future. Sometimes we are just expressing our intentions.

3   Which one of the following sentences expresses an intention about the future and which one has been used to predict the future?
   a   I will go to jail next week.
   b   I shall escape from jail!

As well as using 'will' or 'shall' with present-simple verbs, we can also use these auxiliaries with present-progressive verbs or present-perfect verbs.

4   Fill in the missing sentences in the following table.

Examples of present-tense sentences that use 'will' and 'shall' with different aspects		
	Example sentences using 'will' to predict the future	Example sentences using 'shall' to show intentions about the future emphatically
A sentence in the present simple that uses a modal to talk about the future:	He will go to the party.	I shall go to the party.
A sentence in the present progressive that uses a modal to talk about the future:	He will be going to the party.	a
A sentence in the present perfect that uses a modal to talk about the future:	He will have gone to the party.	b

When we use the modal auxiliary verbs 'will' or 'shall' to refer to the future we say that the sentence is in the 'future mode'. Therefore a sentence such as 'I shall go to the party.' is in the present tense, the simple aspect and the future mode.

5   Give the tense, aspect and mode of your answers to 4 a and b.

Activity J

The following speech was made by a famous black American, Martin Luther King. King made this speech in 1963, when black Americans in the southern states of the United States of America, such as the State of Mississippi, still did not have the right to vote. At this time the black people in the northern states, such as the State of New York, did have the right to vote, but felt that none of the political parties represented their needs.

Read this abridged version of King's speech and answer the questions on page 172.

I have a dream

By Martin Luther King

(Delivered on the steps at the Lincoln Memorial in Washington D.C. on August 28, 1963)

Five score years ago, a great American, in whose symbolic shadow we stand, signed the Emancipation Proclamation. This momentous decree came as a great beacon light of hope to millions of Negro slaves who had been seared in the flames of withering injustice. It came as a joyous daybreak to end the long night of captivity.

But one hundred years later, we must face the tragic fact that the Negro is still not free. One hundred years later, the life of the Negro is still sadly crippled by the manacles of segregation and the chains of discrimination. One hundred years later, the Negro lives on a lonely island of poverty in the midst of a vast ocean of material prosperity. One hundred years later, the Negro is still languishing in the corners of American society and finds himself an exile in his own land. So we have come here today to dramatize an appalling condition.

But there is something that I must say to my people who stand on the warm threshold which leads into the palace of justice. In the process of gaining our rightful place we must not be guilty of wrongful deeds. Let us not seek to satisfy our thirst for freedom by drinking from the cup of bitterness and hatred.

We must forever conduct our struggle on the high plane of dignity and discipline. We must not allow our creative protest to degenerate into physical violence. Again and again we must rise to the majestic heights of meeting physical force with soul force. The marvelous new militancy which has engulfed the Negro community must not lead us to a distrust of all white people, for many of our white brothers, as evidenced by their presence here today, have come to realize that their destiny is tied up with our destiny and their freedom is inextricably bound to our freedom. We cannot walk alone.

And as we walk, we must make the pledge that we shall march ahead. We cannot turn back. There are those who are asking the devotees of civil rights, 'When will you be satisfied?' We can never be satisfied as long as our bodies, heavy with the fatigue of travel, cannot gain lodging in the motels of the highways and the hotels of the cities. We cannot be satisfied as long as the Negro's basic mobility is from a smaller ghetto to a larger one. We can never be satisfied as long as a Negro in Mississippi cannot vote and a Negro in New York believes he has nothing for which to vote. No, no, we are not satisfied, and we will not be satisfied until justice rolls down like waters and righteousness like a mighty stream.

I am not unmindful that some of you have come here out of great trials and tribulations. Some of you have come fresh from narrow cells. Some of you have come from areas where your quest for freedom left you battered by the storms of persecution and staggered by the winds of police brutality. You have been the veterans of creative suffering. Continue to work with the faith that unearned suffering is redemptive.

Go back to Mississippi, go back to Alabama, go back to Georgia, go back to Louisiana, go back to the slums and ghettos of our northern cities, knowing that somehow this situation can and will be changed. Let us not wallow in the valley of despair.

I say to you today, my friends, that in spite of the difficulties and frustrations of the moment, I still have a dream. It is a dream deeply rooted in the American dream.

I have a dream that one day this nation will rise up and live out the true meaning of its creed: 'We hold these truths to be self-evident: that all men are created equal.'

I have a dream that one day on the red hills of Georgia the sons of former slaves and the sons of former slaveowners will be able to sit down together at a table of brotherhood.

I have a dream that one day even the state of Mississippi, a desert state, sweltering with the heat of injustice and oppression, will be transformed into an oasis of freedom and justice.

I have a dream that my four children will one day live in a nation where they will not be judged by the color of their skin but by the content of their character.

I have a dream today.

I have a dream that one day the state of Alabama will be transformed into a situation where little black boys and black girls will be able to join hands with little white boys and white girls and walk together as sisters and brothers.

I have a dream today.

I have a dream that one day every valley shall be exalted, every hill and mountain shall be made low, the rough places will be made plain, and the crooked places will be made straight, and the glory of the Lord shall be revealed, and all flesh shall see it together.

This is our hope. This is the faith with which I return to the South. With this faith we will be able to hew out of the mountain of despair a stone of hope. With this faith we will be able to transform the jangling discords of our nation into a beautiful symphony of brotherhood. With this faith we will be able to work together, to pray together, to struggle together, to go to jail together, to stand up for freedom together, knowing that we will be free one day.

This will be the day when all of God's children will be able to sing with a new meaning, 'My country, 'tis of thee, sweet land of liberty, of thee I sing. Land where my fathers died, land of the pilgrim's pride, from every mountainside, let freedom ring.'

And if America is to be a great nation this must become true. So let freedom ring from the prodigious hilltops of New Hampshire. Let freedom ring from the mighty mountains of New York. Let freedom ring from the heightening Alleghenies of Pennsylvania!

Let freedom ring from the snowcapped Rockies of Colorado!

Let freedom ring from the curvaceous peaks of California!

But not only that; let freedom ring from Stone Mountain of Georgia!

Let freedom ring from Lookout Mountain of Tennessee!

Let freedom ring from every hill and every molehill of Mississippi. From every mountainside, let freedom ring.

When we let freedom ring, when we let it ring from every village and every hamlet, from every state and every city, we will be able to speed up that day when all of God's children, black men and white men, Jews and Gentiles, Protestants and Catholics, will be able to join hands and sing in the words of the old Negro spiritual, 'Free at last! Free at last! Thank God Almighty, we are free at last!'

1   The word 'King' has a capital letter. Is this because it is:
    a   a royal title?
    b   a surname?
    c   a place name?
2   What tense is the first paragraph written in?
3   What tense is the rest of the speech written in?
4   What American word does King use to refer to a black person?
5   In paragraphs 3–5 King uses the auxiliary verb 'must' a number of times. Is he using it:
    a   to show social necessity?
    b   to show physical necessity?
    c   to declare an explanation?
6   King tells his audience to go home 'knowing that somehow this situation can and will be changed.' Some words are implied in this quotation from paragraph 7. Written out more fully, this quotation would be:
    a   knowing that somehow this situation can be changed and will be changed.
    b   knowing that somehow this situation can change and will be changed.
    c   knowing that somehow this situation can to change and will be changed.
7   In the above quotation, the auxiliary verb 'can' means:
    a   'tin'.
    b   'shall'.
    c   'is able to'.
8   In the same quotation above, the auxiliary verb 'will' is part of:
    a   an intention.
    b   a prediction.
    c   a suggestion.
    d   an invitation.
    e   a command.
    f   a request.
9   In paragraphs 9–13 King uses the auxiliary verb 'will' a number of times. Why does he use the word 'will'?
10 In paragraph 15 King uses the auxiliary verb 'shall' instead of 'will'. Is this because:
    a   the sentences have a first-person subject.
    b   he wants to predict the future of the landscape, which cannot think about its own future.
    c   he wants this paragraph to have a traditional, biblical sound.
11 Near the end of his speech King speaks of songs of freedom ringing through the land. The words 'let freedom ring' could be translated as:
    a   allow songs of freedom to be sung.
    b   rent property to free people.
    c   telephone the news to everyone.
12 Paragraph 14 and paragraph 16 are only one sentence long. They both say: 'I have a dream today.' Because they are short these two paragraphs have a lot of impact. When most of the speech is about King's dream of the future, why does he emphasise the present in these two paragraphs?

Adverbs and adjectives showing degrees of likelihood

When we talk about the future we are making a prediction. That prediction might be right or it might be wrong. We can show how much confidence we have in our prediction by inserting an adjective or an adverb of likelihood into our sentence.

Adverbs of likelihood
The following adverbs show different degrees of likelihood:
- definitely/surely/certainly – we use one of these adverbs when we know something will happen
- likely/probably – we use one of these adverbs when we know that something will probably happen, but we are not absolutely sure
- possibly – we use this adverb when something might happen.

1   Which of the following sentences matches each of the pictures below?
    a   It will definitely rain tonight.
    b   It will probably rain tonight.
    c   It will possibly rain tonight.

Adjectives of likelihood
The following adjectives show five different degrees of likelihood:
- definite/sure/certain – we use one of these adjectives when we know something will happen
- likely/probable – we use one of these adjectives when we know that something will probably happen, but we are not absolutely sure
- possible – we use this adjective when something might happen
- unlikely/improbable – we use one of these adjectives when we know something will probably not happen
- impossible – we use this adjective when we know something will definitely not happen.

2   Insert one of the above adjectives into each of the following sentences.
    a   He will win the race. It's a _____ thing, because he is the only person who is running.
    b   It is _____ for us to live if there is no oxygen for us to breathe.
    c   It is _____ that my mother will cook supper tonight, because she always has in the past.
    d   It is _____ that I will get an MP3 player for Christmas, as my father has just been retrenched and money is scarce.
    e   It is _____ that it will rain tonight, as there are clouds in the sky.

Using the adverb 'not' in statements or commands

Before we discuss how to use 'not' in commands, we must first revise the rules about using 'not' in statements.

Using 'not' in statements

To make a sentence that has a multiword verb negative, put 'not' after the auxiliary verb.

If a sentence has just one verb and we want to change it into the negative, we have to check if that verb is a form of the verb 'be'. If it is a form of the verb 'be' we can put 'not' after the verb. If the single verb is not a form of the verb 'be', then we need to insert a form of the dummy auxiliary 'do' in front of 'not'.

1   Change the following sentences to mean the opposite of what they mean now. Do this by inserting 'not', and a dummy auxiliary verb if necessary.

   a   I am looking.
   b   I have looked.
   c   I must look.
   d   I may look.
   e   I can look.
   f   I will look.
   g   I shall look.
   h   I do look.
   i   I like most people.
   j   I am angry.
   k   Aliens exist.
   l   They are guilty of theft.
   m   We were there.
   n   Often animals trample the things underneath their feet.
   o   The judge is wise.
   p   The man judges accused people.

Using 'not' in commands

When we make a command the invisible subject is always 'you', although this could be either singular or plural. When the command is positive we use a finite verb that matches this invisible subject. Look at the following examples.

When we make a negative command we must use a form of the dummy auxiliary verb 'do', but the form we use is always 'do', because this is the finite form that matches the invisible subject 'you'. The verb 'do' must go before the adverb 'not'. Look at the following examples.

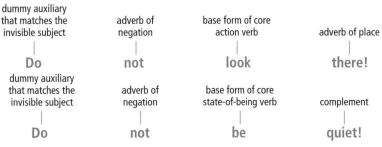

2   Change the following positive commands into negative commands by inserting the auxiliary verb 'do' and the adverb 'not'.
   a   Go to the shops.
   b   Be polite to them.
   c   Throw the ball to me!
   d   Be nasty.
   e   Smoke cigarettes.
   f   Be friendly to strangers.
   g   Give your leftover food to the dogs.
   h   Judge other people.

In the past, speakers of English used to make negative commands without using the dummy auxiliary 'do'. You may come across this construction in traditional Christian prayers. For example, when reading the Lord's Prayer people make the following request to God: 'Lead us not into temptation.' However, people no longer speak like this to each other, and a more modern translation of this line would be 'Do not lead us into temptation.'

As you saw on page 164, we can use 'do' in positive statements as well. However, in these cases it is not a dummy auxiliary verb but an auxiliary verb that shows emphasis.

3   Insert 'do' and an exclamation mark into the following commands for emphasis.
   a   Be quiet.
   b   Go away.
   c   Give them to me.

Talking about the future without using auxiliary verbs

We can talk about the future without needing to use an auxiliary verb. To do this we use the present tense in a way that implies that we are talking about the future.

Using the present simple and an adverb of time to talk about the future

To talk about the future we can use a present-simple verb with an adverb of time that indicates some time in the future. An example is shown below.

	present-simple verb	adverb of time indicating some future time
He	arrives	tomorrow.

This box contains some adverbs of time that can be used to refer to the future. It also contains some adverbial phrases of time that can be used to refer to the future.

Some adverbs of time that refer to the future		
tomorrow	soon	shortly
Some adverbial phrases of time that refer to the future		
tomorrow morning	tomorrow afternoon	tomorrow evening
in a moment	the day after tomorrow	a week from tomorrow
next week	next fortnight	next month next year
this coming Sunday	this coming week	this coming month

1   To refer to the future, insert an appropriate adverb of time or an adverbial phrase of time from the box into the following present-simple sentences.
   a   We drive to Saldhana Bay _____.
   b   Sukie comes _____.
   c   _____ Charl leaves for the airport.
   d   _____ we go home.

The adverb or adverbial phrase can be inserted at the beginning of the sentence or at the end of the sentence. (In more complicated sentences these could also appear between certain other phrases in the sentence.)

Using the present progressive and an adverb of time to talk about the future

To talk about the future we can also use a present-progressive verb with an adverb of time that indicates some time in the future. An example is shown below.

verb showing present tense	verb showing progressive aspect	adverb of time indicating some future time
He is	arriving	tomorrow.

2 To refer to the future, rewrite the following sentences by making the verb in brackets into a present-perfect verb. The adverb/adverbial phrase of time has already been inserted for you.

a The officials _____ _____ next month. (arrive)

b My mother _____ _____ next week. (come)

c The television programme _____ _____ in a moment. (finish)

d Next year the cost of living _____ _____. (increase)

Using the present progressive and an infinitive to talk about the future

We can also use a present-progressive form of a verb combined with an infinitive to talk about the future. This is most often done when the present-progressive verb is a form of the verb 'go'.

Here is an example of a present-progressive form of the verb 'go' combined with an infinitive, which is being used to talk about the future.

verb showing present tense	verb showing progressive aspect	infinitive	
He is	going	to be	there for the wedding.

3 To refer to the future, rewrite the following sentences by making the first verb in brackets into a present-perfect verb and the second verb in brackets into an infinitive.

a We (go) (leave) this party.

b He (go) (be) a doctor.

c They (go) (stay) with friends.

d She (go) (go) overseas.

Sometimes the conjunction also indicates that a subordinate clause is referring to the future. For example, the conjunction 'so' in the following sentence shows that the subordinate clause is referring to future consequences.

Eat everything on your plate, so you have lots of energy.

4 Insert the appropriate conjunction into this sentence to emphasise that the subordinate clause, which is in the present tense, is referring to the future.

Go to bed early, _____ you can have a good long sleep.

Using punctuation to mean 'and' or 'or'

Using commas or semi-colons to mean 'and'
When we write a list we usually use a comma (,) instead of 'and' between each item in the list, except before the last item. This is shown in the examples below.

I like VWs, BMWs, Volvos and Toyotas.

1 Punctuate the following sentences.
    a i watch *Backstage Isidingo* and *Sewende Laan*
    b i enjoy swimming running dancing and cycling

When most of the items in the list are phrases we use a semi-colon instead of a comma between each item. This is shown in the following example.

I watch: Lekgotleng le Modise; The Weakest Link; Days of our Lives; *and* Bold & Beautiful.

When we use semi-colons in this way we also often introduce the list with a colon (:), as shown above. For clarity, when using semi-colons to separate items in a list we usually also put one before the 'and' that adds the last item to the list, particularly if some of the items include the word 'and'.

2 Punctuate the following sentences.
    a i like watching television with my cousin jogging alone at sunrise and hanging out with Thandaza and Michael
    b i enjoy sticking photographs in my scrapbook drawing borders around them with coloured pens and putting stickers and comments all over the pages

If some of the items in a list include commas already then we should use semi-colons between the items in the list, as in the following example.

I like: muffins with butter, cheese and mustard; banana, apple and peaunut butter smoothies; energy bars; and energy drinks.

3 Punctuate the following sentence.
    i enjoy making model aeroplanes ships and cars building things out of wood and shooting stones marbles and berries out of my catapault

Using a forward slash to mean 'or'
We use a forward slash (/) to mean 'or'. This is often used when we do not know if a person is male or female, as in the example below.

When the doctor arrives, we will ask him/her how long you will be in hospital.

4 Punctuate the following sentence.
    if the patient is shy he she may not want to talk about his her problem

Using auxiliary verbs in the past tense

Auxiliary verbs have irregular past-tense forms. The easiest ones to change into the past tense are shown below.

Present-tense form of auxiliary verb	Past-tense form of auxiliary verb
am/is	was
are	were
have/has	had
do/does	did

1 Rewrite the following sentences into the past tense. Keep the same aspect as in the original.

  a I am eating some noodles.
  b He is going to the shops.
  c They are travelling in a train.
  d We have been to the museum.
  e She has shown us her homework.
  f You do not love me.
  g He does not know the truth.

Some of the modal auxiliary verbs can be more difficult to change into the past tense. Look at the table below.

Present-tense form of modal auxiliary verb	Past-tense form of modal auxiliary verb
can	could
will/shall	would
may	might
must	(There is none.)

We use 'would' as the past-tense form of 'shall' as well as 'will'.

There is no past-tense form of 'must', but other ways of showing obligation in the past tense are shown in the answers to question 6 on page 219.

2. Using the table as a guide, rewrite the following sentences into the past tense.

  a When I am fit I can run 10km without stopping.
  b These days, when I visit my grandmother for supper I will wear formal clothes.
  c He says he shall go immediately.
  d The teacher says I may leave the room.
  e The weather report says it may rain this evening.

When we use past-tense auxiliary verbs we often use join them with the conjunction 'when'.

3. Join the subordinate clauses on the left with an appropriate main clause on the right.

Subordinate clause	Main clause
a When we were young,	we could hear strange noises coming from outside.
b When we were hiding in the cupboard,	we tried to learn their language.
c When the English people arrived on our island	we could not understand the reasons for our parents divorce.

The indicative mood and the subjunctive mood

The indicative mood

The indicative mood shows that we are talking about real situations. Most sentences are in the indicative mood.

1   Match each of the following sentences on the left with the appropriate reason on the right for why a sentence can be classified as being in the indicative mood.

Sentence	Reason why this sentence can be classified as being in the indicative mood
a You must go home now.	It describes a real situation.
b We are on our way to school.	It asks a question about a real possibility.
c We will win.	It gives a definite instruction.
d He may live for a few more years.	It refers to a definite intention regarding the future.
e Is supper ready yet?	It refers to a real possibility.

Although some of the sentences in this table talk about possibilities, these are the kinds of possibilities that are firmly rooted in the present reality. The subjunctive mood, on the other hand, talks about possibilities that are removed from the present reality.

The subjunctive mood

Sentences are in the subjunctive mood when they talk about situations that do not exist and are not likely to exist (hypothetical situations). See the example below the picture.

> The situation shown in this picture is a hypothetical situation, so the subjunctive mood is used to talk about it.

If aliens arrived on Earth, I would try to learn their language.

When we use the subjunctive mood we are trying to show that it is something different from the indicative mood. Therefore we avoid using normal present-tense verbs, because these refer to situations that exist. We have to use verbs that do not show the present tense. But, thankfully, English does not require us to learn a whole new set of verb forms. Instead, it uses forms that we already know, but they are used for a new purpose.

So, if we need to use a form of the verb 'be', we use 'were'. And if we need to use almost any other verb, we change it into the form we would use in the past tense.

2   Complete the following subjunctive sentences by adding the appropriate form of the verb 'be'.
   a   If I _____ a teacher, I would be pleasant to my learners.
   b   If he _____ to go to university, we would need to pay his fees.
   c   I would be hurt if our relationship _____ to end now.
3   Rewrite the following indicative sentences into the subjunctive mood.
   a   We will do it, if you ask nicely.
   b   If she jumps on the bed, she will break it.
   c   I will go to the doctor, if I can get out of bed.

Although the verb form 'may' can refer to a possible situation, it cannot indicate the subjunctive mood as it already indicates the present tense. Therefore we use the indicative form 'may' to refer to a likely possibility, and we use the subjunctive form 'might' to refer to an unlikely possibility.

4   Rewrite the following sentences so that they suggest that the action is unlikely. (Change them from the indicative mood into the subjunctive mood.)
   a   My brother may help me with my homework.
   b   We may get free tickets to the concert.

In the subjunctive mood, we can use the conjunction 'if' to join two clauses. Alternatively, if the first clause was a subordinate clause and it had an auxiliary verb, we could leave out the conjunction and move the auxiliary verb in front of the subject, as shown in the following example.

   If you were to give her flowers, she would forgive you.
   Were you to give her flowers, she would forgive you.

5   Rewrite the following subjunctive sentences so that they are joined without the use of a conjunction.
   a   If he were a mechanic, he would fix his own car.
   b   If she had known the truth, she would have told it to me.
6   The following extract is from a famous poem called 'The Wasteland' by T.S. Eliot.
   a   Underline the words that indicate the subjunctive mood.
   b   Why has the poet used the subjunctive mood?

Here is no water but only rock
Rock and no water and the sandy road
The road winding above among the mountains
Which are mountains of rock without water
If there were water we should stop and drink
Amongst the rock one cannot stop or think …
            If there were water
            And no rock
            If there were rock
            And also water
            And water
            A spring
            A pool among the rock
            If there were the sound of water only …
            Drip drop drip drop drop drop drop
            But there is no water …

Direct speech, quotations and quotation marks

When we want to show exactly what a person says we put that person's words into quotation marks. This technique is called 'direct speech' because, when we read it, it is as if the person is talking directly in front of us. We usually introduce the words in quotation marks by showing who is speaking, as shown in the example below.

Zwiitani says, 'Always be honest.'
Johan said, 'Tell the truth.'

The words outside the brackets can be written in the present tense or the past tense. The following table shows the past simple and the present simple forms of the irregular verb 'say'.

The verb 'to say'		Simple aspect	
		Past tense	Present tense
First person singular:	I	said	say
Second person singular:	you	said	say
Third person singular:	he/she/it	said	says
First person plural:	we	said	say
Second person plural:	you	said	say
Third person plural:	they	said	say

1   Rewrite the following words as direct speech inside single quotation marks. Use the present tense, as if you were repeating what was said to someone who had not heard the speaker(s) properly.

I like skate-boarding.

We enjoy skateboarding.

a   Begin by writing: Robbie …   b   Begin by writing: The boys …

Although we sometimes use the present tense in front of direct speech, stories are normally written in the past tense, and writers of stories usually introduce any direct speech using the past tense. However, the words inside the quotation marks can be in either the present or the past tense.

When we write film scripts or play scripts we do not use quotation marks. We write the character's name in capital letters and then we put the words that that character says after a colon, as shown below.

ROBBIE: I like skateboarding.

2   Rewrite the words in question 1 b as a line from a play script.

3   Using the past tense of the verb 'say', introduce the following words in quotation marks.
    a   I (say), 'I was there yesterday.'
    b   You (say), 'I am sad.'
    c   She (say), 'I will go to the shops.'

Non-fiction essays are normally written in the present tense, because we are expressing what we think at the moment. When we refer to what somebody has written on the topic that we are discussing we usually also use the present tense. This is because when people write their opinions down using the present tense, we always read them in the present tense. So whenever we open their books it is as if they are still speaking.

4   a   What form of the verb 'say' should be used in the following statement.

In his autobiography, *Long Walk to Freedom*, Nelson Mandela (say), 'I am no more virtuous or self-sacrificing than the next man, but I found that I could not even enjoy the poor and limited freedoms I was allowed when I knew my people were not free.'

However, when we are referring to a person's written words, rather than using a form of the verb 'say', it is even better to use:
● He writes …
● She states …
● He observes …
● She notes …

This is because 'say' is normally used to refer to someone speaking rather than someone writing.
    When we use the present tense in this way to refer to something that was written in the past we say that we are using 'the historical present'.

5   Rewrite your answer to 4 using one of the verbs suggested above that would be appropriate in this context.

When we use direct speech we must follow these rules regarding punctuation:
● Use single quotation marks to enclose the direct speech.
● Put a comma between the introductory part of the sentence and the part in quotation marks.
● If the quoted words are a full sentence, put a punctuation mark that may be used to end a sentence inside the close quotation marks, and do not add a full stop.
● If the quoted words are not a full sentence, put a full stop after the quotation marks.

6   Write the words in this speech bubble as direct speech. Introduce the direct speech using a verb in the past tense.

I usually finish books quite quickly, but *Long Walk to Freedom* is a very long book.

Changing direct speech into indirect speech

When we report what someone has said without quotation marks we call this indirect speech. But when we use indirect speech we have to make some changes to what the person said, as shown in the examples below.

direct speech

Jessica Gumede said, 'I usually finish books quite quickly, but Long Walk to Freedom *is a very long book.'*

indirect speech

Jessica Gumede said that she usually finished books quite quickly, but Long Walk to Freedom *was a very long book.*

direct speech

Victoria Wylie said, 'Mmm, this slice of cake is delicious, Mum. You must have made it today.'

indirect speech

Victoria Wylie exclaimed in enjoyment that that slice of cake was delicious. She added that her mother must have made it that day.

When a sentence changes into indirect speech a number of things happen:
1   If the sentence inside the quotation marks was a statement, the comma that came before the quotation marks is replaced by the word 'that'.
2   If the sentence inside the quotation marks was a command, the comma that came before the quotation marks is replaced by 'that', and we must insert the appropriate subject ('I'/'we'/'you'/'he'/'she'/'it'/'they').
3   If the sentence inside the quotation marks was a question, the comma that came before the quotation marks is replaced by the word 'whether'.
4   The quotation marks disappear.
5   First person pronouns and determiners changes into the appropriate third person pronouns and determiners.
6   Verbs in the present simple change to verbs in the past simple.
7   Verbs in the present progressive change to verbs in the past progressive.
8   Verbs in the present perfect change to verbs in the past perfect.
9   Verbs in the past simple change to verbs in the past perfect.
10 Verbs in the past perfect do not change.
11 Adverbs of time change so that they refer to a more distant time.
12 Adverbs of place change so that they refer to a more distant place.
13 Exclamation marks, question marks and ellipsis marks are replaced by full stops.
14 Exclamations are removed and an explanation of the noise is given instead, or we use a verb that communicates the same feeling as the exclamation instead of just using 'said'.
15 If the sentence does not start with who is speaking, change the word order so that it does.
16 If the sentence containing the direct speech does not use a form of the verb 'say' to describe how the speaker is speaking, but uses a different verb instead, then use the same verb when you introduce the indirect sentence.
17 If the sentence containing direct speech begins 'let us', drop these two words and use an introductory verb that conveys a similar meaning, such as a form of 'suggest' or 'invite'.

1   Rewrite the following sentences as indirect speech.
    a   Frank said, 'I enjoy surfing.'
    b   You declared, 'I am phoning the police.'
    c   We suggested, 'Hide with us.'
    d   Claire asked, 'Am I early?'
    e   Mr van der Merwe commanded, 'Boys, wait outside my office!'
    f   Azwindini said, 'I have been to the church before.'

The following table shows how adverbs of time and place change when a sentence is rewritten in indirect speech.

Adverbial phrase of time used in direct speech	Adverbial phrase of time used in indirect speech
now	then
today	that day
this morning	that morning
this afternoon	that afternoon
yesterday	the previous day
last week	the previous week
last month	the previous month
tomorrow	the next day
tomorrow morning	the next morning
Adverbial phrase of place used in direct speech	**Adverbial phrase of place used in indirect speech**
here	there
this/that	that
these/those	those

2   Rewrite the following sentences as indirect speech.
    a   He said, 'I am cycling to that church tomorrow.'
    b   Robyn suggested to her mother, 'Let us go to the cinema this evening.'
    c   Britney said, 'I arrived here this morning.'
    d   My teacher said, 'Class, you have homework today.'

The following table gives the meanings of different noises and exclamations people make.

Noises and exclamations showing surprise	Gosh!	… exclaimed in surprise …
Noises and exclamations showing fear	Argh!	… exclaimed in fear …
Noises and exclamations showing enjoyment or anticipated enjoyment	Mmm! Yum!	… exclaimed in enjoyment …/ … exclaimed in anticipation …
Noises and exclamations showing anger	Grrr (or swear words)	… exclaimed in anger …

3   Rewrite the following sentences as indirect speech.
    a   'Gosh,' said Tatum, 'Rev. Steiner, your choir sings beautifully.'
    b   'Argh!' Kyle called. 'It is coming to get me.'
    c   'Grrr,' muttered Mr van der Merwe, 'I thought I told you to wait outside my office.'

Sometimes it is possible to shorten indirect speech that includes people's exclamations, as indicated in the second possible answers given to each of the questions 3 a–c.

More uses for quotation marks

When we are referring to a word instead of using it in a normal way we can write it in italics or use single quotation marks on either side of it. The following sentence shows an example of quotation marks being used in this way.

The word 'happy' is an antonym of the word 'sad'.

When we don't like a word or it makes us uncomfortable but we still use it then we can use single quotation marks around it to show our discomfort with that word as in the following example.

There was a time when 'non-white' people were not allowed to live in this suburb.

Another way in which we use quotation marks is to indicate an ironic use of words as in the following example.

My brother claimed he was too 'busy' to help me.

Quotation marks are sometimes used for a nickname that has been used as part of an actual name, for example:

Tsweu 'Chippa' Mokoro isn't like most guys.

1 Why are the words in the following sentences in quotation marks?
   a When we write negative statements we usually use the adverb 'not'.
   b During the apartheid years, the 'coloured' people were not privileged in the way that white people were.
   c The Latin sentence '*Temet nosce*' means 'Know yourself'.
   d Sipho 'Hotstix' Mabuse is a famous South African singer
   e He said he thought it was 'normal' to eat breakfast in the evening.

Subordinate clauses that act like objects or subjects

On page 147 we practised using the relative pronoun 'that' in subordinate clauses. This pronoun was the subject of the subordinate clause, as in the example below.

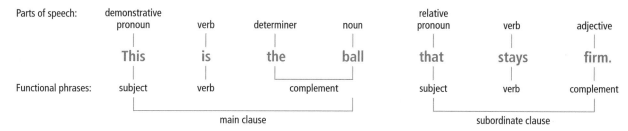

However, we can also use the relative pronoun 'that' in a complex sentence that is constructed in a different way.

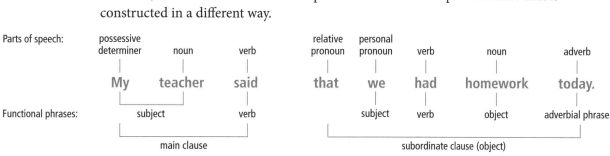

The first example above has two clauses that can be easily separated. However, in the second example the relative pronoun 'that' shows that the subordinate clause is the object of the main clause.

1 Identify the subordinate clause in the following sentences.
   a He says that the workers should work together.
   b Give presents that you would like to receive.

When speaking quickly, sometimes people leave out the relative pronoun 'that' in this type of complex sentence. This makes it harder to understand the sentence.

2 Insert the relative pronoun 'that' into the following sentences.
   a He says he cannot find the right person.
   b She thinks she knows the truth.

A subordinate clause can also be made into the subject of a sentence, although this only happens in rare situations. Look at the following example.

3 Identify the subordinate clause in the following sentence.
   That John is a liar, is totally incorrect.

Activity K

Because languages are always changing, different varieties of English have been spoken at different times in history. We can compare how English has changed over time by looking at how one section of the Bible has been translated into English at different times.

The following two texts are both translations of the words of Jesus, as recorded in Matthew chapter 7, verses 1–12, but they have been translated into English at different points in time. The text on this page is a twentieth-century translation. The text on the following page is from the seventeenth century.

The original Christian Bible was written partly in Hebrew and partly in Greek.

Judging others

1 "Do not judge others, so that God will not judge you, 2 for God will judge you in the same way as you judge others, and he will apply to you the same rules you apply to others. 3 Why, then, do you look at the speck in your brother's eye, and pay no attention to the log in your own eye? 4 How dare you say to your brother, 'Please let me take that speck out of your eye', when you have a log in your own eye? 5 You hypocrite! First take the log out of your own eye, and then you will be able to see clearly to take the speck out of your brother's eye.

6 "Do not give what is holy to dogs – they will only turn and attack you. Do not throw your pearls in front of pigs – they will only trample them underfoot.

Ask, seek, knock

7 "Ask, and you will receive; seek, and you will find; knock, and the door will be opened to you. 8 For everyone who asks will receive, and anyone who seeks will find, and the door will be opened to him who knocks. 9 Would any of you who are fathers give your son a stone when he asks for bread? 10 Or would you give him a snake when he asks for a fish? 11 Bad as you are, you know how to give good things to your children. How much more, then, will your Father in heaven give good things to those who ask him?

12 "Do for others what you want them to do for you: this is the meaning of the Law of Moses and of the teachings of the prophets.

From: *Holy Bible*: Good News Edition, 1983.

---

1 Answer the following questions based on the first text, which is the more modern translation.

a In verse 1, identify the auxiliary verb, which the translator used to show that Jesus is talking about the future.

b In verse 1, identify the adverbs of negation (the same word used twice). Say where these adverbs of negation are positioned in relation to the auxiliary verbs.

c In verse 1, what word is used for the second-person personal pronoun?

d In verse 4, what word is used for the second-person possessive determiner?

e In verse 7, identify the auxiliary verb that is used three times to show that Jesus is predicting future consequences of particular actions.

f In verse 7, what punctuation marks are used?

g In verses 9 and 10, the subjunctive mood is used in questions. What word, used twice, indicates that Jesus is referring to a possible situation rather than one that will definitely happen?

h Why are some words in this text written in bold letters?

> Matthew chapter 7, verses 1–12
>
> 1 Judge not, that ye not be judged.
> 2 For with what judgment ye judge, ye shall be judged; and with what measure ye mete, it shall be measured to you again.
> 3 And why beholdest thou the mote that is in thy brother's eye, but considerest not the beam that is in thine own eye?
> 4 Or how wilt thou say to thy brother, Let me pull out the mote out of thine eye; and, behold, a beam is in thine own eye?
> 5 Thou hypocrite, first cast out the beam out of thine own eye; and then thou shalt see clearly to cast out the mote of thy brother's eye.
> 6 Give not that which is holy unto the dogs, neither cast ye your pearls before swine, lest they trample them under their feet, and turn again and rend you.
> 7 Ask, and it shall be given you; seek, and ye shall find; knock, and it shall be opened unto you:
> 8 For every one that asketh receiveth; and he that seeketh findeth; and to him that knocketh it shall be opened.
> 9 Or what man is there of you, whom if his son ask for bread, will he give him a stone?
> 10 Or if he ask a fish, will he give him a serpent?
> 11 If ye then, being evil, know how to give good gifts unto your children, how much more shall your Father which is in heaven give good things to them that ask him?
> 12 Therefore all things whatsoever ye would that men should do to you, do ye even so to them: for this is the law and the prophets.
>
> From: *The King James Bible*, first published in 1611

2 Answer the following questions by comparing this second, older translation, with the more modern version.

  a In this older translation there are no auxiliary verbs in verse 1. How does it refer to the future?

  b In the seventeenth century, were there different rules to today's rules about where English-speakers could place 'not' in a sentence? Support your answer by referring to verse 1.

  c In verse 1 of this older translation, what word is used as the second-person personal pronoun?

  d In verse 4 of this older translation, what two different words are used for the second-person possessive pronoun?

  e In verse 7 of this older translation, identify the auxiliary verb that the translator has used to show that Jesus was talking about the future.

  f What punctuation marks in the later text, indicating direct speech, have not been used in this earlier translation?

  g In verses 9 and 10 of this older translation there is no modal auxiliary that indicates this sentence is in the subjunctive mood. How have verbs been used to indicate the subjunctive mood?

  h What old-fashioned word is used instead of the word 'snake' in the seventeenth-century translation?

  i Neither translation uses the subjunctive mood in the rhetorical question in verse 11. Why not?

Contractions using apostrophes to show letters are missing

We often shorten two words into one word. When we shorten or contract words in this way we call them contractions. We use an apostrophe to show where letters have been left out.

Contractions of personal pronouns and present-tense forms of the verb 'be'	
I am	I'm
you are	you're
he is	he's
she is	she's
it is	it's
we are	we're
they are	they're

We do not often make the past-tense forms of the verb 'be' into contractions because these would sound just like the present-tense contractions, and this could be confusing.

1   Rewrite the following sentences using contractions where these are allowed.
   a   She is leaving now.
   b   I am so proud!
   c   You are very popular.
   d   It is an aeroplane!

When 'it's' is written with an apostrophe it always means 'it is'. The possessive pronoun, as in 'its food', never has an apostrophe.

Contractions of relative pronouns and verbs			
that is	that's		
what is	what's	what are	what're
which is	which's	which are	which're
who is	who's	who are	who're
there is	there's	there are	there're
here is	here's	here are	here're

The contraction 'who's' always means 'who is', 'who was' or 'who has'. The word 'whose' acts as the relative determiner (as discussed on page 145).

2   Rewrite the following sentences using contractions where these are allowed.
   a   Which is my bag?
   b   There is no door in this wall.
   c   Here are some sweets.
   d   What is that?

Contractions of personal pronouns and present-tense forms of the verb 'have'		Contractions of personal pronouns and past tense forms of the verb 'have'	
I have	I've	I had	I'd
you have	you've	you had	you'd
he has	he's	he had	he'd
she has	she's	she had	she'd
it has	it's	it had	it'd
we have	we've	we had	we'd
they have	they've	they had	they'd

In informal English we often use a contraction of a form of the verb 'have' and the adverb 'not' in front of the word 'got'. This comes from American English. The phrases 'I have' and 'I have got' mean the same thing. Therefore a phrase such as 'I've got' means the same as 'I've'. The effect of using 'got' with a contraction in this way is that it makes your language sound more informal.

3 Rewrite the following sentences using contractions where these are allowed.
   a They have got a big car.
   b He is a doctor.
   c We had already left when the fire started.
   d I had no idea what was happening.

Contractions of present-tense auxiliary verbs and 'not'		Contractions of 'did' and 'not', past tense auxiliary verbs and 'not', and subjunctive forms of auxiliary verbs and 'not'	
can not	can't	could not	couldn't
may not	mayn't	might not	mightn't
must not	mustn't		
will not	won't	would not	wouldn't
shall not	shan't	should not	shouldn't
do not	don't	did not	didn't
does not	doesn't		

4 Rewrite the following sentences out using contractions where these are allowed.
   a I must not fail this examination.
   b We will not be going away this holiday.
   c She does not have feelings for you.
   d David could not come although he wanted to.
   e They should not have told her secret to everybody.
   f Do not do that!
5 We have not discussed how to contract the following phrases. Suggest contractions for them.
   a need not
   b ought not

Making questions by changing word order or adding 'do'

Making questions by changing the word order of a statement

If the verb in a statement is a form of the verb 'be', then we can change that statement into a question by changing the word order. We also need to add a question mark. Look at the following example.

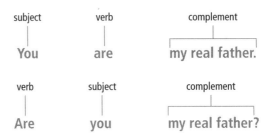

1 Change the following statements into questions.
   a You are unhappy.
   b They were left behind in the forest.
   c I am pretty.

If the first verb in a statement is an auxiliary verb, we can change that statement into a question by changing the word order as in the following example.

2 Change the following statements into questions.
   a You could come with me.
   b He may go out this evening.
   c The girl on the swing is swinging quite high.
   d He has already torn the letter up.
   e You do have to go.

If the statement has two clauses, only change the order of the main clause.

3 Change the following statements into questions. If necessary, swap the clauses around so that the main clause comes first.
   a The teacher would notice if our essays were exactly the same.
   b You would still love me if I were ugly.
   c If you call him, he will come.

These kinds of questions are normally answered by people saying 'yes' or 'no'.

Making questions by adding the auxiliary verb 'do' into a statement
We may also make statements into questions by adding a form of the auxiliary verb 'do' before the subject. This auxiliary verb must match the subject. The finite verb in the statement then changes into the base form of this verb. We also need to add a question mark. Look at the following examples.

When a participle, such as 'shopping', is being used as a noun, then we do not treat it as a verb.

When changing present tense sentences into questions, we add either 'do' or 'does', depending on which word matches the subject. When changing past tense sentences into questions, we always add 'did'.

4   Change the following statements into questions.
 a She likes cycling.
 b He does it by himself.
 c We worked quickly.
 d I just did it.

We use this way of making statements into questions when there is only one verb in the statement, and when this verb is not a form of the verb 'be'.

5   Change the following statements into questions by adding a form of the verb 'do' or by changing the word order, whichever way is correct.
 a *Umkonto we Sizwe* was a resistance movement during apartheid.
 b An oracle can predict the future.
 c You have had a bad experience.
 d He is looking at the spoon.

When questions are made by changing the word order of a statement or by adding a form of 'do' in a statement, they become the kind of questions that we answer by saying 'yes' or 'no'.

Making questions using interrogative determiners or interrogative pronouns

The kinds of questions discussed on pages 192 and 193 are called 'yes-no questions', because they are normally answered by people saying 'yes' or 'no'. We can also ask more specific questions by using interrogative determiners or interrogative pronouns.

Making questions using interrogative determiners
Look at the following examples.

The interrogative determiner 'whose' can be used with the relative pronouns 'that' or 'those' when the items being referred to belong to someone. The answer to a 'whose' question will be a possessive adjective (such as 'Lance's').

When we change a statement into a question in this way we:
● put the interrogative determiner at the beginning of the sentence
● put the noun after the interrogative determiner
● put the verb next, without changing it
● put the relative determiner next
● put a question mark at the end of the sentence.

1   Change the following statements into questions and put the answer in brackets afterwards.
   a   That car is my mother's.
   b   That magazine is Bonnie's.
   c   Those earrings are Tumi's.

We may also use the interrogative determiners 'what' or 'which' to start a question. We use them when we are asking for information other than who owns something, as shown in the following sentences.

That book is Long Walk to Freedom.
What book is that?/Which book is that?

We use 'which' is we are asking 'which of the pair/group'. Otherwise we use 'what'.

2   Change the following statements into questions.
   a   That film is called *The Fast and the Furious*.
   b   The left shoe has a hole in it.

Making questions using interrogative pronouns

While interrogative determiners come before nouns, interrogative pronouns are used instead of nouns. Many pronouns that you already know can be used as interrogative pronouns. ('Interrogate' means 'ask questions'.)

Here is a table showing interrogative pronouns.

Interrogative pronouns to do with:	
one person or many people	who
thing owned by someone	whose
things	what
one of a pair or specific group of things	which
time	when
place	where
reason	why
way of doing things (manner)	how

We put interrogative pronouns at the front of questions.

3   Change the following sentences into questions that start with an interrogative pronoun. Put the answers in brackets afterwards.
   a   She is Michelle.
   b   It is hers.
   c   It is a mountain bike.
   d   Caitlin is the quieter sister.
   e   The game starts at 2 p.m.
   f   It is being played at Auckland Park.
   g   We are watching it to improve our own performance.
   h   They will show it to the public through the medium of television.
   i   I write with my right hand.
4   Insert the correct interrogative pronoun into each of the spaces in the following question. Use each interrogative pronoun from the table only once.
   a   '_____ is that girl with the hat on?'
   b   '_____ do you get the CD out the CD player?'
   c   '_____ is your favourite flavour of ice cream?'
   d   '_____ do you prefer: chocolate or strawberry milkshakes?'
   e   '_____ are you going to arrive at the party?'
   f   '_____ dog is that? It seems to be lost.'
   g   '_____ are humans on Earth?'
   h   '_____ do you go to school?'

Making questions by using a rising tone or a question tag

Making questions by using a rising tone

When we speak we can make a statement into a question just by changing our voice so that it rises at the end of the sentence. When we write this kind of question we just add a question mark.

Question: You are walking to the shops?

Making questions by using a tag question after a statement

We can also make a statement into a question by adding a tag question at the end of the statement, as shown below.

You are coming to the party, aren't you?
You aren't coming to the party, are you?

The tag question uses the same subject and the same verb as the statement, but these are swapped around. Sometimes 'not' or a contraction of 'not' is inserted into the tag question, but this depends on whether the statement is positive or negative. If the statement is positive the tag question must be negative. If the statement is negative the tag question must be positive. (When speaking, use a falling tone with positive tags and a rising tone with negative tags.)

1   Add tag questions to the following statements. Use contractions wherever possible in your tag questions.
    a   You must go, …
    b   I may not go, …
    c   He will believe me, …
    d   They do not know how to play soccer, …

When a noun is used as the subject of the statement, use the appropriate pronoun in the tag question.

2   Add tag questions to the following statements, using contractions wherever possible.
    a   George will want coffee, …
    b   The learners do not understand algebra, …

We can also use the word 'right?' as a positive question tag or the phrase 'or am I wrong?' as a negative question tag. However, in the case of these question tags, you do not need to match a positive question tag to a negative statement or a negative question tag to a positive statement. They can both be used with either kind of statement.

3   a   Use one of the alternative tags to complete sentence 2 a above.
    b   Use one of the alternative tags to complete sentence 2 b above.

Reflexive pronouns

If the subject of a sentence is the same person (or thing) as the object of a sentence, then we use a reflexive pronoun as the object.

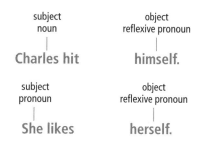

If the subject of a sentence is the same person (or thing) as the complement of a sentence, then we use a reflexive pronoun as the complement.

This means he is not acting normally

To make a reflexive pronoun we usually add 'self' or 'selves' either to the forms of personal pronouns that can act as objects or to the possessive forms of pronouns.

	Personal pronoun that acts as an object	Possessive pronoun	Reflexive pronoun
First person singular	me	my	myself
Second person singular	you	your	yourself
Third person singular	him/her/it	his/her/its	himself/herself/itself
First person plural	us	our	ourselves
Second person plural	you	your	yourselves
Third person plural	them	their	themselves

1   Insert the correct reflexive pronoun into the sentences below.
   a   I looked at _____ in the mirror.
   b   She cannot control _____ when she has drunk alcohol.
   c   You are acting strangely tonight; you are not _____.
   d   If we do not understand _____, how can we understand the people around us?

First-conditional sentences

When we talk about something that is or was possible but not definite, we use a conditional sentence. We show the degree of possibility by the verbs we use in a sentence.

When we talk about situations that are likely to happen, we use a first-conditional sentence, as in the example below.

If you wash the outside of the car, I will vacuum its upholstery.

The first clause is in the present simple and has only one verb. The second clause is also in the present simple, but it uses the auxiliary 'will' and the base form of the core action verb 'vacuum'. The conjunction 'if' is at the beginning of the sentence.

1   Rewrite the following sentences using the pattern shown above. Change the verbs in brackets. If necessary, insert a dummy auxiliary (as discussed on page 165).
    a   If he (do) his homework, she (make) him some dessert.
    b   If you (make) your bed, I (give) you your pocket money.
    c   If I (be, not) tired, I (play) cards with you.
    d   If you (make, not) your bed, I (give, not) you your pocket money.
    e   If he (do, not) his homework, she (make, not) him any dessert.

Although we normally put the subordinate clause introduced by 'if' at the front of the sentence, we can also change the clauses round, as in the following example sentence.

I will vaccum its upholstery, if you wash the outside of the car.

2   Rewrite the following sentences by moving the main clause to the front of each sentence.
    a   If he says anything to her, it will all go horribly wrong.
    b   If he buys this car, he will struggle with the car repayments every month.
    c   If you are rude, I will not let you in my room.

Although we are talking about a hypothetical situation, we do not use the subjunctive mood in a first-conditional sentence. Using the indicative mood makes the suggestion in a first-conditional sentence seem likely to come true. Using the subjunctive mood would make the suggestion seem unlikely to come true.

3   The feminist slogan 'You strike a woman, you strike a rock' became the title of a play. Rewrite this slogan as a grammatically correct first-conditional sentence.

Second-conditional sentences

When we talk about situations that are possible but unlikely we use a second-conditional sentence. A second-conditional sentence is made up of two past simple clauses joined by 'if'. We normally put the subordinate clause introduced by 'if' at the beginning of the sentence. Look at the following example.

If you cleaned the whole house tonight, I would feel very grateful.

In the sentence above, the first clause is written in the past simple and has only one verb. The second clause is also in the past simple, but it uses the auxiliary 'would' and the base form of the core action verb 'feel'. The sentence is in the past because it is in the subjunctive mood, which we must use to talk about unlikely situations.

1   Rewrite the following sentences using the pattern shown above. Change the verbs in brackets. If necessary, insert a dummy auxiliary.
    a   If you (study) for five hours, I (let) you watch a television programme.
    b   If he (do) a double somersault from the diving board, he (win) the prize.
    c   If she (say, not) anything, people (call, not) her rude.

Second-conditional sentences are written in the past tense (because they are in the subjunctive mood) but we use them to refer to the present.

If we are asking someone to help us it is more polite to use the second conditional than the first conditional, because it does not sound like we are expecting the other person to say 'yes'.

2   Rewrite the following first-conditional sentences as second-conditional sentences in order to make them more polite.
    a   If you give me a lift to town, I will be very appreciative.
    b   If you drive the car, I can relax in the passenger seat.
    c   If you read the story, I can close my eyes and just listen.

Third-conditional sentences

When we talk about situations that are extremely unlikely we use third-conditional sentences. Third-conditional sentences are made up of two past perfect clauses joined by 'if'. Look at the following example.

If you had given me an invitation, I would have come to the party.

The first clause is written in the past perfect and has two verbs: the perfect auxiliary and the participle showing the perfect aspect. The second clause is also in the past perfect, but it uses the auxiliary 'would', the base form of 'have' and the participle showing the perfect aspect, which also shows the core action 'come'.

1   Rewrite the following sentences using the pattern shown in the example above. Change the verbs in brackets. If necessary, insert a dummy auxiliary.
    a   If she (keep) my secret, I (keep) hers.
    b   If you (ask) me to the dance, I (be) the happiest girl in the world.
    c   If the leader (promise) the soldiers enough weapons, they (find) energy to continue fighting.
    d   If I (wear) that dress, I (seem, not) slim.
    e   If I (tell) you the truth, you (go, not) on holiday with them.

Third-conditional sentences are written in the past tense and we use them to refer to the past. The reason that the situations that they refer to are very unlikely to happen is that these situations are in the past and the events mentioned have not happened, so now it is impossible for them to happen.

2   Say whether the following situations should be described using first-, second- or third-conditional sentences.
    a   the possibility that Chippa Mokoro continues to play in the PSL, resulting in him being very happy
    b   the possibility that Chippa Mokoro plays for a team in the United Kingdom's Premier League, resulting in him being very rich
    c   the possibility that Chippa Mokoro played for a team in the United Kingdom's Premier League when he was fifteen, resulting in him being very surprised
3   Rewrite the following sentences using the correct kind of conditional sentence.
    a   If Chippa (continue) to play in the PSL, he (be) happy.
    b   If Chippa (play) for a team in the United Kingdom's Premier Leaugue, he (be) very rich.
    c   If, at age fifteen, Chippa (play) for a team in the United Kingdom's Premier League, he (be) very surprised.

Conditional questions

Because all conditional sentences have an auxiliary verb, we can make conditional statements into questions by changing the word order of these sentences.

To change a first conditional sentence from being a statement into being a question, we must start by making sure that the main clause is at the beginning of the question. (We may need to swap the nouns and pronouns if we move clauses around.) Then we must change the word order of the main clause. This process is shown in the examples below.

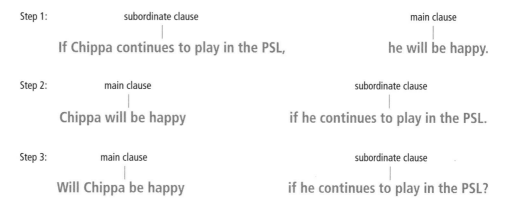

Step 1:   subordinate clause   main clause

If Chippa continues to play in the PSL,   he will be happy.

Step 2:   main clause   subordinate clause

Chippa will be happy   if he continues to play in the PSL.

Step 3:   main clause   subordinate clause

Will Chippa be happy   if he continues to play in the PSL?

1 Change the following first conditional statements into first conditional questions.
   a If you knock, someone will open the door.
   b If that bomb explodes, we will all die.

To change a second conditional statement into a second conditional question, make sure the main clause comes first in the sentence and change the word order in this main clause. (You may need to swap the nouns and pronouns if you move clauses around.)

2 Change the following second conditional statements into second conditional questions.
   a If you knocked, someone would open that door.
   b If that bomb exploded, we would all die.
   c If Chippa played for a team in the United Kingdom's Premier League, he would be very rich.

To change a third conditional statement into a third conditional question, make sure the main clause comes first in the sentence and change the word order in this main clause. (We may need to swap the nouns and pronouns if we move clauses around.)

3 Change the following third conditional statements into third conditional questions.
   a If you had knocked, someone would have opened that door.
   b If that bomb had exploded, we would all have died.
   c If, at age fifteen, Chippa had played for a team in the United Kingdom's Premier League, he would have been very surprised.

Dummy subjects

All English sentences have to have a subject and a finite verb, for example, 'We left.' But sometimes we only want to communicate one fact, and that fact can be contained in either the subject or the verb. For example, look at the picture below.

If we wanted to describe the weather in this picture we could use the subject 'rain' or the verb 'is raining'. But we don't really need to say 'Rain is raining', because then we would be repeating ourselves, and that would be bad style. What we actually say to describe situations such as this is that 'It is raining.'

When classified as a part of speech, the word 'it' is a pronoun, but here it is not standing in place of a noun that has already been mentioned. It has been used because the pattern of the sentence required a subject, and the pronoun 'it' is a rather neutral word that has little effect on the meaning of the sentence. When 'it' is used in this way we call it a 'dummy subject'.

1   Identify the dummy subjects in the following sentences.
   a   It is important to study for your examinations.
   b   It is a long way to Lilongwe.
   c   It was not the dog that was hurt; it was the driver.

We can also use the word 'there' as a dummy subject. We normally use the dummy subject 'there' when we want to use the sentence pattern subject-verb-complement because it feels more comfortable than the concise sentence pattern subject-verb.

For example, the verb 'be' and the verb 'exist' mean very similar things. But while forms of the verb 'exist' do not need to be followed by either an object or a complement, the verb 'be' needs to be followed by a complement. When using forms of the verb 'be' we often use a noun as the complement and 'there' as a dummy subject.

2   Rewrite the following sentences using the dummy subject 'there' and a form of the verb 'be'.
    a   A girl exists in our soccer team.
    b   Sugar exists in the tin.
    c   Stars exist in the sky.
    d   No answer exists.
    e   No milk exists in the fridge.

We can also use a dummy subject in a question if the verb is a form of the verb 'be' or if there is an auxiliary verb. Look at the following examples.

3   Rewrite the following sentences as questions.
    a   It is raining.
    b   There is no sugar in my coffee.
    c   It is not far to go.
    d   There seems to be no explanation.
    e   There is going to be trouble.

Activity L

On pages 205–207 there is an extract from the film script of *The Matrix*. *The Matrix* is a science-fiction film about a fictional future, when machines have taken over the world and humans are controlled by these machines. In this film, a small group of humans are fighting against the more powerful machines.

Morpheus is the leader of this resistance movement. Neo is a young man who has just joined Morpheus's resistance movement. Trinity is one of Morpheus's loyal followers, and she has fallen in love with Neo although he does not know this yet. The Oracle is a kind of prophetess. She can predict the future, although her prophecies do not always mean what they seem to mean.

1 Why are the first three sentences written in italics?
2 What words have been contracted in the following lines?
  a MORPHEUS: We're here. Neo, come with me.
  b MORPHEUS: Yes. She's very old. She's been with us since the beginning.
3 Is the following statement meant to be understood literally or figuratively?
  'She can help you to find the path.' [line 14]
4 When people talk they often do not use full sentences. People leave out words if they know that the person listening to them will know what the full sentence would be even though they do not say it.
  Rewrite the following lines as full sentences.
  a That I would find The One. [line 18]
  b What truth? [line 33]
  c Be right with you. [line 42]
  d Smell good, don't they? [line 48]
  e What vase? [line 52]
  f Who? [line 62]
  g Not too bright though. [line 63]
5 Questions are made by changing statements in some way. How were statements changed to make the following questions?
  a 'She helped you?' [line 15]
  b 'What did she tell you?' [line 17]
  c 'Not quite what you were expecting, right?' [line 46]
6 Rewrite the following sentence without using a dummy subject.
  'There is no spoon.' [line 34]
7 In line 51 four different types of punctuation marks are used. Name each one and say why it is used.
8 a In line 59 the Oracle says to Neo 'What's really going to bake your noodle later on is, would you still have broken it if I hadn't said anything ...' Is the part of the sentence after the comma an example of a first conditional, a second conditional or a third conditional?
  b Why is there no question mark at the end of this sentence?
9 The Oracle translates '*Temet nosce*' as 'Know thyself'. [line 67]
  a What modern reflexive pronoun would usually be used in this phrase instead of 'thyself'?
  b Why do you think the writer of the script wanted the Oracle to use the old-fashioned reflexive pronoun 'thyself'?

10 What tense and aspect are the following sentences written in?

 a 'The Oracle will see you now.' [line 39]

 b 'You're going to have to make a choice.' [line 92]

11 Both of the sentences in the question above refer to the future. In each sentence, what grammatical construction is used to refer to the future?

12 Why is the interrogative determiner 'which' used in the following sentence, rather than the interrogative determiner 'what'?

 'One of you is going to die … which one … will be up to you ..' [line 93]

13 Is the Oracle comparing two things or contrasting two things in the following sentence?

 'You have a good soul … and I hate giving good people bad news ..' [line 95]

Morpheus, leader of the resistance movement, is driving Neo, the newest recruit, to visit the Oracle. Trinity is with them.
 Morpheus stops the car in front of an apartment building.
MORPHEUS: We're here. Neo, come with me.
Trinity stays in the car while Morpheus and Neo walk into an apartment building, and then into an elevator.
5 NEO: So is this the same Oracle that made the prophecy?
MORPHEUS: Yes. She's very old. She's been with us since the beginning.
NEO: The beginning?
MORPHEUS: Of the Resistance.
NEO: And she knows, what, everything?
10 MORPHEUS: (*smiling*) She would say, she knows enough.
NEO: And she's never wrong?
MORPHEUS: Try not to think of it in terms of right and wrong …
They get out the elevator, and start to walk down the corridor.
MORPHEUS: She is a guide, Neo. She can help you to find the path.
15 NEO: She helped you?
MORPHEUS: Yes.
NEO: What did she tell you?
MORPHEUS: (*smiling*) That I would find The One.

They arrive at the door to the Oracle's apartment. Neo waits for Morpheus to open the door. Morpheus shakes his head.
20 MORPHEUS: I told you, I can only show you the door. You're the one who has to walk through it.
Neo puts his hand on the door handle, just about to open it, when a Priestess opens the door, and smiles at him.
PRIESTESS: Hello, Neo. You're right on time ...
She leads him and Morpheus inside.
PRIESTESS: Make yourself at home, Morpheus.
25 *Morpheus stays by the door.*
PRIESTESS: These are the other potentials ... you can wait here.
Neo looks around the room, and sees he is the only adult there. Most of the children's heads are shaved. Some are playing, others meditating, or practising their gift. Neo watches in amazement as a little girl levitates wooden alphabet blocks. He turns around, and sees a skinny bald boy sitting on the floor, holding a spoon, which sways and twists as he bends it with his mind.
30 *Neo crosses over to him, and sits in front of him, interested. The boy looks at Neo as he picks up a spoon and tries to imitate the boy's actions. Despite his best efforts, Neo cannot make it bend.*
SPOON BOY: Do not try and bend the spoon ... that's impossible. Instead, only try to realize the truth ...
NEO: What truth?
SPOON BOY: There is no spoon.
35 NEO: There is no spoon?
SPOON BOY: Then you will see, it is not the spoon that bends; it is only yourself.
Neo gets the spoon and looks at it. This time he is able to bend it with his mind. It bends, curls round, and bends again. He is fascinated. Just then, the Priestess walks up behind him and he jumps.

PRIESTESS: The Oracle will see you now.
40 *Neo loses concentration and the spoon stays bent. He smiles at the Spoon Boy and gets up. He walks into the nearby room, a kitchen. A woman is huddled beside the oven, peering inside through the cracked door.*
ORACLE: I know, you're Neo. Be right with you.
Neo looks around the room. It is an ordinary kitchen with a small table and two chairs.
NEO: You're the Oracle?
45 ORACLE: Bingo ...
ORACLE: (*turning to face Neo*) Not quite what you were expecting, right?
She turns back to the oven.
ORACLE: Almost done! Smell good, don't they?
Neo smiles politely and nods.
50 NEO: Yeah.
ORACLE: I'd ask you to sit down ... but you're not going to anyway. And don't worry about the vase.
NEO: What vase?
Neo knocks over a vase, which falls to the floor and breaks.
ORACLE: That vase.
55 NEO: I'm sorry.
ORACLE: I said "Don't worry about it". I'll get one of my kids to fix it.
NEO: How ... how did you know?
ORACLE: Ohhh.
ORACLE: (*smiling*) What's really going to bake your noodle later on is, would you still have broken it if I hadn't said anything ...

60 *The Oracle gets up and walks up to him.*
ORACLE: You're cuter than I thought ... I can see why she likes you ...
NEO: Who?
ORACLE: Not too bright though.
She grins at him.
65 ORACLE: So what do you think, do you think you're the One?
NEO: I don't know, I honestly don't know.
The Oracle looks above the kitchen door, where the words 'Temet nosce' *are written.*
ORACLE: You know what that means? It's Latin. Means 'Know thyself' ... I'm going to let you in on a little secret ... Being the One is just like being in love. No one can tell you you're in love, you just know it. Through and through. Balls to bones.
70 (*She pauses.*) Well, I'd better have a look at you.
She holds onto the side of his face with her hands.
ORACLE: Open your mouth, say 'Ahhh!'
NEO: Ahhh.
ORACLE: Okay. Now I'm supposed to say ... 'Hmm, that's interesting',
75 but then you say ...
NEO: But...what?
ORACLE: But you already know what I'm going to tell you.
NEO: I'm not The One ...
He looks slightly disappointed.
80 ORACLE: Sorry, kid. You got the gift, but it looks like you're waiting for something ...
NEO: What?
ORACLE: Your next life maybe, who knows? That's the way these things go.
Neo starts laughing in an ironic manner.
NEO: Morpheus ... he, he almost had me convinced ...
85 ORACLE: Poor Morpheus ... without him ... we're lost.
NEO: What do you mean, without him?
ORACLE: Are you sure you want to hear this?
Neo nods.
ORACLE: Morpheus believes in you, Neo. And no one, not even you, not even me, can convince him otherwise. He believes it so
90 blindly, that he's going to sacrifice his life, to save yours.
NEO: (*looking shocked*) What?
ORACLE: You're going to have to make a choice. In one hand, you'll have Morpheus's life ... and in the other hand, you'll have your own. One of you is going to die ... which one ... will be up to you...
Neo is speechless with shock.
95 ORACLE: I'm sorry, kiddo, I really am. You have a good soul ... and I hate giving good people bad news ....
Neo looks down.
ORACLE: Oh, don't worry about it ... As soon as you step outside that door, you'll start feeling better. You'll remember you don't believe in any of this ... you're in control of your own life ... remember?
She holds out a tray of oatmeal cookies to Neo.
100 ORACLE: Here, take a cookie ... I promise, by the time you're done eating it, you'll feel right as rain ...
Neo slowly reaches out and takes a cookie, then walks out the door to Morpheus.

Extended metaphors and visual metaphors

Extended metaphors

A metaphor is a comparison that is made without using a comparing word. When a writer uses this metaphor for longer than one sentence we call the metaphor an 'extended metaphor'.

1   There is an extended metaphor in the following text.
    a   What is being compared to what and why?
    b   Why would this metaphor be called an extended metaphor?

Learners are delicate plants. They need to be watered with encouragement. They need to feel the warm rays of praise on their leaves. A teacher must make sure that learners are happy in their environment, because only then will they flourish and grow.

Visual metaphors

When something refers to something else by the way that it is designed, we say that it is a visual metaphor. The perfume bottle in the following perfume review is a visual metaphor.

Highly explosive

Flowerbomb wasn't going to be subtle, of that we could be certain. But what the first perfume from Dutch design duo Viktor & Rolf would actually smell like was anybody's guess. Well, the scent is finally here, and the name is perfect. Flowerbomb, from R495, features rose, freesia, orchid, orange and jasmine sambac, with an undercurrent of patchouli.

FLOWER BOMB
VIKTOR & ROLF

FLOWER BOMB
VIKTOR & ROLF

2   a   What is the bottle designed to look like? (Hint: see page 19.)
    b   Why has the designer chosen to use this visual metaphor?

Cause and effect

A story can simply list events as long as it uses full sentences. Technically, the following sentences are a story.

The king died. The queen died.

However, a good story has a plot. A plot is the underlying structure of the story and it connects causes and effects. The following story has a plot because the two events are linked with the underlined adverbial phrase of reason.

The king died. The queen died <u>of grief</u>.

We can also add in conjunctions such as the one underlined here to link a cause and an effect.

The queen died of grief <u>because</u> her husband, the king, had recently died.

1 Join each of the following pairs of sentences using the conjunction in brackets. Remove any unnecessary words when you join the sentences, and replace repeated nouns with appropriate pronouns.
   a In the past the land in France was divided up between the nobles. (so)
      Most of the other people farmed on the nobles' land and had to obey them.
   b Grégoire Ponceludon de Malavoy was a kind nobleman. (therefore)
      Grégoire Ponceludon de Malavoy wanted to help the people in his community.
   c Dombes was in a flat area in France. (therefore)
      When it rained the water did not flow away in rivers.
   d Mosquitoes, which breed in water, bred easily in Dombes. (because)
      The rainwater formed swamps.
   e People in Dombes often died of malaria. (because)
      Mosquitoes gave the people in Dombes this disease.
   f De Malavoy did not want people in his community to get malaria. (therefore)
      De Malavoy wanted to drain the water out of the swamps.
   g De Malavoy designed a way of draining the swamps but he did not have enough money to make his invention work. (therefore)
      De Malavoy became very frustrated.
   h De Malavoy went to the Palace of Versailles. (because)
      De Malavoy wanted to meet the King of France.
   i The King of France had lots of money. (because)
      He charged the ordinary French people high taxes.
   j The king gave money to witty nobles who amused him. (so)
      De Malavoy tried to make a clever joke in front of the king.

2 a Now look at the pairs of sentences above. For each pair decide which sentence was the cause, and which sentence was the effect. Write down the letter of those sentences where the cause was the first sentence.
   b What conjunctions did you use to join the sentences where the cause came before the effect?

Making puns and playing with words

When we use a word in a way that shows it is a homophone or a homonym, then we are making a pun.

For example, on page 109 the title of the article on Nike is 'Heart and sole'. This is a pun because the word 'sole' is a homophone of the word 'soul'. The word 'sole' refers to the bottom part of a shoe, and the article is about a company that makes sports shoes. The word 'soul' is often used in the idiomatic phrase 'to put your heart and sole into something', which means to be totally involved in something (to be trying your hardest to make something work). The title 'heart and sole' refers to the word 'sole' because that is how the third word is spelt, but it also refers to the idiom 'heart and soul' because it sounds the same as this idiom. The writer has intentionally made the title refer to both homophones in order to seem clever. Puns are clever, and they are considered a kind of joke, although they are not usually laugh-out-loud funny.

1   Read the following extract from the film script of *Ridicule*. What word in this extract means both 'topic' and 'person who is ruled over by the king'?

The French king, a countess, and some of the king's assistants are walking through the palace gardens. De Malavoy, an engineer, is waiting and hoping to meet the king. He knows that if he can meet and impress the king, the king might help him by giving him money for his engineering project.

KING: (*to the countess*) Is this the man you spoke of?

(*to De Malavoy*) They say you have great wit.

DE MALAVOY: Sire?

KING: Indeed, yes! The countess sings its praises. Come. Show us. Be witty this minute! Use me, for example.

DE MALAVOY (*hesitating, trying hard to think of a joke*): Sire, the king is not a subject.

KING (*smiling*): 'The king is not a subject.' Admirable!

Most memorable. De Malavoy may join us.

I hear you have a hydrographic project.

DE MALAVOY: To drain the Dombes swamps, Sire.

KING: We'll discuss it. Speak to my secretary.

---

2   Complete the following analysis of the above pun by filling in the missing words.

The nobleman, De Malavoy, has made a _____ (a) by using the word
'_____ (b)', which has _____ (c) different meanings in this context.
When the king suggests that De Malavoy should say something witty about him,
he is suggesting that he be the subject of De Malavoy's joke. So when De Malavoy
_____ (d) 'the king is not a subject', the word 'subject' means both 'a person who must obey the king' _____ (e) 'a topic of conversation'.

Round brackets and square brackets

Round brackets

We usually use round brackets to add extra information into a text. In many cases we can choose whether to put information inside commas, dashes or round brackets. However, of all these options, round brackets remove the information from the main flow of the sentence the most.

My parents were married on 14 February 1967, and were divorced ten years later.
My parents were married on 14 February 1967 – and were divorced ten years later.
My parents were married on 14 February 1967 (and were divorced ten years later).

The extra information in round brackets can be part of a sentence, as shown above, or it can be a full sentence, as shown below. However, if the words inside the round brackets are a full sentence then the full stop must go inside the brackets.

My parents were married on 14 February 1967. (They were divorced ten years later.)

We should not put a lot of information into round brackets. If the information does not fit into the main flow of the article, it should probably be deleted or put in a footnote.

1   Insert round brackets into the following pieces of text as appropriate. Remove any other unnecessary punctuation marks.
    a   My brother is going to the navy, which means I will have my own bedroom.
    b   Knowing my father was going to lose his temper, and not wanting to be there when he did, I slipped off quietly after supper.
    c   The rosy glow of sunset flatters everyone. This time of day is sometimes called 'the hour of the beautiful people'.

We often also use round brackets when we note what books we have referred to in an essay. We normally put the date these books were published into round brackets.

Square brackets

Square brackets are rarely used. We only use them when we are quoting an incomplete section of someone's speech/text and we need to clarify something. For example, if someone uses a pronoun when speaking, we might need to explain that pronoun when we quote only a section of that person's whole speech.

Luke: My mother is a kind person. I love her.
Luke said, 'I love [my mother]'.

The square brackets indicate what words were not in the original statement, showing these have simply been inserted to make the meaning of the original statement clear. Some authors insert square brackets instead of other, vague words (as in the example above). Some authors insert square brackets alongside the other vague words.

2   a   Why were square brackets used in the article on page 109, in the sentence 'It's the difference between being another player or an MVP [most valued player]'?
    b   Have the square brackets been added to the existing text or do they replace a part of the existing text?

Writing present-tense sentences in the passive voice

Most sentences are written in the active voice, as in the following sentence.

The subject is doing the action to the object.

When we rewrite active sentences as passive sentences the object of the active sentence becomes the subject of the passive sentence, as in the following example.

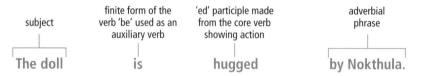

The passive sentence uses an 'ed' participle, which is usually used to show the perfect aspect. However, in this case it is a participle used to show the passive voice, and the auxiliary verb 'is' is a passive auxiliary verb. Therefore this passive sentence is not in the perfect aspect, just as its active equivalent above is not in the perfect aspect.

We should label the passive sentence as follows.

When we change a sentence from the active voice to the passive voice we:
- make the direct object of the active sentence the subject of the passive sentence, changing its form if necessary
- put a finite form of the verb 'be' after the new subject, which acts as a passive auxiliary verb
- change the core verb showing action into a passive participle, which follows the same rules as participle that show the perfect aspect
- add the preposition 'by'
- add the noun/pronoun that was the subject of the active sentence, changing its form if necessary so that it can form the adverbial phrase with the preposition 'by'.

1 Change the following present-tense active sentences into passive sentences.
  a The husband and wife accept the results.
  b We like that dog.
  c John meets his girlfriend.
  d The silicone enriches the hair gel.

The following table shows how present-tense sentences in the active voice are changed into the passive voice.

Tense and aspect	Active voice	Passive voice
Present simple	I translate the book.	The book is translated by me.
Present progressive	I am translating the book.	The book is being translated by me.
Present perfect	I have translated the book.	The book has been translated by me.

2 Change the following present-tense active sentences into present-tense passive sentences.
   a I eat breakfast.
   b I am eating breakfast.
   c I have eaten breakfast.

Look at how passive sentences in the present progressive and the present perfect can be labelled.

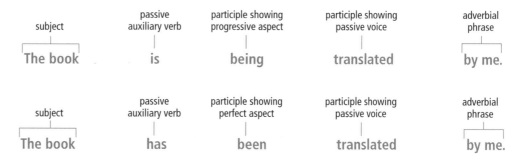

You should notice that the passive auxiliary verb can be a form of 'be' or 'has'. It is a form of 'be' when it is immediately in front of a participle showing the passive voice or the progressive aspect, but it is a form of 'have' when is it is immediately in front of a participle showing the perfect aspect.

3 Insert the correct passive auxiliary into the following passive sentences.
   a

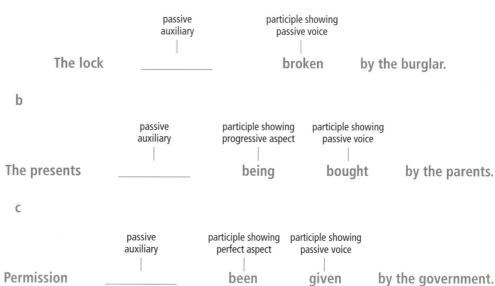

Writing past-tense sentences in the passive voice

Look at how the following past-tense sentence changes from the active voice to the passive voice.

Nokthula hugged the doll.
The doll was hugged by Nokthula.

When changing a sentence in the active voice into a sentence in the passive voice, we follow the rules on pages 212, but we use an auxiliary verb that is in the past tense.

1   Change the following active past-tense sentences into past-tense passive sentences. Use the passive auxiliary verb 'was' or 'were' in each of these sentences.
    a   I translated the book.
    b   You flew the aeroplane.
    c   Miranda tore the packet.
    d   We spilled our cool drinks.
    e   You invited me to the party.
    f   The children saw the seagulls at the beach.

The following table shows how past-tense sentences in the active voice are changed into the passive voice.

Tense and aspect	Active voice	Passive voice
Past simple	I translated the book.	The book was translated by me.
Past progressive	I was translating the book.	The book was being translated by me.
Past perfect	I had translated the book.	The book had been translated by me.

Although technically possible, it is too awkward to change a past-perfect-progressive sentence from the active voice to the passive voice.

2   Change the following past-tense active sentences into past-tense passive sentences.
    a   I ate breakfast.
    b   I was eating breakfast.
    c   I had eaten breakfast.

Note that we change only transitive verbs into the passive voice. It is not possible to change sentences around in this way if the verb is an intransitive verb. For example, we cannot apply the rules used above to the active sentence: 'She laughed.' There must be a direct object in the active sentence in order for us to change this active sentence into a passive sentence.

We can also not make sentences with a subject-verb-complement pattern into passive sentences.

Look at how passive sentences in the past progressive and the past perfect can be labelled.

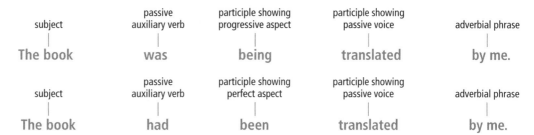

In past-tense passive sentences we use the passive auxiliary verb 'was' or 'were' when the auxiliary verb is immediately in front of a participle showing the passive voice or the progressive aspect, but we use the passive auxiliary 'had' when this auxiliary verb is immediately in front of a participle showing the perfect aspect.

3   Identify the aspect of the following active past-tense sentences. Then rewrite the sentences in the passive voice, following the appropriate pattern from the table on page 214.
    a   He liked my sister.
    b   Kayleigh threw the ball.
    c   My mother was spending the money.
    d   We were enjoying the play.
    e   All the learners had passed the test.
    f   He had eaten his chocolate.
    g   She was washing the clothes.
    h   They had expected bad news.
4   Some of these sentences are in the present tense, and some are in the past tense, but they are all in the passive voice. Rewrite them as active sentences.
    a   A long explanation was given by the naughty boy.
    b   The clothes had been dried by the sun.
    c   Good behaviour was expected by my grandmother.
    d   Full attendance is required by the school.
5   Label the different parts of the following sentences.
    a   The ball is kicked by the players.
    b   The ball was being kicked by the players.

Using the passive voice to avoid mentioning who did something

When we write statements in the active voice we have to say who did the action, as shown in the following examples.

Kabelo kicked the ball.
David spilled the juice yesterday.

When we write these statements as passive sentences they look like this.

The ball was kicked by Kabelo.
The juice was spilled by David yesterday.

But, while the names of the people doing the actions cannot be removed from the active sentences, they can be removed from the passive sentences, as shown in the following examples.

The ball was kicked.
The juice was spilled yesterday.

So, when we do not want to mention who did something, we write it in the passive voice and leave out the part that shows who did the action.
  Note that adverbs (such as 'yesterday') or adverbial phrases (such as 'the day before yesterday) can remain the same when you change a sentence from the active to the passive voice.

1 Rewrite the following passive sentences without the part that shows who did the action.
  a The rugby ball was dropped by Wayne.
  b The sheet was torn by the child.
  c The keys were lost by me yesterday.
  d The competition has been won already by an elderly woman.
2 Rewrite the following active sentences as passive sentences that do not show who did the action.
  a David spilled the juice on the chair.
  b The Prime Minister of the United Kingdom had made mistakes.
  c The government has raised the taxes.
  d Lily stole a packet of sweets from the shop.
3 In which of the following sentences would the government prefer that reference to the government be left out?
  a Thousands of houses were built by the government last year.
  b Millions of rand were spent irresponsibly by the government last year.

Using the passive voice to change what comes first in a sentence, or to remove obvious information

We should normally use active sentences because they are clearer than passive sentences and easier to read. However, sometimes we can make a paragraph flow better by writing one of its sentences in the passive voice, because this reorders the words in that sentence in a useful way.

Look at the following examples.

active sentence → A good example of a South African icon is Nelson Mandela. The apartheid government imprisoned him for many years. ← active sentence

active sentence → A good example of a South African icon is Nelson Mandela. He was imprisoned by the apartheid government for many years. ← passive sentence

The second paragraph is constructed in a better way than the first paragraph, because the pronoun 'he' comes at the start of the second sentence, immediately linking this sentence to the one that has come before. In contrast, readers of the first paragraph have to wait until they are more then halfway through the second sentence before they can see the connection between these sentences.

1 Change the second sentence in the following paragraphs into a passive sentence so that these paragraphs flow better.

   a A useful resource is the *Cambridge Advanced Learner's Dictionary*. Learners of English throughout the world use this dictionary.

   b Tashiana is now five years old. Her mother bore her on 4 July 2005.

When we are talking about babies being born, we very rarely use the active voice, because it is obvious that the baby was born by his/her mother, and the passive voice allows us to leave out this obvious information.

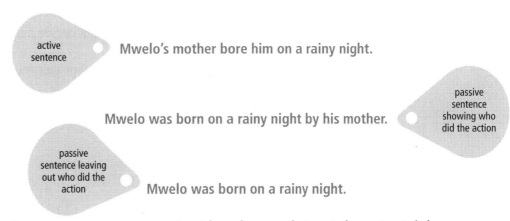

active sentence → Mwelo's mother bore him on a rainy night.

Mwelo was born on a rainy night by his mother. ← passive sentence showing who did the action

passive sentence leaving out who did the action → Mwelo was born on a rainy night.

2 Rewrite your answer to question 1 b so that any obvious information is left out.

Different ways of talking about obligation

When we are obliged to do something we can express this in a number of different ways. Some of these ways are shown below.

subject	modal auxiliary verb	base verb showing action	direct object	adverb of time
I	must	do	my homework	now.

subject	modal auxiliary verb	base verb showing action	direct object	adverb of time
I	should	do	my homework	now.

subject	finite verb	infinitive showing action	direct object	adverb of time
I	have	to do	my homework	now.

subject	finite verb	infinitive showing action	direct object	adverb of time
I	ought	to do	my homework	now.

As shown above, some verbs are used as auxiliary verb-base verb combinations, while others are finite verb-infinitive combinations. We do not use 'must' and 'should' with infinitives, and we do not use 'ought' or a form of 'have' with the base form of a verb.

1 Rewrite each of the following sentences in three other ways.
   a I ought to do my homework now.
   b We ought to brush our teeth before bedtime.

There is a slight difference in meaning between the above four ways of talking about obligation. When we use 'must' or a form of 'have' we are communicating a very strong sense of obligation, and we are also communicating the feeling that we are planning to follow this sense of obligation. However, when we use 'should ...' and 'ought to ...' we are communicating the fact that we feel we are obliged to do something, but that we do not really want to do this thing. In particular, because 'should' puts a sentence into the subjunctive voice, the use of this verb emphasises that although the subject of the sentence must do something this subject might decide not to.

2 Rewrite the following sentences so that the speaker sounds more definite and gives a more powerful message.
   a I should stay in bed if I feel sick.
   b He ought to wear a seatbelt when driving a car.

When we talk about an obligation not to do something, we usually insert 'not' after the auxiliary/finite verb, as shown in the following examples.

I must not lie.   *I should not lie.*   *I ought not to lie.*

We do not use 'not' with 'have' in order to show obligation.

3 Correct the mistakes in the following sentences.
   a I have not to make a mess.
   b She should not to drink so much of the juice.

Another two ways of talking about obligation are shown below.

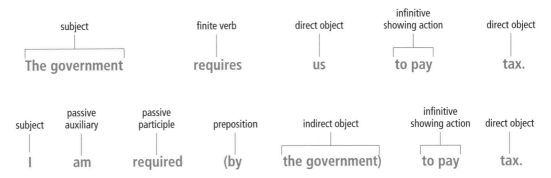

The first example above is written in the active voice. The second example above is written in the passive voice. When using the verb 'require' we usually use the passive voice and leave out the part of the sentence that shows who is doing the action.

4 Rewrite the following sentences in the passive voice to show obligation. Do not mention who is requiring you to do the action.
   a My school requires learners to wear black shoes and white socks.
   b The manager of the public swimming pool requires all swimmers to wear a swimming cap.
   c The police require drivers to show their driver's licences at the road block.
   d Publishers require script writers to write stage directions in italics.

Just as we can use a passive construction based on the word 'require' we can also use a passive construction based on the word 'oblige'. In this case the thing that obliges us is our own moral code, and does not need to be mentioned.

> There is no past form of 'I must do it.' One of the other options needs to be used instead.

5 Rewrite the following sentences using 'obliged' instead of ' required'.
   a I am required to support my parents in their old age.
   b I am required to pay for the things that I damaged.

The following table shows how to refer to past obligations in the first-person voice.

> We usually use the first three past-tense options when we talk about actions we were obliged to do and did do, and we use the other two options to talk about things we were obliged to do but did not do.

How to refer to your present obligations in the first-person	How to refer to your past obligations in the first-person
I am required to do it.	I was required to do it.
I am obliged to do it.	I was obliged to do it.
I have to do it.	I had to do it.
I ought to do it.	I ought to have done it.
I should do it.	I should have done it.

6 Complete the following sentences.
   a I _____ leave school to support my family.
   b I _____ refused to drink any alcohol.

Using a thesaurus

Imagine you wanted to write a thank-you letter, but you didn't know how to fill a whole page with words unless you wrote the word 'thank-you' over and over again. You could then use a thesaurus, which is a book of synonyms, to find different ways of saying how thankful you were. In this way you could make a thank-you letter fill a whole page.

When using a thesaurus:
Firstly, look up the word you know in the back of the thesaurus. For example, you could look up 'thank'.

> **thank** 837.6 be grateful, 878.9 reward
> **thankful** 765.4 satisfied, 837.4 grateful
> **thankfully** 765.13 with satisfaction, 837.8
>   gratefully
> **thankfulness** 765.1 satisfaction, 837.1
>   gratitude
> **thank God** 837.7 give thanks, 837.9 thank you

Secondly, choose the word or phrase that means the same as the word that you are interested in, and go to the section given just before that synonym. For example, you could look up 'be grateful', which is a synonym for 'thank', in section 837.6. If you look at the sections listed for 'thankful', 'thankfully', 'thankfulness', and 'thank God' you will notice that the section 837 is referred to a lot. This indicates it will have many useful words, some of which will not be a verb such as 'thank', but which will related in meaning to this word.

Thirdly, choose the words and phrases that you would like to use. For example, you could note down the following from section 837.6 (shown on page 221):
- be grateful
- appreciate
- express gratitude
- say thank you.

You could also note down the following useful words from section 837 as a whole.
- appreciation
- sincere thanks
- indebted
- much obliged
- with gratitude
- with a grateful heart
- as a token of one's gratitude.

Before using the new words in your thank-you letter, check their exact meanings by looking them up in your dictionary.

837   Gratitude

NOUNS

1 **gratitude**, gratefulness, thankfulness, appreciation, appreciativeness, obligation, sense (*or* feeling) of obligation, sense (*or* feeling) of indebtedness, awareness, mindfulness, cognizance

_ *851 Approval, 812 Celebration, 228 Motive*

2 **thanks**, thank you, grateful thanks, hearty thanks, sincere thanks, thanksgiving, Eucharist, blessing, benediction, Magnificat, Te Deum, prayer, prayer of thanks, paean, praise, hymn, grace, grace before meals

3 **recognition**, acknowledgment, credit, credit line, credits, by-line, thank-you letter, thank-you card (*or* note), bread-and-butter letter, thank offering, thank-you gift (*or* present), reward, tip, bonus, gratuity, token of one's gratitude, recognition of one's services, leaving present, retirement gift, parting gift, gold watch, vote of thanks, tribute, praise, testimonial, applause, round of applause, golden handshake (Inf)

_ *878 Reward*

ADJECTIVES

4 **grateful**, thankful, appreciative, pleased, gratified, pleased as punch, indebted, beholden, obliged, much obliged, under obligation, obligated, mindful of obligations, in one's debt, owing a favour

5 **thanking**, blessing, praising, crediting, giving credit, cognizant of, acknowledging

VERBS

6 **be grateful**, be thankful, feel (*or* have) an obligation, appreciate, express gratitude, thank, give thanks, express thanks, render thanks, return thanks, say thank you, receive with grateful thanks, receive with open arms, return a favour, show gratitude, show appreciation, reward, tip, give a bonus, acknowledge, express acknowledgements, pay tribute, praise, recognize, applaud, give a (big) hand, give three cheers, give credit, attribute

7 **give thanks**, say grace, bless, say a prayer of thanks, thank (*or* bless) one's lucky stars, count one's blessings, thank God, praise heaven, be thankful for small mercies

ADVERBS

8 **gratefully**, with gratitude, thankfully, with (special) thanks, appreciatively, to express appreciation(s), with a grateful heart, from a sense of obligation, in recognition of one's service(s), as a token of one's gratitude

INTERJECTIONS

9 **thank you**!, thank you very much!, bless you!, much obliged!, thank heaven!, thank God!, thank goodness!, heaven be praised!, Allah be praised!, gramercy! (Arch), thanks! (Inf), many thanks! (Inf), thanks a lot! (Inf), ta! (Inf), cheers! (Inf)

1 In the thank-you letter on page 230, which words give the sense that the writer is saying 'thank you'?

Activity M

Read the following extract from Nelson Mandela's autobiography, *Long Walk to Freedom*, and then answer the questions that follow.

I was not born with a hunger to be free. I was born free – free in every way that I could know. Free to run in the fields near my mother's hut, free to swim in the clear stream that ran through my village, free to roast mielies under the stars and ride the broad backs of slow-moving bulls. As long as I obeyed my father and abided by the customs of my tribe, I was not troubled by the laws of man or God.

It was only when I began to learn that my boyhood freedom was an illusion, when I discovered as a young man that my freedom had already been taken from me, that I began to hunger for it. At first, as a student, I wanted freedom only for myself, the transitory freedoms of being able to stay out at night, read what I pleased and go where I chose. Later, as a young man in Johannesburg, I yearned for the basic and honourable freedoms of achieving my potential, of earning my keep, of marrying and having a family – the freedom not to be obstructed in a lawful life.

But then I slowly saw that not only was I not free, but my brothers and sisters were not free. I saw that it was not just my freedom that was curtailed, but the freedom of everybody who looked like I did. That is when I joined the African National Congress, and that is when the hunger for my own freedom became the greater hunger for the freedom of my people. It was this desire for the freedom of my people to live their lives with dignity and self-respect that animated my life, that transformed a frightened young man into a bold one, that drove a law-abiding attorney to become a criminal, that turned a family-loving man to live like a monk. I am no more virtuous or self-sacrificing than the next man, but I found that I could not even enjoy the poor and limited freedoms I was allowed when I knew my people were not free. Freedom is indivisible; the chains on any one of my people were the chains on all of them, the chains on all of my people were the chains on me.

It was during those long and lonely years that my hunger for the freedom of my own people became a hunger for the freedom of all people, white and black. I knew as well as I knew anything that the oppressor must be liberated just as surely as the oppressed. A man who takes away another man's freedom is a prisoner of hatred; he is locked behind the bars of prejudice and narrow-mindedness. I am not truly free if I am taking away someone else's freedom, just as surely as I am not free when my freedom is taken from me. The oppressed and the oppressor alike are robbed of their humanity.

When I walked out of prison, that was my mission, to liberate the oppressed and the oppressor both. Some say that has now been achieved. But I know that is not the case. The truth is that we are not yet free; we have merely achieved the freedom to be free, the right not to be oppressed. We have not taken the final step of our journey, but the first step on a longer and even more difficult road. For to be free is not merely to cast off one's chains, but to live in a way that respects and enhances the freedom of others. The true test of our devotion to freedom is just beginning.

I have walked that long road to freedom. I have tried not to falter; I have made missteps along the way. But I have discovered the secret that after climbing a great hill, one only finds that there are many more hills to climb. I have taken a moment here to rest, to steal a view of the glorious vista that surrounds me, to look back on the distance I have come. But I can rest only for a moment, for with freedom come responsibilities, and dare not linger, for my long walk is not yet ended.

1 a In paragraph 1, is the first sentence a positive sentence or a negative sentence?
  b Can this sentence be understood literally or must it be understood figuratively? Why?
  c Is this sentence written in the active voice or the passive voice?
2 In paragraph 2 Mandela says 'I discovered as a young man that my freedom had already been taken from me.' He uses the passive voice here because:
  a he can focus on the person who received the action
  b he can leave out who did the action to avoid sounding accusatory, and because it is obvious who is responsible for the situation
  c he can put the pronoun 'I' at the front of the clause
  d a, b and c are true.
3 In paragraph 3 Mandela gives a cause and an effect. The effect was that he changed his behaviour. What was the cause of this?
4 In paragraph 3 Mandela uses the noun 'monk'. What is the female equivalent of a monk?
5 In paragraph 4 Mandela uses the verb 'liberated'. Is this:
  a a finite verb showing that the sentence is in the past tense
  b an auxiliary verb
  c a participle showing that the sentence is in the perfect aspect
  d a participle showing that the sentence is in the passive voice.
6 In paragraph 5 the adverb 'just' is used to mean:
  a fair
  b only
  c recently.
7 Does Mandela believe that the liberation of both the oppressed and the oppressor has been achieved?
8 Rewrite the following sentence using square brackets in the place of 'that' to clarify what is being referred to.
  Mandela writes, 'Some say that has now been achieved.' [paragraph 5]
9 In the last paragraph does Mandela use:
  a an extended metaphor
  b a visual metaphor
  c a pun
  d jargon.
10 Explain why he has used this metaphor.

Examples of some of the texts that you could be required to write

SMS

An SMS is a short typed message sent from one cellular phone to another. The abbreviation SMS means 'short message service'.

You should only write one short paragraph for an SMS. This information about the sender is added automatically to the end of your message.

hi, gr8 party. met yr friend Gina. Pls ask 4 her cell no 4 me as she is v hot ta. jerry

Sender: JERRY
+2782908110

Because SMSs must be very short to fit on a cell phone's screen, people usually do not use full sentences. In this SMS the writer has left out the subjects of the sentences.

There are many abbreviations used only in SMSs. For example:	cell – cellular
	no – number
g8 – great	4 – for
yr – your	v – very
pls – please	ta – thanks

E-mail message

At the top of an email you must fill in the email address of the person to whom you are writing, the email address of anyone else you might want to receive this email, and the subject of the email.

Emails often only have one real paragraph, because they usually deal with only one idea. If the writer wants to deal with more than one topic he/she normally sends two emails, and uses the subject line to indicate that they have different topics.

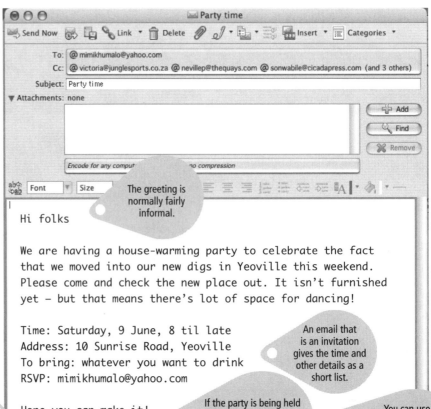

The greeting is normally fairly informal.

An email that is an invitation gives the time and other details as a short list.

End with a friendly comment.

If the party is being held by many people, give all their names at the end of the email, even if only one person writes the email.

You can use abbreviations and exclamation marks in emails to friends, but avoid exclamation marks in more formal emails.

Friendly letter of apology

505 Thorniebrae Court
York Street
Green Point
8025
15 December 2007

Dear Rachel

I really enjoyed seeing you again during our girls' night out on Saturday evening. However, I realise that I probably offended you when I suggested you were homosexual. I know that Sarah and yourself just enjoy walking arm-in-arm and that is all there is to it. I do not think either one of you are homosexual. (Although if any of my friends were, I would not mind that either.)

I was just teasing you, and trying to make everyone laugh. But I always wanted to laugh with you, not at you. Looking back I can see that I went too far, and I will try to be more sensitive in future.

I am truly sorry if your feelings were hurt.

Your friend,

Emily-Rose

Formal letter of application

Formal letters are normally used in business contexts and can be written for many purposes: to order goods, to complain, to promote a new product, etc. In an examination the formal letter you are most likely be asked to write is a letter applying for a job.

Write your address, your contact details and the date on the right-hand side.

19 Protea Road
Pretoria West
0183
Telephone number: (012) 679 5400
Email: vincef@excite.com
11 June 2008

Write the company's address on the left-hand side, with the title of the person you are writing to at the top.

The Manager
Fixit Hardware Store
20 Station Road
Garsfontein
0042

Write the subject of your letter in the centre of the page and underline it.

<u>Application for the post of sales assistant</u>

If you know the name of the person to whom you are writing, write 'Dear' and then write their name in a formal way. If you do not know their name, write 'Dear Sir/Madam'.

Dear Mr de Villiers

I am responding to the advertisement for a sales assistant that appeared in the June edition of the *Mr Fixit* magazine. The advertisement stated that your company was looking for a young person to work in your hardware store, and I would like to apply for this position. I think I have both the knowledge and the people skills that the advertisement said were required.

Write when you saw the job advertisement and say that you would like to apply for the job.

Write two or three paragraphs about why you think you would be perfect for the job.

I enjoy do-it-yourself projects and studied Design and Technology at school, excelling in all parts of this learning area. I have a good general knowledge of tools and materials. I have made a number of pieces of furniture for my family's house and I also am in charge of maintaining the plumbing and fixing any cracks or leaks.

I also enjoy working with people and I believe I would be good at assisting customers with their purchases. While at school I started and ran the Rocket Club, which offered after-school workshops on how to make air-powered rockets out of 2l plastic bottles, as well as workshops that focused on making paper gliders and kites. I enjoyed helping other people select materials and found that they respected my advice.

I am happy working with other people, and I enjoy the camaraderie that comes when people work together as part of a team. My experiences playing for my school's first rugby team have taught me the importance of supporting others, and listening to what they have to say.

Ask to be considered for an interview.

I am sure I could be an asset to your shop, and I hope you would consider interviewing me for the position you advertised.

Please find my CV and a character reference from my Grade 12 form teacher is attached.

Say that a CV and a reference is attached, and remember to attach these.

If you have never met the person to whom you are writing, write 'Yours faithfully,'. If you have met the person to whom you are writing, write 'Yours sincerely'.

Write your full name by hand.

Yours faithfully,

Vince Falcone

Print your name and title.

Mr Vince Falcone

Curriculum vitae

Vince Falcone
Curriculum Vitae

Print your name and italicise the word 'Curriculum Vitae'. Put these words in a large font at the top of the page, in the centre.

Print your sub-headings in bold.

Personal Details
Full Name: Vincent Leonardo Falcone
Address: 19 Protea Road, Pretoria West, 0183, South Africa
Telephone Number: (012) 670 4453
E-mail: vincef@excite.com
Age: 18 years
Nationality: South African
Health: Excellent
Driver's License: Light Motor Vehicle

Use colons when you list your personal details and your educational details.

Educational Details
Secondary Education: Uitsig Hoër Skool, 2003–2007
Best Subject and Percentage Achieved: Design and Technology, 80%
Academic Prizes: Design and Technology Prize, 2007; Pretoria West Trophy for Woodwork
Sports Achievements: player on the school's first rugby team

Select the educational details that you include so that you sound like an achiever.

Work Experience
I have performed a number of handyman tasks for people that live in our neighbourhood, such as installing shelving and putting up a diamond-mesh fence.

Try to include a paragraph showing that you have some work experience.

Hobbies
I enjoy making furniture, carving wooden animals and playing rugby.

When mentioning hobbies, think of ones that are related to the job that you are applying for.

Contactable Referee
Mr van der Vliet
Design and Technology teacher, Uitsig Hoër Skool
Tel: (012) 671-0290
Email: vlietie@intekom.co.za

Make sure that your contactable referee would be happy to be contacted by your prospective employer.

Attached Reference
Please find attached a written reference from my Grade 12 form teacher, Mrs Theron.

Mention that you have attached a reference and, in real-life situations, attach this reference with a paperclip or staple. In examination situations you would not be expected to actually attach a reference, but you should still write that you have.

Business letter thanking client

The following letter is from an architect to a client for whom he designed a house. Other people who are planning to build their own home have contacted the architect, and he arranged for these people to visit this completed house. In this letter the architect is thanking the client for allowing him to bring prospective clients to the house. Because the people were impressed with what they saw, some of them have hired the architect to design their houses.

A business letter is a formal letter that is sent to a business contact.

The sender's address is written on the top right. If the company has a name, you should use this instead of your own name.

Madywabe Architecture
177 Biermann Avenue
Rosebank
2132
Tel: (011) 280 9343
E-mail: nmadywabe@intekom.co.za
15 October 2008

Mr and Mrs Jacob Koch
Eagle's Nest
Acacia Drive
Gardenview
2174

You should write the name and address of the client on the left, below your own address.

If you know the name of the client/s you should use it. Use their titles and surnames to create a formal tone.

Divide your text into paragraphs.

Dear Mr and Mrs Koch

You have kindly allowed a number of our firm's prospective clients to view your house and I am very grateful to you for being so accommodating. I am aware that having a group of strangers walk through your home is no small inconvenience, yet you have allowed this to happen on three occasions.

Say what your are thanking them for.

I would like to say that in all cases our prospective clients were very impressed, both with our design and with Mrs Koch's decorating skills. The adjectives they used to describe your home were 'gracious' and 'stately', which confirms for me that we achieved the overall tone that we all tried so hard to create.

Say something nice about their firm/family/house etc., as relevant.

We were not expecting to be served snacks and drinks on your porch, so this was a pleasant surprise. Your hospitality was very much appreciated.

Be thorough and think of everything they have done for you and mention it.

As a consequence of these visits, two of the prospective clients have become actual clients, and we are designing houses for them at the moment.

I hope that Eagle's Nest always remains a happy home and a beautiful venue in which to entertain.

End with a positive wish for the future. Your last paragraph should be one sentence long.

With sincere thanks,

Nelson Madywabe

Nelson Madywabe

You can end by saying 'Yours sincerely' or by adapting this standard phrase to 'With sincere thanks'.

Sign your name in pen above its printed form.

Letter to the press

A letter to the press can also be called a letter to the editor.

PO Box 1199
Howard Place
Pinelands
7450
1 November 2006

As with any formal letter, you must write your address and the date on the right, and then, after leaving a line, write the editor's work address on the left.

The Editor
DRUM
PO Box 653284
Benmore
2010

If you don't know the name of the editor, write 'Dear Sir/Madam'.

Dear Sir/Madam,

If the letter is printed in the magazine or newspaper, the editor will only include the title, the paragraphs, and your printed name. The editor might put the name of your town, city or province that you wrote in your address after your name. If you don't want people to know your name write 'Anonymous' instead of your name.

Soccer stardom no easy road

Write the heading in bold and centre it.

Too many young men dream of becoming soccer stars because they have some talent in this area, and none anywhere else. They choose to focus on this dream to the exclusion of all other career options, and then are left high and dry when they find they are not good enough to make it in the tough world of professional soccer.

Be clear and concise about what you want to say. Like when writing an argumentative essay, have a clear opinion on the topic. There is not space to discuss every aspect of an issue in a letter to the press.

DRUM's article on Chippa Mokoro, 'Eyes on the Future', which was published on 26 October 2006, emphasised some important facts. Firstly, it takes lots of hard work and dedication to become a professional soccer player. Secondly, it is not a career that you can follow for your whole life.

If you are referring to an article that was printed in the magazine or newspaper give the name of the article and the date.

Mokoro has the dedication required to be a success in the PSL, and he has the entrepreneurial vision that will carry him when his playing days are over. I wish more young men were as sensible as he is.

End with a clear message.

Yours faithfully,

Lekoloane Lisoga

Lekoloane Lisoga

In business letters, if you do not personally know the person to whom you are writing you should end by saying 'Yours faithfully', and then sign your name and print it clearly.

Narrative essay

Stripped of my Powers
By Dwayn Daniels

Boy, I felt spiffy with my new shoes. Picture it, me wearing my brand-new, space-age, air-pocket technology, Trace 4x4 Power takkies. My mother looked proud too, although she didn't like the price. But then, you get what you pay for.

After the whole of Access Park had seen me in my new takkies I decided that it was time to take them home to show my neighbourhood. So off we motored back home to Kensington.

As soon as I got home I was out the door. When my mother asked me where I was going I simply replied, 'I'm going to the shop, Mommy, don't stress. It's cool.' With a bounce and a roll I was off to the 'Bubby shop' on the corner, next to the fisheries.

Passing the goons that hover outside the shop, I greeted them like I was the president, and then I smoothly slid past them. I was surprised how friendly these gangsters were today, considering I'm their entertainment on other days.

'Hello, Uncle Gammie,' I said on entering the shop. My hands were in my pockets, not only to be cool, but also to pull up my trouser pipes, showing off my new shoes.

'Hey, but that's a nice pair of takkies,' said the old man, straightening ever so slightly to peer over the counter top.

'Thank you Uncle Gammie, I didn't think anyone would notice,' I replied. I bought a packet of 50c chips and told Uncle Gammie I'd see him later.

Before I left though, he told me that I should look after my shoes. 'New takkies have a habit of walking away from their owners,' he said.

Misunderstanding him, I said, 'Ag, don't be silly, Uncle Gammie, I won't forget these anywhere.'

The old man chuckled to himself and said something in Afrikaans under his breath.

I left the shop and was almost off the pavement when the main gangster stopped me. I was quite surprised, because he never talked or even laughed when the rest of the goons were taunting passers-by. But he was especially friendly today; he even put his arm around

---

Annotations (margin notes):

Write your title after you have finished the first draft of your essay. Try to think of something catchy that uses, for example, a pun or alliteration, but still refers to the topic of the essay.

It is safest to write your whole essay in the past tense. If you change tense as you go you could easily make mistakes.

Many writers give an indication about what is going to happen to the main character, although the main character does not realise it yet. This helps build the story to a climax.

Give lots of little details as you tell your story.

Here the title is a pun because 'to be stripped of one's powers' is an idiom meaning 'to have the powers that come with a particular job taken away', but the word 'powers' also refers to the brand of Power takkies that the main character is showing off.

This essay uses a casual style as if the teenager is speaking to a friend about what happened to him. This can be an effective way to evoke a sense of place, because readers will associate the language the speaker uses with a particular community or geographic area.

If using direct speech, every time a new person speaks you need to start a new paragraph.

my shoulder and talked to me as if we were old friends. After his every sentence, the other goons would laugh and grin. I didn't get the joke, but I felt I should laugh with them.

The main gangster complimented me on my shoes. 'Check here, brother, that's a nice pair of shoes. What size are they?'

'Size 8,' I replied.

'What a coincidence. I'm also an 8!' he said. 'You mind if I try them on quickly?'

'Excuse me?' I questioned him.

'*Haal af!*' he shouted. I felt my cheeks get warm all of a sudden. I realised he had smacked me fast and hard in the face.

As quickly as I had put those shoes on for the first time, my Trace 4x4 Power takkies were removed. (It seems you don't always get what you pay for.)

Walking home in my socks I felt terrible, lower than low, but when I told my mother what happened and saw her face, then I felt even worse.

Next time I get new shoes … some time in the distant future … I'll put my hands in my pocket – and pull my trouser pipes down.

Particularly when the reader expects the climax, you need to make it exciting so he/she is not disappointed.

Indicate what the moral of the story is without actually saying it like a boring school teacher.

Try and emphasise the disaster by presenting an extra angle on it.

234

Discursive essay

Do the advantages of technology outweigh the disadvantages?

By Lana Jacobs

A discursive essay discusses both sides of an issue. It is far more balanced than an argumentative essay.

In your first paragraph discuss what the topic means and make it sound interesting.

We live in the twenty-first century where, for many us, our lives are ruled by computers, wireless technology, infrared sensors, pebble-bed reactors, satellite tracking and bar codes. A wealthy person with many technological devices can sit under the warm glow of a halogen light and talk to friends around the globe using the Internet, while a microwave cooks a full meal and the fridge indicates it is out of milk. All this makes us feel advanced, but this lifestyle must be powered by electricity or batteries, so what happens when the power disappears and the lights go out?

The recent power shortages have made me realise how much our lives are disrupted when our technological gadgets no longer work. Businesses that depend on computers cannot run, causing huge amounts of money to be lost. Without fridges, freezers or ovens, restaurants cannot open and food goes bad. Hospitals have to use emergency batteries for essential services, and have to postpone non-essential operations. Life in the cities grinds to a standstill.

Discuss one point of view giving examples.

A new idea requires a new paragraph.

Few of us that use technology have a clue how to fix it when it breaks down. Our new technologies have stunted our growth. We no longer have basic skills because we have become reliant on technology to help us survive. How do we sell goods to customers without a cash register? How do we wash stained clothes without a washing machine? How do we keep food fresh without a fridge? How do we entertain ourselves without a television? How do we work without a computer? The answers to these questions exist, but many of us do not know them. While our ancestors were resourceful and independent, today's consumers are not.

Through technology we have also opened up the doors to a different kind of war, and to genocide. For example, the nuclear bombs that were dropped on Hiroshima and Nagasaki killed millions of people. The gassing of the Jews by the Nazis and the present-day shootings of Christians in Darfur have both been made possible by technology.

However, we cannot ignore the advantages of technology. It has provided us with knowledge and power. Technology has aided us in the cure of diseases, provided new jobs and eliminated many boring and dangerous ones. It has allowed us to understand the world around us. Because of better schooling and a vibrant media young people today know so much more. Because of advances in telecommunications rural people often now get the opportunity to learn new skills that are not taught by teachers in their area. Technology can make life much easier, safer and more interesting.

While it is easy to romanticise the past, the realty was that without technology most people's lives were dominated by drudgery. They had a range of basic skills, but they had to use them so often that there was no time for leisure. Even if television had existed centuries ago, few people would have had time to watch it.

People are divided about whether the pros of technology outweigh the cons. While I do not believe they do, I also understand why many other people do believe that there are more advantages than disadvantages to technology. The list of benefits is long, and we may not experience too many tragedies in the future. However, I would just like to leave today's smug and self-satisfied consumers with this question: 'What will you do if the lights go out?'

Always use a formal register and a clear style.

Discuss the other point of view, giving examples.

A discursive essay may choose a side at the end of the essay, but should not say that it is the only answer.

Your conclusion should have impact, but should not introduce new information. Find a punchy way to sum up the two sides of the subject.

Argumentative essay

Football disregards the borders between nations

Give your essay a title that summarises your position on the topic.

By Wayne Stynder

Write whether your essay is an argument for or against the motion. Then put a colon and write out the motion in full.

Argument against the motion: It is ridiculous that people in South Africa support English football clubs.

Your introductory paragraph should state your opinion strongly and convincingly.

While people who are not lovers of 'the beautiful game' might find it ridiculous that South Africans watch and support English football clubs, any football fan would disagree.

Your essay does not have to be made up of only facts. Here is some rhetorical language, such as a political speaker might use. It makes the essay sound interesting and effective.

Football is the most widely played sport in the world. From Japan to Ghana, from New Zealand to Iceland, football enjoys immense popularity, and for people in one country to support teams in a far-off land is part of the universal spirit of football.

Your second paragraph should make your opinon sound like the only reasonable opinion on the topic.

In the third paragraph introduce a possible objection to your position, but only mention one that you can demonstrate to be wrong. Then spend the rest of the paragraph demonstrating that it is wrong.

Some people say it is unpatriotic for South Africans to support teams from a foreign country, such as England. But those uninformed people who say this have probably never seen a game played by two clubs in the English Premier League. The players in this league have been drawn from all over the world, so although the teams are named after particular areas in England, the teams are made up of international players, including South Africans.

Give additional reasons why you are correct in your next paragraphs.

It is a pleasure to watch games played by clubs in the English Premier League, because these are played by the world's best players. In addition to this, the standard of refereeing is excellent, and so are the facilities.

Your style should be forceful but elegant.

Some people support a club, not for who is playing, but for how the team performs. But whether it is a foreign or local club, it is always football that is being supported, and that, to me, is patriotism. Soccer fans have their own nationality, and anywhere that football is played, they are supporting their 'nation'.

Your register should be formal.

If you want to tell a story to illustrate a point, it must be short enough to fit into one paragraph.

The ability of football to unite people even during the darkest hours was underlined one Christmas Day during World War I, when the British and the German soldiers put down their weapons and ran onto no-man's land and started playing a friendly game of 'footie'.

In conclusion, I would like to remind people that all over the world 'the beautiful game' remains the same, whether it is South African soccer or English football. If you are supporting Orlando Pirates or Liverpool it should not really matter where they are playing, but how they are playing, and that you are supporting them through thick and thin.

Your concluding paragraph should not introduce a new idea but should summarise your position in a convincing way.

Play script

If your play has more than one scene, number each scene. This is an abridged extract from *Woza Albert!* by Percy Mtwa, Mbongeni Ngema and Barney Simon, which has 26 scenes.

A film script is written in the same way as a play script, but refers to different tools, such as cameras instead of curtains.

Scene Eleven

Lights up bright on a barber's open-air store. Percy – the barber – is sitting on a box, Mbongeni – the customer – between his knees. Auntie Dudu's shawl is now the barber's sheet.

In italics, describe who and what is on the stage at the beginning of the scene.

PERCY: Ehh, French cut? German cut? Cheese cut?

MBONGENI: Cheese cut.

PERCY: Cheese cut – all off!

MBONGENI (*settling*): That's nice … How much is a cheese cut?

PERCY: Seventy-five cents.

MBONGENI: Aaay! Last week my cousin was here and it was fifty cents.

PERCY: Hey, you've got very big hair my friend. (*He begins cutting hair.*)

MBONGENI (*squirming nervously during the – mimed – clipping, relaxing at the end of a run*): That's nice. What machine is this?

PERCY: Oh, it's number ten …

MBONGENI: Number ten? Ohhh.

PERCY: Though it's a very old clipper.

MBONGENI: That's nice. (*more cutting, more squirming*) That's nice. Where's your daughter now?

PERCY: Ohh, she's in university.

MBONGENI: University? That's nice. What standard is she doing in university?

PERCY (*clipping*): Ohhh, she's doing LLLLLB. I don't know, it's some very high standard.

MBONGENI: Oh yeah, LLB.

PERCY (*confirming with pleasure*): Uh huh, LLB.

MBONGENI: That's nice! I remember my school principal failed seven times LLB!

PERCY: Ohhh, I see! I understand it's a very high standard. (*The clipper gets caught in Mbongeni's hair. He struggles.*)

MBONGENI: EEEEeeeeiiiiii!

Blackout.

Always show who says each line. Write the character's name in capital letters and then put a colon.

When describing the behaviour or tone of voice of a character during the scene, use italics in brackets.

If your stage has lights you can write 'Blackout.' at the end of the scene. This will show the scene is over. If your stage has curtains, you can write 'Curtains close.', which will have the same effect. If your stage has neither lights nor curtains, your characters can simply leave the stage in order to indicate the end of a scene.

Formal report

For attention: Mr Wandani (Headmaster)

Title: Sign language course (4 March 2007)

<u>Terms of reference:</u> This report refers to the introductory Sign Language course held by Mrs September at the Mary Kihn School for the Hearing Impaired. This took place on 4 March 2007.

<u>Procedure:</u>

a At 08h00, two cars, driven by Mr Smit and Mrs Ndlovu, took eight learners from Willow Tree High School to the Mary Kihn School for the Hearing Impaired.

b We arrived at 08h30 and were welcomed by Mrs September, who was running the Sign Language course. We learned about the challenges that deaf and partially hearing people face, and some of the strategies they have developed to overcome these problems.

c At 10h00 we had tea and biscuits.

d After tea we learned some basic signs and how to sign the letters of the alphabet.

e Between 12h00 and 12h30 we ate our packed lunches.

f At 12h30 we were taught more signs so that we could prepare to hold a conversation in sign language.

g At 13h30 some of the deaf learners at the school came to our room to have a conversation with us in sign language. We had simple conversations with them about our ages and our hobbies.

h At 14h30 Mr Smit and Mrs Ndlovu took all the Willow Tree learners back to Willow Tree High School.

<u>Conclusion:</u> The outing was educational and enjoyable, although we learnt only a few signs and were not able to have very long conversations using these signs.

<u>Recommendations:</u>

a Learners interested in learning sign language should attend classes on a weekly basis, for a small fee.

b A few learners should report to the school about the outing during a general assembly, and show the school some of the signs that they learned.

<u>Date:</u> 15 March 2007   <u>Signed:</u>   *Jasper Davids*
                                         Mr Jasper Davids

Newspaper report

Monday, 30 October 2006

Nigerian air crash kills 97

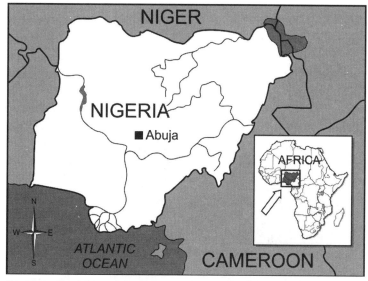

This image shows the crash location.

Abuja. – Seven survived when a Nigerian airliner carrying 104 people crashed in a storm yesterday just after taking off from the airport in the capital.

The dead included the man regarded as the spiritual leader of Muslims in Nigeria, Sultan Maccido, authorities said.

Debris from the shattered plane, body parts and personal belongings of passengers were strewn over an area the size of a soccer field where the plane went down in a wooded location, an Associated Press reporter on the scene said.

The crash site was about 3km from the end of the runway at the airport in Abuja.

Smoke rose from the plane's mangled and smouldering fuselage as rescue workers pulled out burning corpses.

About 50 bodies were gathered in a corner of the site.

The tail of the plane was hanging from a tree. – **Sapa-AP, Reuters and dpa**

240

Magazine article

A noble profession

Story by GRACE KHUZWAYO • Photos by BRETT FLORENS

Say who
wrote the article
and who took the
photographs.

Magazine
articles are not
normally about breaking
news stories. They are
well-researched articles about
relevant topics. Sometimes
they are written far in
advance to tie in
with particular
occasions.

Unless the magazine
article is an interview feature
about one person, it should show
the different perspectives of at
least two people. This article show
two different nurses that do quite
different jobs. The fact that one
is a man is unusual and
interesting, which is why
the article starts off
with his story.

May 12 was National Nurses Day. With this in mind, *BONA* did the rounds with two nurses based at Netcare Umhlanga Hospital in KZN to find out more about this caring profession ...

Brian's story

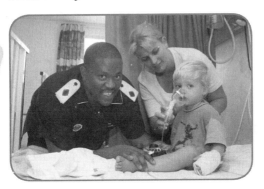

Who says nursing's only for women? Not Brian Khambule.

When people first meet Brian Khambule they're usually very surprised to find out he's a nurse. This tall, well-built man looks as if he belongs on a rugby field rather than doing the rounds in a hospital ward!

> Want to do some good? Become a nurse! You'll also never be without a job!

But when you see him interacting with his small patients it becomes obvious that this compassionate, gentle man is clearly suited to his profession.

Since 2003 Brian has been staff nurse in the paediatric (children's) ward. "I wanted to become a doctor, but there wasn't enough mony for me to go to university," he says.

"After training as a nursing assistant, I joined Netcare and, after further study,

qualified as a staff – or 'enrolled' – nurse."

Brian's duties include administering medication and injections, serving meals, making beds and assisting senior nurses and doctors.

Most importantly, Brian's always there to comfort children who are frightened or in pain.

While there are very sad times when a small patient passes away, there're also the rewarding times when a critically ill child recovers and goes home fit and healthy.

"I feel honoured to have done something towards healing one little innocent soul. That's really what nursing is all about," says Brian.

Pearl's story

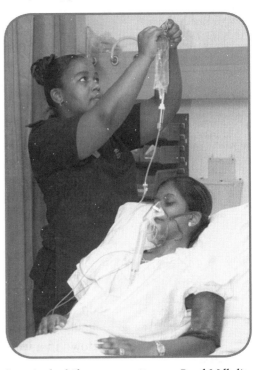

In a single shift trauma unit nurse Pearl Mdluli can find herself dealing with anything from a child with a cough to gunshot victims ...

Sister Pearl Mdluli works in the trauma unit, where it's almost always busy as medical staff rush to tend to patients brought in by ambulances.

The casualty section also forms part of this unit and in the space of a day Pearl can find herself dealing with anything from a child with a cough to gunshot victims, accidents on building sites to critically injured victims of a motor accident.

"I've always wanted work in a trauma unit so I was very excited when this position came up," says Pearl, who qualified in 2003.

Emotions often run high as staff try to calm hysterical relatives of the patients.

Career opportunities

A growing shortage of nurses both here and in many countries overseas makes nursing a wise career choice for those suited to the profession.

"A qualification in nursing is a passport to the world and you'll never battle to find work," says Eileen Brannigan, national nursing director, Netcare.

"Be warned, though," she adds. "The reality is that nursing is not the glamorous job it's often portrayed to be on TV."

"It's about hard work and, as with all jobs, there are unpleasant aspects to it – but it's also about compassion and caring, about helping and healing and the rewards are plentiful."

The South Africa Nursing Council (SANC) can be contacted on 012-420-1000. You can also find comprehensive information and a list of registered training centres on their website: www.sanc.co.za.

Levels of nursing qualifications
There are three levels:
First: Enrolled nursing auxiliary (ENA) or nursing assistant. This is a one-year course.

Second: Enrolled nurse, also known as a staff nurse – a two-year course.
Third: Professional nurse also known as Sister – a four-year course.

A professional nurse is qualified in general nursing and as a midwife, psychiatric nurse and community health nurse.

Once you have your basic qualifications you can decide which group of patients you would like to work with, such as children, the elderly, trauma victims and so on.

Matric is required for the four-year course, and a minimum of Grade 10 for the shorter courses. School leavers with subjects such as biology, science and maths generally have a better chance of being selected.

What you can earn
Much depends on the size and type of the hospital. An enrolled nursing assistant will usually earn between R3 500 and R5 000 a month and an enrolled nurse between R4 500 and R7 000.

The starting salary of a registered nurse is around R6 800, rising to around R17 000 depending on speciality and seniority.

Where to train
Training is offered at government and private nursing colleges and at universities. Part of the training includes practical skills in a hospital.

All training institutions must be registered with the South African Nursing Council (SANC) and students are strongly advised to check with the council before deciding on a course.

Some training institutions are operating illegally as they're not registered with SANC and "qualifications" from these places will not be recognised.

SANC can be contacted at 021-412-1000. You can also find comprehensive information and a list of registered training centres at their website: www.sanc.co.za.

Magazine articles use sub-headings to break up the text into manageable sections.

Boxes add visual interest and highlight certain pieces of information.

242

Obituary

September 5, 1997

Mother Teresa dead at 87

'Saint on Earth' suffered heart failure, malaria

CALCUTTA, India (CNN) – The legendary nun Mother Teresa has died at age 87. She reportedly died of cardiac arrest in her religious order's headquarters in eastern India, Friday. The spokeswoman for Missionaries of Charity said the Roman Catholic nun died at 9:30 p.m.

Mother Teresa spent her life taking care of those she lovingly called 'the poorest of the poor'. Young and old alike revered the Roman Catholic nun, who became known as a 'saint on Earth'.

Mother Teresa said she saw Christ in the faces of the poor, the outcast, the maimed and the dying. She felt they all deserved what she called 'the delicate love of God'.

Wherever she went, her message was the same: 'Love the poor.' 'I think it is really important that we all realize they are our brothers and sisters, and we owe that love and care and concern,' she once said.

The diminutive nun took her message of care and concern around the world. She regularly visited the victims of major disasters, praying for their recovery and helping raise money for their care.

Mother Teresa's 'Missionaries of Charity' grew from 12 original followers to thousands of sisters working in 450 centres around the world.

Calcutta, India, was Mother Teresa's adopted home. It's where she began her work with the poor, where she earned the nickname 'the saint of the gutters'.

Early start

Mother Teresa was born Agnes Gonxha Bojaxhiu to Albanian parents on August 27, 1910, in what's now Macedonia, part of the former Yugoslavia. She was 18 years old when she went to Dublin, Ireland, to take her vows and become a nun of Loretto, a teaching order that ran convent schools in India. She took the name 'Sister Teresa' after Saint Teresa of Lisieux, the patroness of missionaries.

Mother Teresa's tireless efforts on behalf of world peace brought her a number of important humanitarian awards, including the Nobel Peace Prize in 1979. She said such earthly rewards were important only if they helped her help the world's needy. 'Pray together and we stay together, and if we stay together, we'll love each other as God himself loves you,' Mother Teresa once said.

The small nun with the large heart worked tirelessly to the very end, despite illness in her later years. She was hospitalized in early 1996 after breaking her collarbone in a fall at her Calcutta headquarters.

She received a pacemaker in 1989. In 1983, Mother Teresa suffered a heart attack while meeting Pope John Paul II in Rome.

Mother Teresa's message of love and of hope reached millions. It is a message she prayed would not end when her time on earth was over.

Correspondent Al Hinman, the *Associated Press* and *Reuters* contributed to this report.

Film review

Film review: Get rich or die tryin'
Drama. 2006. 134 min. With 50 Cent, Viola Davis.
Director: Jim Sheridan. Age restriction 16.

In the US this film caused controversy because it supposedly glorifies violence and gangsterism. Far from it – it's more of a case of 50 Cent trying to glorify himself with a romanticized version of his life story.

Marcus wants to make it as a rapper but his plans go awry when his mother's murder makes him an orphan. He becomes a drug dealer on the streets of the Bronx in New York and writes lyrics about his experiences. It takes a brush with death for him to realise his future lies in words and not gangs.

The plot is standard – a gangster breaks from his youthful life of crime to triumph as a rapper – but there's vitality in the details. These include a startling, brutal fight by naked men in a prison shower and also the comic-book moment of transformation when a razor blade is thrown into Marcus's cell, encouraging him to kill himself; instead, he uses it to carve his rhymes into the walls.

The story is predicable but 50 Cent turns in a fair performance – and the soundtrack kicks butt.

Write the words 'Film review' and a colon before giving the name of the film that you are reviewing.

In your introductory paragraph say something interesting about the film.

In the third paragraph, give your opinion on the film and compare it to others in its genre by saying whether it is 'standard and predicable' or 'original and groundbreaking'.

This review uses an informal register. Before choosing your register, discuss with your teacher where your review would be read. The context in which it will be read will indicate how formal or informal it should be.

Give the genre of the film, the date it was released, its length, the main ators and actresses, and the age restriction, if it has one.

Your second paragraph should summarise most of the story but not its ending. If this is an unexpected twist then say this, but don't spoil the film for your readers by saying what the twist is.

Summarise your opinion of the film in the last paragraph.

Your style should be informative, analytical and interesting. To write a good review you need to have strong opinions about the film.

Agenda for a meeting

Write the title in bold or in large letters, in the top centre of the page.

Under the subheading 'Agenda' list the topics to be discussed. Number these topics, and make the last topic 'Any other business'.

Write the name and title of the person who wrote the agenda.

Write the date, time and place of the meeting. This does not need to be in a full sentence.

**Agenda of Willow Tree High School
Rugby Teams' Annual General Meeting**

Monday 10 May 2007 in Mr Smit's classroom at 1 p.m.

Agenda

1   Minutes of the previous meeting
2   Volunteer coaches for junior teams
3   Sponsors for first team's tour
4   End-of-season braai
5   Any other business

Gerhardt Louw
Secretary

Minutes of a meeting

Write the title in bold or in large letters, in the top centre of the page.

**Minutes of Willow Tree High School
Rugby Teams' Annual General Meeting**

A general meeting was held on Monday 10 May 2007 in Mr Smit's classroom at 1 p.m.

Write the date, time and place of the meeting. Use a full sentence, and write in the past tense and the passive voice.

Under the sub-heading 'Present' write the initials and the surnames of the people who came to the meeting.

Present	Apologies
J. Jackson, I. Nel, F. Kruger, T. Du Plessis, P. Anastasiadis, P. Kokoshka, M. Magagula, F. van Wyk (Captain of First Team), G. Louw (Secretary).	D. du Plessis

Under the sub-heading 'Apologies' write the names of anyone who sent his/her apologies. These can be in a box, as shown here, but do not need to be in a box.

Number the topics based on the numbering system used in the agenda. Use the same sub-headings for these topics and underline them.

1   Minutes of previous meeting
    The minutes of the meeting held on 4 May 2006 were taken as read and signed.
2   Volunteer coaches for junior teams
    Ian Nel and Paul Kokoshka volunteered to coach the U14 rugby teams. Mandla Magagule and Fritz van Wyk volunteered to coach the U16 teams.
3   Sponsors for first team's tour
    It was decided that Fritz van Wyk would ask Spike's Grill for sponsorship. Jeffrey Jackson's father, who owns T-shirts for Africa, had already offered to print T-shirts for all the learners going on tour this year.
4   End-of-season braai
    It was decided this would be held at the pavilion on 20 August 2007 between 5pm and 8pm.
5   Any other business
    5.1   Second-hand rugby clothes will now be sold through the school's second-hand shop.

Use full sentences under each topic. These sentences are often written in the passive voice, but they do not have to be.

Any other topics that were discussed should be numbered as sub-sections of the last topic.

Interview dialogue

Namibia: **President Pohamba speaks**

Namibia's president, Hifikepunye Pohamba, has been in office for a year and a half. He has a clear vision as to where he wants to take his country. **Omar Ben Yedder** went to interview him in Windhoek. Here are excerpts:

Omar Ben Yedder: You've been in power for over a year now. What has life been like at the top?

President Pohamba: I must say that it has been a very interesting first year, a year of successes and challenges. I took office from my colleague, the founding president of the republic, Sam Nujoma,

a man I had known for the past 16 years, with whom I had worked, a man with a lot of energy, whose boots were always going to be difficult to fill.

But I am lucky in the sense that I have the ruling party, Swapo, as a shelter or protection.

Omar: What about the opposition? Are they playing their role as a constitutional opposition, and giving you a good run for your money?

Pohamba: That name 'opposition' means a lot. They work as opposition because they oppose whatever you do, otherwise they lose their *raison d'être*. In our situation, considering the cooperation that I am receiving from the opposition members of parliament, I feel that we should add the word 'constructive' to their name – constructive opposition. I call them here, to State House, and we sit down, not as people opposing one another across the political divide, but as Namibians. We discuss the socio-economic challenges facing our country and the possible solutions They follow their party line. That does not bother me, insofar as they cooperate with me as head of state. That's why I say maybe we should refer to people like these as progressive or constructive opposition.

Omar: Your economy is heavily dependent on diamonds. Is Namibia getting a fair deal from the diamond mining companies operating here? At the moment, most of the diamonds are exported in their raw form to be polished elsewhere in Antwerp or London. Why can't Namibia polish its own diamonds here and make a larger margin on the added value?

Pohamba: What a good question. Namibia has diamonds. We mine diamonds. But until recently we had no polishing factories here. Now we have three, but they are not enough. So the mining companies still export the diamonds in their raw form to I don't know where, but I know it's not somewhere in Namibia.

The value addition you mentioned is at the very top of our policy list. We want it done here. Our wish is to have Namibian produce processed here. It is very important. First you provide jobs for the people and secondly you get better prices abroad because of the value-addition. It is a win-win situation for all.

Full-sentence summaries

Full-sentence summaries are summaries that are made up of a number of full sentences.

The sentences should be joined together into a paragraph.

Add words so that the sentences link together in a new paragraph.

What President Pohamba said

Give your summary an appropriate title.

President Pohamba has had an eventful first year in office, but Swapo is very supportive of him. In addition, the opposition is being very constructive. Namibia's economy is benefiting from three new diamond-polishing factories, but the president wants more to be established in Namibia to create jobs and wealth.

Only include the main points of the text you are summarising. Do not include examples.

As a general rule, write one sentence for each paragraph from the original text. But you cannot just quote a sentence, you need to rewrite it so that it fits into your summary and your summary flows nicely.

Try to make last sentence a concluding one.

Point-form summaries

Point-form summaries are bulleted lists of the main points in a text.

Write the points in a sensible order, but do not add linking words.

Give your summary an appropriate title and then use a colon to introduce the bullets.

President Pohamba said:

- first year of presidency interesting and challenging
- Swapo supportive
- opposition party constructive
- three diamond-polishing factories created
- more such factories needed to create jobs and wealth.

The points should not be full sentences. Avoid wasting space using finite verbs.

Use one full stop at the very end.

Only include the main points of the text you are summarising. Do not include examples.

The last sentence does not need to be a concluding sentence.

As a general rule, write one point for each paragraph from the original text.

Answers

Exercise 1

Parts of speech	Sentence a	Sentence b	Sentence c	Sentence d
nouns	band South Africa	Junior Theo Thembi Lebo song	Thembi Lebo	Sun City
pronouns				they
determiners	the	the		
adjectives	popular	new		
verbs	was	learnt	danced	liked
adverbs		carefully	beautifully	
prepositions	in			
conjunctions		and	and	

Exercise 2

1

Concrete nouns		Abstract nouns
Proper nouns	**Common nouns**	
Thembi North Sea Jazz Festival Boom Shaka Nike Johannesburg Christianity Greeks Islam	people car music church friend performance fashion religion believer	victory pride grief kindness

2 The Greeks worshipped Nike, a goddess of victory, before they converted to Christianity.

Exercise 3

1 a girls
  b believers
  c lengths
2 a wives
  b brooches
  c manageresses
  d splashes
3 a The learners looked at the bacteria under the microscopes.
  b We can continue playing only when you throw the two dice.
  c The planets rotate on their axes.
4 a music
  b grief

5 a pride
  b flock
  c herd
  d library

Exercise 4

1 cock, chickens
  b cow, calf
  c cub
  d bull, cow.
2 a actress
  b director/directress
  c waiter, waitress
3 a It is used as a way of being rude about where the man lives.
  b It is used as a way of showing affection.
  c It is used to show that something is physically small.

Exercise 5

1 a awful
  b outstanding
  c poor
  d excellent
2 a The small Malawian boy was adopted by the American superstar named Madonna.
  b The cylindrical gold tube had a red lipstick inside.
  c Because large European cities are so full of traffic, many people cycle to work or take the train.

d   The AIDS symbol had been used on the <u>square</u> <u>Zulu</u> brooches.

e   We use a <u>large</u>, <u>black</u>, <u>iron</u> pot to make potjiekos in.

Exercise 6

1 a   Naledi is <u>short</u>, but Jeff is <u>shorter</u> and Natalie is the <u>shortest</u> of them all.

b   Lance Armstrong is the <u>fastest</u> cyclist in the world.

c   Lebo Mathosa was <u>famous</u>, but Brenda Fassie was <u>more famous</u>.

d   Of all the teachers at the school, Mr Khumalo is the <u>tallest</u>.

e   She was chosen to act the main part in the film. I think she is the <u>luckiest</u> girl alive.

f   I am <u>older</u> than my sister, but she dresses up in such formal clothing that she seems <u>more sophisticated</u>.

Exercise 7

1 a   Tumi is being compared to a block of ice to show how unfriendly she was to her husband.

b   Rikki is being compared to a giant to show that he is bigger than his friends.

c   Christopher is being compared to a bear with a sore head to show that he is in a bad mood.

d   The secret about the murder is being compared to a timebomb to show that eventually people will find out what the secret is, and then there will be lots of trouble.

2 a   Bandile is being compared to a bomb with a short fuse, to show that he loses his temper quickly.

b   Learners are being compared to trains, to show that they work better when following the correct procedures.

c   The insults are being compared to many bombs, to show that they were nasty and there were a lot of them.

d   The dander is being compared to dynamite to show that she has lots of energy and attracts a lot of attention.

Exercise 8

1 a   email, fax

b   bike, trike

2 a   PSL

b   ANC, DA

c   BMW/Beemer, Merc, VW

3 a   Mr, Mrs

b   Dr, Prof.

4   COSATU

Exercise 9

1

	Column A	Column B
a	place	area
b	vocalist	singer
c	aeroplane	jet
d	clothing	apparel
e	sneaker	trainer
f	level	degree
g	base	pedestal
h	device	gadget
i	fragrance	perfume
j	explosion	blast
k	form	shape
l	era	age
m	confidence	self-esteem
n	grief	sorrow
o	stress	tension
p	commitment	dedication
q	snake	serpent

2

	Column A	Column B
a	real	genuine
b	provocative	controversial
c	core	inner
d	fragile	breakable
e	fashionable	trendy
f	virtuous	good
g	tiny	minute
h	abstract	theoretical
i	tender	gentle
j	likely	probable
k	lucky	fortunate
l	witty	funny
m	simple	basic
n	perfect	flawless
o	talented	gifted
p	convincing	persuasive

3

	Column A	Column B
a	enhance	improve
b	move	transfer
c	express	tell
d	act	perform
e	want	desire
f	change	alter
g	complain	protest
h	make	construct
i	leave	quit
j	teach	educate
k	allow	let
l	govern	control
m	retrench	fire
n	incorporate	include
o	suppose	think
p	hit	strike
q	look	gaze
r	tear	rupture

4

	Column A	Column B
a	solo	alone
b	frequently	often
c	constantly	always
d	quickly	promptly
e	simply	just
f	now	immediately
g	also	too
h	tenderly	carefully
i	internationally	worldwide

Exercise 10

1

	Column A	Column B
a	fantastic to watch	spectacular
b	say it does not exist, will not happen or is not true	deny
c	friends and acquaintances of a similar age	peers
d	not at a good time	untimely
e	based on the old ways of doing things	traditional
f	to begin something enthusiastically; to set something into motion	launch

g	suggest someone by name for a particular title	nominate
h	ongoing public argument about provocative subject	controversy
i	drops of water left outside after a cool night	dew
j	an almost godlike person that is so well-known that he/she starts to represent a particular era	icon
k	religious object or lucky object	amulet
l	huge group of similarly aged people who do not necessarily know each other but experience the same era	generation
m	an article that announces the death of someone and summarises their life	obituary
n	possible to get	available
o	easily breakable	fragile
p	expensive car that is so long it contains a little room so that passengers can sit facing each other and have a party	limousine
q	a person who expects the worst from other people	cynic
r	long car for transporting coffins	hearse

2 a limousine
   b hearse

Activity A

1 Lebo Mathosa
2 a popular
   b an almost godlike person that is so well-known that she starts to represent a particular era
3 a singer
   b sorrow
   c reason
4 It is the name of a band./It is a proper noun.
5 She started her career as a singer separate from Boom Shaka in 2000 …
6 SAMA
7 a rhythm and blues
   b African National Congress Youth League
   c Communist Youth League
8 a a noun
   b feminine
9 The newspaper was comparing her to everyone else who had performed that year.
10 She is being compared to a bomb blast/explosion.

11 No. This comment is reported immediately after
we are told that Lebo had a good sense of humour.
Therefore we know it was a joke.

12 c

Exercise 11

1

Column A	Column B
a self	other
b captivity	freedom
c life	death
d cause	effect
e light	darkness
f truth	lie
g base	top
h atheist	believer
i immigrant	exile
j justice	injustice
k victory	failure
l capitalist	communist
m democracy	monarchy
n comrade	opponent
m king	subject
n right	responsibility
o employer	employee
p oppressor	oppressed

2

Column A	Column B
a give	receive
b assemble	disperse
c come	go
d construct	destroy
e raise	lower
f approve	veto
g connect	disconnect
h help	obstruct
i progress	regress
j laugh	groan
k advance	retreat

3

Column A	Column B
a equal	unequal
b subtle	unsubtle
c movable	immovable
d convincing	unconvincing
e local	global
f convenient	inconvenient
g recognisable	unrecognisable
h genuine	false
i perfect	imperfect
j domestic	public
k certain	uncertain
l expected	unexpected
m possible	impossible
n fashionable	unfashionable
o extravagant	pennypinching
p respectful	abusive
q urban	rural
r usual	unusual
s respectful	flippant
t early	late
u absent	present
v divisible	indivisible
w visible	invisible

4

Column A	Column B
a here	there
b well	badly
c largely	slightly
d yesterday	tomorrow
e sincerely	ironically
f verbally	physically
g commonly	rarely
h full	empty
i extravagantly	cheaply
j completely	incompletely
k similarly	alternatively
l literally	metaphorically
m seriously	jokingly

Exercise 12

1 a ironic
b sarcastic

2 'You look really pretty. Seriously!'

Exercise 13

1 a 'Where have you been,' asked Susie when her
mother fetched her from school. "I've been
waiting <u>forever</u>!'
 b 'I've asked you a <u>million times</u> to clean your
room,' said Ma Masinga to her son.
2 a rhetorical question

Exercise 14

1 a smell
 b scent
2 a capitalist
 b flog
 c corporate
 d wheel and deal
 e racket
3 positive connotations
4 a orthodox
 b dogma
 c fanatic
 d principles
 e superstition

Exercise 15

1 a a
 b the
 c an
 d an
2 a some
 b any
3 a There is no cow.
 b There is no milk.

Exercise 16

1 a he
 b you, I

Exercise 17

1 a you
 b she
 c I
 d It
2 a We
 b you

 c We
3 a she
 b She
 c He
 d he
 e they
 f We
4 a them
 b him
 c me
 d him
 e you
 f us
 g you
 h me

Exercise 18

1 a my
 b my/our
 c your
 d her
 e your

Exercise 19

1 a mine
 b mine/ours
 c yours
 d hers
 e theirs

Exercise 20

1 The poem has four beats in each line.
2 roses are red/sugar is sweet

Activity B

1 flawless
2 They have positive connotations.
3 a ten
 b In line 1 she wants to use a word that means
'flower' but has one syllable. In line 5 she wants
to use a word that means 'flower' but has three
syllables.
4 a first-person plural pronoun that comes before
the verb/first-person plural pronoun that acts as
the subject of its clause

b first-person singular possessive determiner
5 alliteration
6 'One perfect rose'
7 'Why is it no one ever sent me yet/One perfect limousine, do you suppose?'
8 limousines
9 It is meant in an ironic way.
10 abab abab abab

Exercise 21

1 a this
   b that
   c Those
   d these

Exercise 22

1 a these
   b these
   c those
   d this
   e that

Exercise 23

1 a noun
   b advancement to an improved state
2 a no
   b When we use the word 'progress' as a noun we pronounce it slightly differently to when we use it as a verb.
3 a The first syllable is stressed.
   b The second syllable is stressed.
4 regress
5 a progression
   b progress
6 She wants to feel she is progressing to where she wants to be in life, but she does not know where she wants to be, so she cannot even attempt to go there.

Exercise 24

2 Old English
3 liberty, French and Latin
4 a freedom
   b liberty

Exercise 25

1 The apartheid government was unprogressive, while the ANC government is progressive.
2 a *phōnē* (sound)
   b *cyclus* (wheel)
   c *pēs* (foot)
   d *centum* (hundred)
   e *pēs* (foot)
   f *tupos* (image)
   g *stereos* (solid) + *phōnē* (sound)

Exercise 26

1 a **ex**-wife
   b **tele**vision
   c **un**usual
   d **co**workers
   e **en**velope
   f **homo**sexuality
   g **tran**slate
   h **super**market
   i ***über**mensch*
   j **archi**tect
   k **mono**cycle, **bi**cycle, **tri**cycle
   l **motor**car
   m **motor**bike
   n **milli**pedes
   o **multi**word
   p **hyper**-allergic
2 a beautiful
   b happier
   c better
   d excellent
   e terrible
   f wooden, plastic
   g German
   h victorious
   i highest
   j flawless
   k nocturnal
   l explosive
3 a shocking
   b curved
   c scented
   d typed

256

Exercise 27

1 a over
  b from, to, in
  c on
  d under/below
  e above
2 a to
  b of
3 a throughout
  b over
  c during
  d after
  e until
  f since
  g before
  h between
  i in
  j on

Exercise 28

1 a my lucky little sister's new CD
  b Jonathan's wonderful silver bicycle
  c the hungry teenager's chocolate ice cream
  d Cindi September's black limousine
2 a The American sportswear company's slogan is 'Just do it!'
  b Nike's slogan is 'Just do it!'
3 a Jeremy's bicycle is broken.
  b Ntombi's bag is empty.
  c The man's car has two flat tyres.
  d The girl's hair was braided with beads.
4 a It is Jeremy's bicycle.
  b It is Ntombi's empty bag.
  c It is the man's car.
  d It was the girl's hair.
5 a dress
  b dog
  c husband
  d daughter

Exercise 29

1 a In our road all the houses look the same and the houses' doors are all the same as well.
  b Many actresses' families hardly see them when they are working on a film.

c There is a nurse at the clinic that helps with women's medical problems.
  d The dice's corners have been worn smooth because they have been used so often.
2 a The car's left back wheel is flat because it went over a nail on the road.
  b A woman's bag was found in the shop and is being kept at the front desk.
  c The wheels' axes are not perfectly parallel; they need to be aligned.
  d The bacteria's environment was destroyed by the strong detergent.

Exercise 30

2 (This is an example of a possible answer, but there are other possible answers.)
*Throughout history, humans have been on the move, so that many historians now talk about the '**routes**' that people have walked, rather than the 'roots' that people have that tie them to one place. All humans originally come from **Africa** (which is why this continent is often called the '**cradle of humankind**'), but over time humans have spread out over the whole world.*
3 a The word is in italics to show that it is from a different language.
  b The word is in italics to show that it is being emphasised.
  c The words are in italics to show that they are the titles of books.
4 The words are in italics to show that they are the titles of films.

Activity C

1 The name is based on the French name, '*La liberté éclairant le monde*', which means 'Liberty Enlightening the World' when it is translated directly into English./ It refers to political freedom, particularly the political independence of the United States of America.
2 This is a key phrase in this webpage.
3 They are written in italics to show that they come from a different language.
4 They are hyperlinks that will take you to another page if you click on them.
5 fortification
6 a a noun meaning 'development'
7 c a noun that means 'the process of being carried somewhere'.

8 a foot
   b hundred
9 a on
   b of
   c from, until, after
10 a again
   b The statue was first assembled in France when it was made. This is the second time it was being assembled.
11 When he was Governor of the State of New York he did not want to spend the state's money on building a base for the statue.
12 It was probably named after a person called 'Bedloe'.
13 base
14 b by sea
15 a Ice Age/Stone Age/Iron Age/Bronze Age/ Industrial Age/etc.
   b era
16 b the symbol that most people associate with the United States
17 United States of America

Exercise 31

1 a look
   b is
   c has
   d jumps
   e is jumping
2 a look
   b be
3 a I look at my big pile of homework.
   b We look at the car.
   c You are a good soccer player.
   d She is a good friend.
   e He has his own room.
   f They have lots of bicycles.

Exercise 32

1 a I looked for my friend in the crowd.
   b He looked proudly at his girlfriend.
   c We danced together.
   d They partied all through the night.
   e You played soccer well.
   f She jumped into the dam for a swim.
2 a I state my opinion clearly.
   b You advertise for a waitress every summer.

   c It crawls across the kitchen floor.
   d We play soccer in the afternoon.
   e She cries with sorrow.
   f They fry some eggs in a pan.
3 a He had a lean body.
   b I was very angry.
   c We were in the car.
   d You were a well-behaved class yesterday.
   e You had a wonderful bicycle.
   f She had a happy childhood.
4 a Yesterday I was in a bad mood.
   b When I was a baby, my father disappeared.
   c Whenever somebody pops a balloon I always jump.
   d In the past cycling was not a fashionable sport.
   e My grandparents were freedom fighters during apartheid.
   f These days companies often use famous soccer players, such as Thierry Henry, in their advertisements.

Exercise 33

1 a am braiding
   b braid
2 a I am looking in the mirror.
   b You are looking out the window.
   c He is looking at the girls.
   d We are looking everywhere for my key.
   e You are always looking behind you.
   f They are looking for their friends in the playground.

Exercise 34

1 a I am being stupid now.
   b You are being sweet today.
   c She is being clumsy today.
   d We are being careful now.
   e You are being very thoughtful today.
   f They are being very formal now.
2 These are just examples of possible answers.
   a I am being stupid now. However, after one cup of coffee I will be able to concentrate.
   b You are being sweet today. But I have heard that this is how you act when you are trying to chat up girls.
   c She is being clumsy today. She is nervous about today's examination.

d We are being careful now. This section of road is very slippery.

e You are being very thoughtful today. I suppose that is because it is my birthday.

f They are being very formal now. But after the speeches everyone will relax and start to party.

3 a They are having a swim after school.

b I am having a meeting.

c She is having a small lunch.

4 a I have a headache.

b I am having a bad day.

c I have a bicycle.

5 a I am stopping the car.

b He is sitting on the bicycle's saddle.

c They are jetting off to France for their holidays.

d The mother is labelling all her son's school clothes.

6 a You are being grumpy today.

b He is riding a mountain bike on the dirt road.

c I am letting my friend use my other car.

d The tennis player is hitting the ball against the practice wall.

e She is admitting to the crime.

f I am having guests tonight.

g He is creating beautiful statues out of metal and wood.

h Dennis is using his brakes to stop the bicycle.

i He is being unusually stupid.

j The film festival is featuring *Tsotsi*, *Twist* and *Yesterday*, as well as many foreign films.

Exercise 35

1 a am listening

b listened

2 a I was looking out the window of the train.

b You were looking at him with an odd expression on your face.

c He was looking left and right.

d We were looking in the biscuit tin.

e You were looking at me in surprise.

f They were looking across the fields at the sunset.

3 a While you were playing soccer, I walked around the field.

b While they were watching television, I made dinner.

c While you were dragging your bag on the pavement, I saw the bottom come off.

d While the hens were squabbling over those breadcrumbs, the duck ate the breadcrumbs.

e While I was looking at the shirt in the shop window, you went in to find out the price.

f While you were listening to me, I explained how I thought he felt.

g While she was explaining the answers on the board, I tickled my friend and made her giggle.

h While we were dancing at the party, someone broke into our car.

i While I was lying in the sunshine, my brother poured a bucket of water over me.

Exercise 36

1 a I was being clumsy.

b You were being very appreciative.

c She was being shy.

d We were being cautious.

e You were being polite guests.

f They were being a good audience.

2 a We were being so naughty that our teacher kept us in after school.

b They were being such an appreciative audience that the performer sang two extra songs.

3 a I was having a small meal.

b You were having a huge, four-course meal.

c She was having a haircut.

d We were having mutton stew.

e You were having a good time together.

f They were having guests for supper.

4 a While I was having fun, I realised that my boyfriend was bored.

b While we were having a swim at the dam, the grown-ups sat around at the house and chatted.

c While she was having the baby, her husband never left her side.

5 a I had a bicycle.

b We had a small house in the countryside.

c He had two tickets to the theatre.

d She had a good sense of humour.

Exercise 37

1

Column A	Column B
a It's no use crying over spilt milk.	We cannot improve a situation by wishing that something had not happened.
b Strike while the iron is hot.	Do things when the opportunity is there and people are ready for action.
c Take time to smell the roses.	Don't be too busy to enjoy life.
d A woman's work is never done.	Women are continually looking after children and their homes, and these tasks need constant attention.
e Dynamite comes in small packages.	Small/short people often have big personalities.

2

Column A	Column B
a 'Man is born free, but is everywhere in chains.' Jean-Jacques Rousseau	This means that there are so many rules in modern society that people cannot do what they want to do.
b 'Workers of the world unite; you have nothing to lose but your chains.' Karl Marx	If workers join together into trade unions they will have more power over their employers, and because they are presently being treated so badly they are not really risking anything.
c 'Freedom's just another word for nothing left to lose.' Mickey Gilley	This means the ties we have to people and places are what are important in life.
d 'Get rich or die tryin'' 50 Cent	This means we must try hard to succeed in life.
e 'Form follows function.' Mies van der Rohe	This means we should design the shapes of things based on what they will be used for.

Exercise 38

1

Column A	Column B
a to add colour	to make something more interesting
b to be larger than life	to have a personality that attracts a lot of attention from other people
c to steal the show	to be a better actor or actress than the main actor/actress
d to drag out a story	to make a story last so long that it gets boring
e to be wheeling and dealing	to be making business deals all the time
f to put someone on a pedestal	to act as if someone is a god/goddess
g to let slip information	to tell a secret without intending to
h to come back from the dead	to come alive again after being dead, or to recover after a serious illness
i to shake off an idea	to make an idea leave your mind
j to have shock factor	to be able to surprise people by doing something unexpected
k to be anybody's guess	to be an answer that nobody knows, or an outcome that nobody can predict
l to strike a chord in people	to say something that other people feel is true and meaningful
m to compete at the top end of a sport	to play against the best players, to race against the elite, etc.
n to be walking through a minefield	to be in a situation where it is hard not to make a mistake or say the wrong thing
o for oppression to be at its height	for government control and intimidation to be at its worst/harshest
p to be king	to be the most important person or thing in a particular area
q to put your heart and soul into something	to do everything you can to make something work
r to strike gold	to find a way of making lots of money

s	to see something in the light of something else	to understand a statement by referring to a different statement which clarifies the meaning of the first statement
t	to throw yourself into a task with your heart and soul	to become totally involved in something
u	to be cast from the same mould as someone else	to have the same values and abilities as someone else
v	to be packed like sardines	to be squashed very closely together like fish in a tin
w	to bake someone's noodle	to confuse someone's brain
x	to cast pearls before swine	to give precious things or valuable knowledge to people who do not appreciate it
y	to turn your back on something	to choose not to do something
z	to feel right as rain	to feel good/to feel perfectly OK

Exercise 39

1 WANTED
2 You could print this word many, many times, until the letters were worn away.
3 type
4 *stereos* – solid
  tupos – image
5 negative
6 negative
7

Proverbs (wise sayings that most people respect)	Clichés (irritating sayings or ideas that people are tired of hearing)	Expressions of a stereotypical attitude to certain groups of people
Don't judge a book by its cover.	Sugar is sweet and so are you.	All black people dance well.
It takes a village to raise a child.	They lived happily ever after.	German people think they are better than people of other nationalities.

Exercise 40

1 a print-ing
  b cli-ché
  c stereo-type/ste-reotype/stere-otype
2 a sixteen-year-old
  b Statue-of-Liberty-type
  c multi-platinum-sellers
  d laugh-out-loud

3

Words that have hyphens after their prefixes		
Words that have hyphens after their prefixes but the prefix has only recently been used with this root word	Words that have hyphens after their prefixes but the prefix does not fit nicely	Words that have hyphens after their prefixes, when the prefix does fit nicely, and has for years, but the hyphen is still used out of habit
hyper-allergic	co-ordinator	self-esteem
multi-national	re-assembled	ex-husband

4 a In South Africa, drivers drive on the left-hand side of the road.
  c Although they were both National Party leaders, F.W. de Klerk was a more forward-thinking person than P.W Botha.
5 a This is a well-written essay.
  b Full-grown lambs are called 'sheep'.

Activity D

1 They have been used as sub-headings.
2 Yes, it is recommended.
3 three
4 at, Victoria and Alfred, eighties, telephone
5 a The word 'orthodox' is used in religious contexts.
  b positive
6 a It is the name of a play.
  b It is a key phrase.
7 b they form a compound adjective.
8 b apartheid was at its worst.
9 While a person is watching the play that person will believe that these actresses actually are the characters that they are acting.

10 It shocked audiences when it first came out because it boldly represented life under apartheid when other plays did not dare to. However, nowadays many plays refer to apartheid's injustice so this play is not unusual and does not surprise audiences by being daring.

11 a the play sometimes seems to go too slowly?

12 a The slogans are being compared to bombs that come often.

   b This shows that the political message in the play is unsubtle.

13 The audience felt that the play told stories that were relevant and true.

14 These words are from a different language.

15 a the present tense

   b the simple aspect

   c The struggle is continuing.

   d When written in the simple aspect the sentence is short and punchy./It is usual to use the simple aspect when talking about an ongoing activity that might not be going on right now (as mentioned at the bottom of page 63).

16 A woman's work is never done.

17 Women are shown as hard-working and family-orientated, but men are shown to be absent or abusive.

Exercise 41

1 a South Africans, adults, English speakers, people who listen to music

   b Americans, adults, English speakers, people who read poetry

2 a South African, English-speaking adults who listen to music

   b American, English-speaking adults who read poetry

3 a No

   b Encyclopaedias are meant to be read by a wide audience.

4 They are interested in watching drama or dance shows at a theatre./They will be in Cape Town during the time these shows are being performed.

Exercise 42

1 a I have looked up into the night sky.

   b You have looked at the television.

   c She has looked at what is in the oven.

   d We have looked for the car keys.

   e You have looked under the table.

   f They have looked out the door.

2 a I have looked at my friend's homework already.

   b He has looked everywhere for you.

Exercise 43

1 a I have been hungry.

   b She has been lucky.

   c You have had a big lunch.

   d He has had a good time.

2 a I have been there.

   b I have had a bad cold.

3 Rewrite the following past simple sentences into the present perfect.

   a I have lost my jacket.

   b She has thrown the ball outside.

   c I have spilled/spilt the bucket of water on the floor.

Exercise 44

1 a to inform

   b to entertain/satirise

   c to protest

Exercise 45

1 a I had looked over the fence.

   b You had looked at the brochures.

   c She had looked for her dog.

   d We had looked at the posters.

   e You had looked everywhere.

   f They had looked for a house to rent.

2 a I had looked for my jersey everywhere, and then I realised I was wearing it.

   b We had looked at all the dresses in the shop, but none of them was suitable for the wedding.

3 knitted

Exercise 46

1 a They had been happy.

   b You had been sad.

   c He had been confident.

2 a I had been very fit, before I spent three months in a hospital bed.

   b We had been very materialistic, until we became

Christians and realised there was more to life than worldly goods.

3 a I had had enough supper.
  b You had had enough of me.
  c She had had enough of all the complaints.
  d We had had enough sweets.
  e You had had enough water.
  f They had had enough sunshine.

4 a I had struck a match.
  b You had met interesting people at university.
  c We had won the game!
  d They had seen the match on television.
  e I had put some money in the collection box.
  f She had torn her jeans on the fence.

5 a I had worn clothes with designer labels, such as Prada, Gucci and Chanel.
  b He had been a good father.
  c They had found ticks on their cows.
  d You had flown to Paris often.
  e We had run to the train station.
  f Jessica and Tashiana had sat on the bench.

6 Rewrite the following present perfect sentences into the past perfect.
  a I had spent all my money.
  b You had had a serious illness.
  c She had kept my secret.

Exercise 47

1 a luckily
  b beautifully
  c tenderly
  d extravagantly
  e realistically
  f well
  g perfectly
  h progressively
  i correctly
2 a sometimes
  b weekly
  c monthly
  d now
  e often
  f forever
  g yearly
  h then
3 a outside
  b inside
  c there

  d here
4 a therefore
  b however/nevertheless
  c however/nevertheless

Exercise 48

1 a more extravagantly
  b better
  c most beautifully
2 a fairly/quite
  b very/really
3 a too
  b slightly

Exercise 49

1 a You are not coming with me.
  b He is not a capitalist.
  c We are not negotiating a deal.
2 a No, I will never love you.
  b No, you will never succeed.
3 a I have got nothing in my lunchbox because I forgot my sandwiches in the fridge.
  b None of my essays got a good mark.
  c No-one knows the answer to that question.
  d Of all the villagers, none was left alive.
  e I told your secret to no-one.
  f Since I put on weight nothing in my wardrobe fits me.

Exercise 50

1 a very formal
  b slightly formal
2 b Thank you for giving me the benefit of your advice.
3 a American youth slang
  b formal English
4 noun, adjective, verb

Activity E

1 They talk about business and make business deals while they play the sport.
2 cycling
3 all the other sports in South Africa
4 It makes it sound as if the money is being spent foolishly.

5 'Form follows function.'

6 a No, if he co-presents it he must have a co-presenter that he works with.

  b It deals with more than one topic, which is why it is called a 'magazine programme'.

7 He almost died of cancer but is healthy again.

8 d a word that means 'person being studied'

9 a It means to be making business deals all the time.

  b They are really moving along on bicycle wheels while they are making business deals.

10 entrepreneurs

11 It means to compete against the best sportspeople who do this sport.

12 a act like they know exactly how to present themselves

13 Interest had grown.

14 Male mountain bikers are more sexy.

15 c to discuss and entertain?

16 a bling

  b He has used it to seem fashionable.

  c It means 'ready to spend lots of money'.

Exercise 51

1 a anecdotal

  b descriptive

  c action-packed

2 a past

  b present

  c past

Exercise 52

2 hate

3 drain, foul, filthy, dirty, stinky, poooooooo

4 She is stereotyping children.

5 Dogs' droppings smell like violets and primroses compared with children!

Exercise 53

1 a question

  b statement

  c question

  d statement

  e question

  f command

  g command

  h command

2 a You do it again!

  b You pass the ball!

  c You aim for the hoop!

  d You try to score now!

3 a order/command

  b instruction

Exercise 54

2 a wealth, power, status

  b job security, service to the community

  c mobility, easiness

  d stimulation, novelty

  e independence, mobility

3 a Yvette

  b Vusi

  c Lerato

  d James

  e Jenny

4 a She has a positive attitude to her community. She thinks the people in her community are worth helping.

  b Jacob has a negative attitude to boredom. He finds it very unpleasant.

5 driving, working on a cruise liner

6 free time to spend with friends and family

7 a mobility, status, wealth

  b They would not like cheap, low-quality equipment.

Exercise 55

1 a The artist has drawn smiling young men.

  b The artist has drawn the young men walking in step, to show that the soliers are a team and to give a feeling of solidarity.

  c The poster has commands on it. Commands sound more powerful and encourage people to act.

  d This makes going to war sound like an adventure.

  e It is encouraging men to join up immediately, otherwise they might change their minds.

2 a It is showing a possible situation in the man's future.

  b Most fathers would like to be able to say that they fought for their country.

  c It makes them feel afraid that when they are asked this question they will not be able to give an answer this makes them sound brave and patriotic.

d It is making people afraid.

e It makes a young man reading the poster feel that he is being addressed directly, that his future children will specifically focus on his achievements, and that he will not be able to hide behind the achievements of others.

3 The one on the left uses a negative image to scare young men.

b The one on the right uses a positive image to attract young men.

4 The first-person pronoun 'you' and the soldier with his pointing finger are both making a direct appeal to the reader. This makes it harder to ignore their message.

5 This poster stereotypes British women as brave and selfless as they send their men to war for the good of their nation. Women reading this poster would feel that they should act in this way as well or they would be being unpatriotic.

Exercise 56

1 clothes
2 Her body is plumper.
3 She is excited, cheerful and friendly rather than aloof.
4 Relo Tsotetsi is modeling the clothes. She is from the band Skwatta Kamp.
5 Instead of sounding aloof/sophisticated this name shows enthusiasm/excitement.

Exercise 57

1 a I don't do much exercise; I only walk.
b I don't buy cheap clothes; I buy only brand names that I trust. However, I buy vegetables from the stalls at the station.
2 Insert the adverb in brackets into the sentence that follows.
a I just walked along to the shops.
b I simply let down the hem to make this skirt longer.
c I merely asked whether you wanted some coffee.
d I only wanted to help./I wanted only to help.
3 a Just do it.
b We should not make any excuses but should get exercising as soon as possible.
c It makes us feel we should respond immediately.

Exercise 58

1

British English nouns	American English nouns
autumn	fall
pharmacy	drugstore
pavement	sidewalk

2

American idiom	Explanation
to give your five cents worth	to say what you think
to talk a dime a dozen	to talk very fast
to feel like a million dollars	to feel very good
to spill the beans	to tell a secret

3 It is an American advertisement. This is evident from the way 'favorite' is spelt without a 'u'.

Exercise 59

1

Column A		Column B	Column C
only	a	just	recently
win against	b	beat	rhythm/syllable
object for creating wind	c	fan	abbreviation for 'fanatic'
beloved	d	dear	expensive
not dark	e	light	not heavy
fungi found on the surface of food or other objects	f	mould	shape you pour liquid into, before it sets into something hard
thick wooden stick	g	club	group of people who get together for a particular purpose
stop living	h	die	object with numbers on, for throwing in games of chance
apartment	i	flat	level
party after a funeral	j	wake	stop sleeping
muscle on the lower part of the leg	k	calf	young cow/bull
climb	l	scale	object you weigh things on
kind, sort	m	type	metal letters
title of a certain level of nobleman, male equivalent of a 'countess'	n	count	record the number of things
topic	o	subject	person who is ruled over by a king or queen

2 a just
  b flat
  c die
3 a type
  b letters, kind/sort
4

Column A	Column B
a dear	beloved
b soul	spirit
c heart	part of your body that pumps your blood
d peek	secret look at something
e lore	knowledge, collected wisdom on a particular topic
f heel	back part of foot
g sight	something you see, or your ability to see
h suede	leather that is not smooth
i golf	game where you hit a little white ball into a far-away hole
j new	not old
k root	part of a plant that is underground
l raise	a verb meaning to make something higher

5

Column A	Column B
a deer	antelope
b sole	flat bottom part of a shoe
c hart	male deer
d peak	top of a mountain
e law	rule
f heal	a verb meaning to make a sick person healthy
g site	place (either physical or on the internet)
h swayed	a verb, the past tense of 'sway', meaning to move gently from side to side
i Golf	model of car made for a famous German brand
j knew	a verb, the past tense of 'know', meaning to understand and remember something
k route	way to get from somewhere to somewhere else
l rays	beams

6 a swayed
  b peak
  c heart, soul
  d site

Exercise 60

1 silicone enriched

Activity F

1 a and
  b This is an article about a company that makes shoes, and shoes have soles, so the writer is playing with words.
2 It is the name of a magazine.
3 Yes. Examples of emotive words from this paragraph include: 'trainer-junkies', 'trip of a lifetime', exclusive' and 'amazing'.
4 a sneaker/sports shoe/takkie
  b addict
  c The people who love trainers are being compared to drug addicts to show how obsessed they are with sports shoes.
5 mobility/novelty/status
6 basketball
7 a He says that he is glad he is only there for a day, showing he would get bored if he stayed longer.
  b It shows that he comes from an urban context.
  c He has made it into a compound adjective.
8 shoes
9 a It still looks good.
  b It is made out of leather. We know this because we are told it is suede, which is a kind of leather.
10 He wants to show that he does not understand all the technical language and has stopped trying to work out what it means.
11 a headquarters
  b high-technology
  c advertisement
12 MVP
13 a The cynic in me wanted to know whether Nike really cared about the sport and those who played it.
  b The writer has chosen to tell his story this way because it sounds more exciting, as if everything is just happening as he is writing.
14 discursive
15 a He wants to give an American feel to the article because it is about a visit to America.
  b It is spelt in the American way because it is part of the American scientist's direct speech. We should not change the spelling of words that appear in quotation marks, and the writer has

extended this rule to how spoken words are spelt.
16 a the Greek goddess of Victory
b The equipment they make helps sportspeople win.
17 Most have positive connotations.
18 He adds the word 'seriously' after his statement.
19 c not stereotype the company, and instead represent the company Nike as being interested in both profits and helping sportspeople play better?
20 The singer is 50 Cent, and the quotation is 'Get rich or die tryin''.

21 a a command
b We should do exercise and not think of excuses not to.
c When people exercise they need appropriate clothes and shoes, and this creates a bigger market for Nike to sell to.
22 a only
b recently
c the use of the past tense
23 It is a metaphor that compares the company Nike to a god, which shows us how strongly he believes in Nike.

Exercise 61

1

Column A		Column B	Column C
sports shoe	a	trainer	person who trains someone else in a sport or a skill
picture of religious figure, painted on wood (common in Greek orthodox and Russian orthodox churches)	b	icon	symbol of an era
go past something	c	pass	piece of paper giving a person permission to enter somewhere
front of head where the eyes, nose and mouth are	d	face	to look in a specific direction, or to be confronted with a specific problem
media that use the printed word	e	press	push
goal	f	aim	point something at something else
hit	g	strike	stopping work temporarily in protest against employers
kind, well-intentioned	h	good	well-made
hollow cylinder	i	tube	train system that uses underground tunnels
outgoing and ready to take risks	j	bold	using thick lines
self-respect and honour	k	pride	group of lions

2 a stopping work temporarily in protest against employers
b kind, well-intentioned
c sports shoe

Exercise 62

1 a look
b strike
c walk
d tear
e keep
f has
g be

2 a verb
b were
c perfect

Exercise 63

1 a I have been looking everywhere for my father.
b You have been looking at that young man very often.
c James has been looking at the car's engine.
d We have been looking for the needle on the floor.
e You have been looking deeply into each other's eyes.
f They have been looking out the window.

2 a Yes, recently I have been looking for my mother in the shebeen all the time.
b Yes, recently Ms Tekateka has been looking at our homework every day.
c Yes, recently they have been looking in their postbox every morning.

Exercise 64

1 a Ewetse has been being violent this evening. (But he will be embarrassed in the morning.)
b We have been being unfair to him. (But now we will be nice to him.)
c He has been being a brat. (But he will change when he becomes older.)
2 a I have been having a good time at school. (This is because I have met many new friends recently.)
b Geoffrey has been having a haircut every month. (So that he can look professional for his new job.)
c They have been having breakfast before 6 o' clock. (So that they can catch the early train.)

Exercise 65

1 a I had been looking in my suitcase.
b She had been looking in the mirror.
c We had been looking for you everywhere.
2 a I had been looking for your name on the list of results. (Then I realised you had not written the examination.)
b You had been looking for his face at the party. (Then you remembered he was in Johannesburg.)
c She had been looking in her cupboard for the dress. (Then she remembered she had outgrown it.)
d We had been looking for mussels on the rocks. (Then we remembered there had been a red tide recently and they would not be edible.)
e They had been looking up at the stars. (Then they found the Southern Cross and worked out which direction was home.)

Exercise 66

1 a Before my mother arrived, we had been being lazy.
c Before I realised his father was HIV-positive, I had been being very flippant about people with AIDS.

2 a Before the doctor arrived, he had been having convulsions.
b Before the teacher walked into the classroom, my friend had been having her sandwiches as a morning snack.
c Before they started to argue, they had been having a romantic walk through the veld.

Exercise 67

1 a yes, present tense
b no
c no
2 trains
3 a No, there is no subject and no tense.
b Yes.
c No, there is no subject and no tense.
d No, there is no subject.
e Yes.
f No, there is no full stop.
g Yes.
h No, there is no subject and no tense.
i No, there is no subject and no tense.
j No, there is no capital letter at the beginning of the sentence.
k Yes.
4 (These are just examples of possible answers.)
a She is dancing.
c I am flying to London.
d The bomb exploded.
f Justin flew to New York.
g No smoking is allowed.
i He had died and gone to heaven.
j She is coming.

Exercise 68

1 a and d
2 a first clause: Most Muslims were shocked by the London bombings
second clause: and they disagreed with the actions of the bombers.
b first clause: Some Christians think that all Muslims are evil
second clause: although most are good and peaceful people.
c first clause: Christians do not believe in suicide
second clause: because it shows a lack of faith in power of God to make things better.

3 a after the bombing
  b fearing death
  c squashed under my shoe

Exercise 69

1 d, b, a, c, e

Exercise 70

a On October 28, 1886, the Statue of Liberty was dedicated by President Grover Cleveland in front of thousands of spectators. (Ironically, it was Cleveland who, as Governor of the State of New York, had earlier vetoed a bill by the New York legislature to contribute $50 000 to the building of the base.)
b Moveable type was expensive. When the letters on the stamps got worn down, the printers had to buy more. William Ged invented a cheaper way of printing. He made a page of movable type, and then he took a mould of this page. Then he cast this page in metal. So instead of printing with the expensive movable type and wearing it down, Ged printed with a solid metal sheet of type. This solid sheet of type was later called a 'stereotype'.
c To refer to the realities of oppression during the political turmoil of the 1980s was daring and risky. Today the play has lost some of its shock factor, but none of its relevance. After 12 years of freedom, the same women are at the same taxi rank, toiling to provide for their children – children still threatened by hunger, their fathers still absent or abusive. Then, the women took a stand against the injustice of apartheid; today the stand is against social injustice. Hope for the future lies in the resilience of these women, in their ability to keep their sense of humour, and their dignity in the face of hardship.
2 a On October 28, 1886, the Statue of Liberty was dedicated by President Grover Cleveland in front of thousands of spectators.
  b William Ged invented a cheaper way of printing.
  c Today the play has lost some of its shock factor, but none of its relevance.

Activity G

1 It is a noun meaning 'line of carriages linked together and pulled along tracks by a locomotive'.
2 explosion
3 tear
4 It shows that the situation went on for a while but was about to change.
5 a phrase
6 They were packed together tightly in a small space, like sardines in a tin.
7 two
8 a whoosh
  b hearing
9 Eventually, staff <u>reached</u> the carriage and <u>led</u> survivors through the train and on to the tracks to King's Cross.
10 'I immediately phoned my partner then my parents, who live in Norfolk, to tell them I was OK. I said to my parents 'I've just got off the train; I've escaped the bomb.' They hadn't even heard what had happened.'
11 The article on page 120 is a general overview of the event. The article on page 123 gives more detail about one part of the disaster and focuses on the experiences of individual people.
12 It indicates that the article is about the experiences of individuals caught in the disaster.

Exercise 71

1 a impartial
  b biased
2 a This is biased against a certain group of people.
  b This is biased towards a certain group of people.
3 a (personal opinion) Yes, the writer calls the Londoners 'innocent' when they are complicit with the British invasion of Muslim countries. / No, the writer seems objective.
  b He quotes from Barot's notebook to show what Barot was planning.
  c (personal opinion) Yes, this phrase is used so often that Christians are starting to think that all Muslims are fanatics. / No, the fact that we use the word 'fanatic ' in front of the word 'Muslim' shows that not all Muslims are fanatics. If all Muslims were fanatics we would not need to use the word 'fanatic' in front of the word 'Muslim'.

Exercise 72

1 a

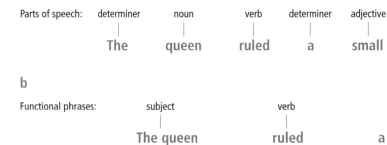

b

Functional phrases: subject   verb   object

The queen   ruled   a small powerful country.

2 a The king decided he would meet her the next day. (functional phrases)
   b Do you think it is good for a country to be ruled by a king? (parts of speech)

Exercise 73

1 a England
   b It
   c Wales, Scotland and Ireland
   d the United Kingdom
   e The people who lived in these places
   f the United Kingdom
   g This area
   h The people of Botswana
2 a the father of Keneilwe
   b the second president of a democratic South Africa
3 a is
   b borders
   c have come
   d come, go
4 a The library <u>is</u> over there.
   b The flock of sheep <u>is</u> grazing in the field.
   c The pride of lions <u>looks</u> at the herd of cattle.
5 a The Botswanan government <u>decides</u> how much money to spend on education.
   b The governments of African countries sometimes <u>meet</u> to plan Africa's future.

Exercise 74

1 a a Polo Playa
   b southern Botswana
   c Michael
   d some carrots
2 a Themba <u>hit</u> the cricket ball.
   b We <u>enjoy</u> ice cream and chocolate sauce.
   c Matome <u>is making</u> Christmas decorations.
   d I <u>have</u> a fast car.
3 a I make delicious pap.
   b I hit my attacker.
   c I enjoy romantic comedies.
   d I have my own television.
4 a When she heard the joke Khanyi laughed.
   b When I said she was pretty Jessica smiled.
   c When Aaron heard the bad news he cried.
   d When Martha got angry she frowned.

Exercise 75

1 a happy
   b ridiculous
   c oppressive
   d convincing
2 a wet
   b such a sunny day
   c a good dancer
   d my dog
3 a to Gauteng (adverbial phrase of place)
   b by bicycle (adverbial phrase of manner)
   c in the morning (adverbial phrase of time)
   d in the village of Riebeek-Kasteel (adverbial phrase of place)
   e more quickly than me (adverbial phrase of degree)
   f very fast (adverbial phrase of intensity)
   g for her Mathematics examination (adverbial phrase of reason)
   h to my sister (adverbial phrase of place)
4 a In some countries people measure distances using feet, yards and miles.
   b People in other countries measure distances in terms of centimetres, metres and kilometres.

5 a

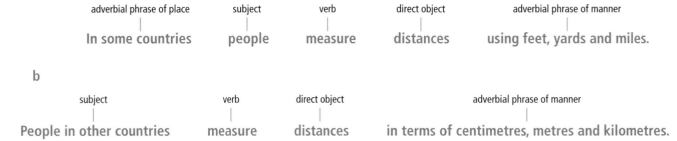

adverbial phrase of place	subject	verb	direct object	adverbial phrase of manner
In some countries	people	measure	distances	using feet, yards and miles.

b

subject	verb	direct object	adverbial phrase of manner
People in other countries	measure	distances	in terms of centimetres, metres and kilometres.

Exercise 76

1 a The boy gave his father the bucket.
  b Thandi told her aunt the news.
  c They took him the present.
2 a her friends
  b her hungry family
  c the striker
3 a I kicked her the ball.
  b She baked him a cake.
4 a I kicked the ball to her.
  b She baked a cake for him.

Exercise 77

1 a to store
  b to put
  c to be
2 a Cecilia wants to go to the zoo.
  b We prefer to go swimming.
3 a Peter is going to go to university.
  b Simon is hoping to become a carpenter.
4 a Zoleka has waited to open the Christmas presents for a long time now, but the rest of the family is still sleeping.
  b The aspiring guitarist has wanted to play with a band for a long time.
5 like, enjoy, want, prefer, go, hope, wait, want

Exercise 78

1 a want
  b hope
2 a Monako intends to be a lawyer when she grows up.
  b I hate to leave my family behind when I go to the mines to work.
  c We wish to incorporate more youthful designs into our advertising campaign.

d Maya loves to eat but she does not gorge on food.
e A man ought to trust his wife, and she ought to give him good reason to do so.
f I plan to study architecture after school.
g Our school hopes to build a new set of classrooms.
h Jeff aspires to have a penthouse and a sports car.
i I will try to arrive on the early train.
j You have to know the truth about who your father is!
k They want to meet the shortlisted candidates.
l He needs to work hard to get ahead in this industry.
m He expects to earn a good salary as an accountant.
n The children fear to enter the haunted house.
o Many young people desire to travel around the world.

Exercise 79

1 a i present simple with gerund
    ii present progressive
  b i present progressive
    ii present simple with gerund
  c i present simple with gerund
    ii present progressive
2 a He goes cycling in all types of weather.
  b We enjoy eating ice cream and chocolate sauce.
  c They like going to the coast on holiday. They like going on holiday to the coast.

Exercise 80

1 a I adore having a hot bath on a cold day.
  b We love eating tomato sauce on everything.
  c She hates seeing people feeling sad.
  d He detests talking to strangers.

e They intend settling in Kimberley.

f Sonwabile tries to save money by switching off unnecessary lights.

g The government anticipates collecting billions of rand in taxes this year.

h Many people fear to go to the dentist.

i I prefer watching comedies to horror films.

2 a I anticipate arriving soon./I expect to arrive soon.

b I expect to leave today./I anticipate leaving today.

c I want to succeed.

3 love, hate, intend, try, fear, like, enjoy, go, prefer

Activity H

1 our Standard Three teacher

2 to know, to be

3 school principals

4 bank-telling

5 a She would have caned her.

b (personal opinion) Yes, a teacher should respond to the actions of each learner without being influenced by that learner's previous behaviour./No, the teacher knew that Monei did not try to say silly things to disrupt the class, therefore she knew it was not appropriate to cane Monei for saying something silly.

6 a beautiful white girl, drinks

b It is always a transitive verb.

7 b gender stereotypes

8 a no

b She was making the sames rules about measurement for all her subjects.

9

subject	verb	adverbial phrase of time
The class	erupted	again.

10 a no

b We cannot put a gerund after the verb 'want'.

Exercise 84

1 a ⟨I would like to become a professional soccer player⟩ ⟨because I want to earn money doing something I enjoy.⟩

b ⟨I will not have a chance of becoming a professional soccer player⟩ ⟨unless I train regularly.⟩

11 a centimetres, metres and kilometres

b airplane

Exercise 81

1 a aching

b whining

c ringing

d striking

2 a spilt

b stricken

c charted

d invited, uninvited

e known, uncharted

3 spilt

Exercise 82

1 a What is your name?

b Stop right there, you thief!

c I see you aren't eating the rest of your chocolate pudding …

Exercise 83

1 a but

b or

c yet

d and

2 a I was travelling up the escalator and I saw my mother travelling down the escalator.

b He is angry or he is drunk.

3 a Justin is a financial disaster. He has neither the ability to earn money nor the ability to save it.

b Samkele is always busy. She is either out with her friends or she is working as a waitress at The Africa Café.

4 a Being dumped by your partner hurts; dumping your partner hurts in a different way.

b She lit the fuse; the bomb exploded.

c (I do score a few goals sometimes)   (**although** I am a natural midfielder.)

d (I would like to play in the PSL)   (**if** I had the opportunity.)

e (I try hardest)   (**when** my team is losing.)

f (I get scared of losing)   (**so** I put extra effort into scoring a goal.)

2 a (**While** I was playing last Saturday,)   (I knew the talent scouts were watching me.)

b (**Until** I get offered a contract by a club,)   (I have to think about other careers.)

c (I was dreaming about playing for Manchester United)   (**before** I realised I have to succeed in South Africa first.)

d (**After** I make a name for myself here,)   (I want to play for Manchester United.)

3 a My mother wants me to go to a technikon **because** she thinks there is no financial security in the world of professional soccer.

b **Although** my father knows she is right, he also understands I have to follow my dream.

Exercise 85

1 a That is the coach whose training methods are unusual.

b This is my friend whose favourite sport is also soccer.

c Those are my classmates, whose favourite team is Orlando Pirates.

d These are my teammates, whose dream is to win the Polar Ice Cup.

2 a That is the player whose style I like.

b This is the goalie whose skill I admire.

Exercise 86

1 a That is the man who works in the Western Deep Level Mines.

b That is the girl who makes her own dresses and skirts.

2 a That is the player whom I admire.

b That is the girl whom I like.

3 a That is the doctor to whom I am very grateful.

b That is my grandmother for whom I painted some pictures.

4 a This is the dress that is torn.

b That is the ball that was lost.

5 a This text is from an encyclopaedia called *Wikipedi*, which is on the Internet and is free for everyone to use.

b Here is a list of some adverbs of place, which say where something is done.

6 a This is the box in which I put all the balls.

b These are the books from which I learned all about nuclear physics.

Exercise 87

1 a That loan shark, whose loan rates are very unreasonable, has a bad reputation.

b My friend, whose debt is getting bigger, does not know what to do.

c My teammates, whose cars were expensive, have asked the banks for car loans.

2 a My friend, who repaid the loan shark, now has a bank loan at a reasonable lending rate.

b I, who hate filling in forms, am struggling to open a bank account.

c My friend, who is very helpful, is helping me go through the process.

3 a The bank that is on the corner of Kerk Street and Hani Street has a good reputation.

b The autobank that is working is on the right.

c The form that I filled in was three pages long.

4 a This shampoo, which is my favourite, makes my hair glossy.

b These CDs, which are very romantic, belong to my sister.

c This shirt, which I caught on barbed wire, is torn.

5 a The MP3 player, which looks very cool, is basically a modern walkman.

b The radio that has a green handle is not as expensive as the others.

c Those people, who are walking towards the train, are gangsters.

d The police, to whom I am very grateful, found my stolen car.

6 a Zimasile, suffering from bad eyesight for years, finally saved up to afford glasses.

b This MP3 player, ideal for people on public transport, can store hundreds of songs.

d Jeremiah, looking for investment opportunities, investigated setting up a pay phone.

e Rayda, realising she was on the wrong train, stepped back onto the platform.

Exercise 88

1 a The goalie jumped left (as) the striker took the free kick, (although) it was too soon to know where way the striker would aim.

b (While) he was jumping, the goalie realised he had guessed incorrectly, (but) it was too late to change direction.

c (Because) the striker had kicked the ball rather high, the shot seemed unlikely to be a goal, (unless) the ball bumped the goal post on its way into the goal box.

2 a The ball bumped the goal post [and] it went into the goal box, [and] the striker was very pleased with himself.

b The striker pulled his shirt over his head with happiness [and] ran round the soccer pitch, [but] then he bumped into one of his teammates.

c His teammate gave him a hug (because) he was also happy, [or] perhaps he just wanted to seem appreciative in front of the crowds.

3 a This is the shirt /that\ I was looking for, /which\ I need to wear for the match.

b An unusual type of abbreviation /that\ is often used in the motor industry is '4x4', /which\ stands for 'four-by-four'.

c This is the group of funny-looking letters, /which\ belong to the huge International Phonetic Alphabet /which\ has a symbol for each sound in every language.

4 a I like ice cream, (although) frozen yoghurt is also nice, [and] it is healthier.

b (When) the midfielders fell back to help the goalie, the opposition team tried harder to score a goal, [but] this never happened.

c We can talk about 'a ceremony organised to respectfully bury a dead person' [or] we can use the word 'funeral', /which\ means the same thing.

5 We, who are all older than him, call him 'Junior', although perhaps it is time to stop.

Exercise 89

1 (Some variations to this answer would be acceptable.)

Dynamite

Bang & Olufsen's latest device is a pocket-friendly MP3 player that stores hours of music, and it's so simple and intuitive to use that you can operate it without taking it out of your pocket. It is stylishly constructed in aluminium and rubber, and the earphones are comfortable and can be used with any Bang & Olufsen audio system. The earphones come with their own specially designed leather carrying case and an extension cord. Don't let its size fool you, because the sound quality is second to none in the portable MP3 arena.

2 a France lost the 2006 World Cup to Italy.
  b After Zidane had been sent off the field, France was playing with only ten men.
  c Italy, which had all its strikers to choose from, scored the most goals during the penalty shootout.

3 *I expected public opinion to be against Zidane – but most people were very sympathetic to his situation.*

Exercise 90

1 a Zee is a lot <u>like</u> his father.
  b Just <u>as</u> his father wanted to be a professional footballer, so does Zee.
  c Zee's father is always reminding him to keep his eyes on the ball, but Zee is actually very focused, and his style of play <u>resembles</u> his father's.
  d Festus is Zee's brother and he is cast <u>from the same mould</u> as Zee and his father.
  f There is <u>not much difference</u> in age between Zee and Festus.
  g Zee has a girlfriend called Julia, and they <u>share</u> an interest in photography.
  h <u>As could be expected</u>, Julia takes many photographs of Zee playing soccer.
  i She likes Zee to wear light colours when she photographs him playing; if he wears dark colours there is <u>little contrast</u> between his clothing and his skin.
  j On Valentine's Day, Zee sent Julia a teddy with 'I love you' written on its T-shirt, which is quite a <u>clichéd</u> thing to do.
  k Julia does not mind if this has been <u>done before</u>;

she is pleased with her teddy.
  l Julia enjoys reading romantic novels, even if they have <u>stereotypical</u> characters.
  m 'The heroines in your novels all seem the <u>same</u>,' commented Zee.
  n 'Don't you get tired of reading stories that are so <u>predictable</u>?' asked Zee.
  o 'No,' smiled Julia, 'I enjoy guessing correctly about what will happen. Now in this novel, I think the man that seems so unfriendly in the beginning is going to fall in love with the heroine, because they have so much <u>in common</u>.'
  p The story did continue <u>as predicted</u>, and ended with the heroine marrying the man who had seemed so unfriendly in the beginning.
  q They say that art <u>imitates</u> life, but sometimes life also imitates art.
  r <u>In a similar way</u> to the gruff heroes of Julia's novels, Zee, who had not always seemed a romantic person, started to talk about marriage.
  s When the big day came, Julia wore a white dress, as is <u>usual</u> for brides.
  t Festus was Zee's best man, and they looked quite <u>alike</u> in their dark suits and white shirts.
  u Even the way that Festus looked at the bride was <u>similar</u> to the way that Zee looked at her …

2 a When she was young, Julia liked the idea of marriage <u>but</u> she was scared she would not be able to be faithful to one man.
  b She was <u>more</u> beautiful than most young woman.
  c When she walked through a crowd men's eyes followed her, <u>even if</u> those men had girlfriends or wives with them.
  d Julia did not have a steady boyfriend for many years, <u>preferring</u> to date a new man every few weeks.
  e <u>However</u> her best friend, Linah, managed to find a nice young man, named Zee.
  f Zee was sport-mad, <u>although</u> he was also good to Linah.
  g He was taciturn to her best friend, Julia, though, and Linah did not understand why he seemed so <u>different</u> when Julia was around.
  h She told him, 'When Julia is here you seem so <u>unlike</u> your usual self.'
  i 'I didn't know I had done anything <u>unusual</u>,' replied Zee.

j 'It's not what you do,' explained Linah, 'it's what you do <u>not</u> do that is strange. You don't smile. You don't make jokes. You don't even meet her eyes.'

k 'Well,' muttered Zee, 'perhaps I don't find her very respectable. <u>In contrast to</u> you, Julia seems to have very loose morals.'

l 'Well, our opinions of Julia do <u>differ</u>,' retorted Linah. 'She is a good friend and you could try to be a little less judgmental.'

m Zee shrugged and joked, '<u>Alternatively</u>, you could get a new best friend.'

n 'That will never happen!' exclaimed Linah. 'She will always be my best friend, whether you like it <u>or</u> not.'

o Linah tried to arrange situations where Zee and Julia did not have to be in each other's company. They did a lot of things with their <u>other</u> friends.

p One day Linah <u>unexpectedly</u> saw Zee and Julia sitting on a park bench together.

q As Linah came up behind them she heard Julia say, in a softer voice <u>than</u> usual, 'But I thought you were in love with Linah.'

r 'Julia, oh, Julia,' Zee murmured, 'when I think about how I feel about you, there is <u>no comparison possible</u>. I have been trying to hide my feelings from myself for too long, but now … now I have my eyes on the ball.'

s As they kissed, Linah gasped and stumbled away from her boyfriend and the person she had <u>previously</u> thought was her best friend.

Activity I

1 a when
  b and
  c but
  d who
  e if
  f because
  g whom
  h which
  i whose
  j before
  k that
  l although
2 paragraphs 2, 3, 4, 18, 19
3 paragraph 8

Exercise 91

1 a suggestion
  b suggestion
  c command
  d command
2 a request
  b invitation
  c invitation
  d request

Exercise 92

1 a The boy can ride a bicycle.
  b The woman can type a letter on the computer.
  c I can swim.
  d The child can eat with a knife and fork.
2 a The man can use a computer.
  b The young man can drive a car.
  c I can make my own clothes.
3 a I cannot walk.
  b We cannot vote.

Exercise 93

1 a My friend may look at my diary.
  b Khutso may go to the party.
  c Zwelinzima may have another plate of food.
2 a My friend may not look at my diary.
  b Khutso may not go to the party.
  c Zwelinzima may not have another plate of food.

Exercise 94

1 a I may be going to Welkom this week.
  b We may be driving to town tomorrow.
2 a They may have gone to church.
  b He may have torn his jeans.

Exercise 95

1 a We must be polite to our grandparents.
  b The boy must click on the arrow to get to the next section of the website.
  c The minister must christen the child.
  d You must use the key to unlock the door.
2 a I must be going home now.
  b We must be leaving now.

Exercise 96

1 a Timothy must have eaten it.
   b S'bu must have left it open.
   c The electricity must be off.
2 a She must have been crying.
   b They must have been travelling at night.
   c She must have been wondering where I was.
3 a It must be my father.
   b He must have found them at the second-hand shop.
   c It must have been a new shopping mall.
   d They must have had an argument last night.

Exercise 97

1 a I do more than one job.
   b She does the washing up every evening.
   c He does little exercise.
2 a She *does know* a lot about cooking, but she uses too many herbs.
   b I *do love* her, but sometimes I need to be alone.

Exercise 98

1 a She does not learn Zulu at school.
   b The waitress does not spill the cocktails often.
   c I do not wear jeans.
2 a Niren and Moses are not going to Gauteng.
   b The boy at the back of the classroom is not Simon.

Exercise 99

1 a Simone is going to the cinema tomorrow.
   b Yesterday she was looking for her pencil case.
   c I am studying for my examinations.
   d Yesterday we were waiting for the bus, but it never came.
   e We were not expecting the bus to come today.
2 a am, are, is
   b was, were
3 a I have eaten enough food already today.
   b Yesterday my brother had not eaten anything until supper.
   c My father has left for work already this morning.
4 a have, has
   b had
5 a, d, f, g

6 a I must attend school although I do not want to.
   b I still do love you!
   c He still does love you.
   d We may not smoke on the train.
   e I can open that using a tin-opener.
7 a We do not want to go.
   b She does not like to read.
8 shall, will
9 modal auxiliaries

Exercise 100

1 a However she will become irritated by John after the wedding.
   b However, she will come to her brother's funeral.
   c But he will pass this year's examination.
   d But tomorrow you will be crying.
   e However will be gone.
   f But it will be stolen in one month.
2 a I shall marry him.
   b We shall go.
   c However soon I shall be gone.
   d This year we shall be travelling by car.
3 a prediction about the future
   b intention about the future
4 a I shall be going to the party.
   b I shall have gone to the party.
5 The answer to 4 a is in the present tense, the progressive aspect and the future mode.
   b The answer to 4 b is in the present tense, the perfect aspect and the future mode.

Activity J

1 b a surname
2 the past tense
3 the present tense
4 Negro
5 a to show social necessity
6 a knowing that somehow this situation can be changed and will be changed.
7 c is able to.
8 b a prediction.
9 It shows his intentions about the future.
10 c he wants this paragraph to have a traditional, biblical sound.
11 a allow songs of freedom to be sung.
12 He knows that his dream of the future will only come true if people work towards that dream in the present.

He wants to emphasise that while equality does not yet exist, there is hope because the dream of it exists./ (or anything similar)

Exercise 101

1 a A
   b C
   c B
2 a definite/sure/certain
   b impossible
   c likely/probable
   d unlikely/improbable
   e possible

Exercise 102

1 a I am not looking.
   b I have not looked.
   c I must not look.
   d I may not look.
   e I cannot look.
   f I will not look.
   g I shall not look.
   h I *do* not look.
   i I do not like most people.
   j I am not angry.
   k Aliens do not exist.
   l They are not guilty of theft.
   m We were not there.
   n Often animals do not trample the things underneath their feet.
   o The judge is not wise.
   p The man does not judge accused people.
2 a Do not go to the shops.
   b Do not be polite to them.
   c Do not throw the ball to me!
   d Do not be nasty.
   e Do not smoke cigarettes.
   f Do not be friendly to strangers.
   g Do not give your leftover food to the dogs.
   h Do not judge other people.
3 a Do be quiet.
   b Do go away.
   c Do give them to me.

Exercise 103

2 a The officials are arriving next month.
   b My mother is coming next week.
   c The television programme is finishing in a moment.
   d Next year the cost of living is increasing.
3 a We are going to leave this party.
   b He is going to be a doctor.
   c They are going to stay with friends.
   d She is going to go overseas.
4 so

Exercise 104

1 a I watch *Backstage*, *Isidingo* and *Sewende Laan*.
   b I enjoy swimming, running, dancing and cycling.
2 a I like: watching television with my cousin; jogging alone at sunrise; and hanging out with Thandaza and Michael.
   b I enjoy: sticking photographs in my scrapbook; drawing borders around them with coloured pens; and putting stickers and comments all over the pages.
3 I enjoy making model aeroplanes, ships and cars; building things out of wood; and shooting stones, marbles and berries out of my catapult.
4 If the patient is shy he/she may not want to talk about his/her problem.

Exercise 105

1 a I was eating some noodles.
   b He was going to the shops.
   c They were travelling in a train.
   d We had been to the museum.
   e She had shown us her homework.
   f You did not love me.
   g He did not know the truth.
2 a When I was fit I could run 10km without stopping.
   b Those days, when visited my grandmother for supper I would wear formal clothes.
   c He said he would go immediately.
   d The teacher said I might leave the room.
   e The weather report said it might rain that evening.
3 a When we were young, we could not understand the reasons for our parents divorce.

 b When we were hiding in the cupboard, we could hear strange noises coming from outside.

 c When the English people arrived on our island, we tried to learn their language.

Exercise 106

1 a gives a definite instruction

 b describes a real situation

 c refers to a definite intention regarding the future

 d refers to a real possibility

 e asks a question about a real possibility

2 a If I were a teacher, I would be pleasant to my learners.

 b If he were to go to university, we would need to pay his fees.

 c I would be hurt if our relationship were to end now.

3 a If she jumped on the bed, she would break it.

 b I would go to the doctor, if I could get out of bed.

 c We would do it, if you asked nicely.

4 a My brother might help me with my homework.

 b We might get free tickets to the concert.

5 a Were he a mechanic, he would fix his own car.

 b Had she had known the truth, she would have told it to me.

6 a Here is no water but only rock
Rock and no water and the sandy road
The road winding above among the mountains
Which are mountains of rock without water
If there <u>were</u> water we <u>should</u> stop and drink
Amongst the rock one cannot stop or think …

    If there <u>were</u> water
    And no rock
    If there <u>were</u> rock
    And also water
    And water
    A spring
    A pool among the rock
    If there <u>were</u> the sound of water only …
    Drip drop drip drop drop drop drop
    But there is no water …

 b The poet has used the subjunctive mood to indicate that he is talking about a hypothetical situation that does not exist in reality.

Exercise 107

1 a Robbie says, 'I like skateboarding.'

 b The boys say, 'We enjoy skateboarding.'

2 THE BOYS: We enjoy skateboarding.

3 a I said, 'I was there yesterday.'

 b You said, 'I am sad.'

 c She said, 'I will go to the shops.'

4 a says

5 writes/states

6 Jessica Gumede said, 'I usually finish books quite quickly, but *Long Walk to Freedom* is a very long book.'

Exercise 108

1 a Frank said that he enjoyed surfing.

 b You declared that you were phoning the police.

 c We suggested that you hid with us.

 d Claire asked whether she was early.

 e Mr van der Merwe commanded the boys to wait outside his office.

 f Azwindini said that he had been to the church before.

2 a He said that he was cycling to that church the next day.

 b Robyn suggested to her mother that they go to the cinema that evening.

 c Britney said that she had arrived there that morning.

 d My teacher said that our class had homework that day.

3 a Tatum exclaimed in surprise and said to Rev. Steiner that his choir sang beautifully./Tatum exclaimed in surprise to Rev. Steiner that his choir sang beautifully.

 b Kyle exclaimed with fear that it was coming to get him./Kyle exclaimed fearfully that it was coming to get him.

 c Mr van der Merwe exclaimed in anger that he had thought he had told them to wait outside his office./Mr van der Merwe exclaimed angrily that he had thought he had told them to wait outside his office.

Exercise 109

1 a to show the word is being referred to and not used in a normal way
  b to show that the writer is uncomfortable with the term
  c to show the words are being referred to and not used in a normal way
  d to show that the word is a nickname or not his real name
  e to show that the word is being used in an ironic sense

Exercise 110

1 a that the workers should work together
  b that you would like to receive
2 a He says that he cannot find the right person.
  b She thinks that she knows the truth.
3 That John is a liar

Activity K

1 a will
  b The adverb of negation is 'not'. This adverb of negation verb is positioned between the auxiliary verb and the base verb.
  c you
  d your
  e will
  f quotation marks, commas, semi-colons and a full stop.
  g would
  h They are sub-headings.
2 a The present simple tense is used to refer to the future. This is combined with the conjunction 'so' that shows that the subordinate clause is indicating future consequences.
  b Yes, in the seventeenth century people could place 'not' after a verb that stood alone, even if that verb was not a form of the verb 'be'. We can see this in the clause 'Judge not'. The adverb 'not' could also be placed in front of a multiword verb in the subjunctive mood. We can see this in the order of the words 'not be judged'.
  c ye
  d thy, thine
  e shall
  f quotation marks

g In both verses, the base form of the verb 'ask' is used without there being an auxiliary verb in front of it.
h serpent
i According to the Bible, God's generosity is not a possibility but a certainty.

Exercise 111

1 a She's leaving now.
  b I'm so proud!
  c You're very popular.
  d It's an aeroplane!
2 a Which's my bag?
  b There's no door in this wall.
  c Here're some sweets.
  d What's that?
3 a They've got a big car.
  b He's a doctor.
  c We'd already left when the fire started.
  d I'd no idea what was happening.
4 a I mustn't fail this examination.
  b We'll not be going away this holiday./We won't be going away this holiday.
  c She doesn't have feelings for you.
  d David couldn't come although he wanted to.
  e They shouldn't have told her secret to everybody.
  f Don't do that!
5 a needn't
  b oughtn't

Exercise 112

1 a Are you unhappy?
  b Were they left behind in the forest?
  c Am I pretty?
2 a Could you come with me?
  b May he go out this evening?
  c Is the girl on the swing swinging quite high?
  d Has he already torn the letter up?
  e Do you have to go?
3 a Would the teacher notice if our essays were exactly the same?
  b Would you still love me if I were ugly?
  c Will he come if you call him?
4 a Does she like cycling?
  b Does he do it by himself?
  c Did we work quickly?
  d Did I just do it?

5 a Was *Umkonto we Sizwe* a resistance movement during apartheid?
  b Can an oracle predict the future?
  c Have you had a bad experience?
  d Is he looking at the spoon?

Exercise 113

1 a Whose car is that. (my mother's)
  b Whose magazine is that? (Bonnie's)
  c Whose earrings are those? (Tumi's)
2 a What film is that? (*The Fast and the Furious*)
  b Which shoe has a hole in it? (the left shoe)
3 a Who is she? (Michelle)
  b Whose is it? (hers)
  c What is it? (a mountain bike)
  d Who is the quieter sister? (Caitlin)
  e When does the game start? (at 2 p.m.)
  f Where it is being played? (Auckland Park)
  g Why are we watching it? (to improve our own performance)
  h How will they show it to the public? (through the medium of television)
  i Which hand do you write with? (my right hand)
4 a 'Who is that girl with the hat on?'
  b 'How do you get the CD out the CD player?'
  c 'What is your favourite flavour of ice cream?'
  d 'Which do you prefer: chocolate or strawberry milkshakes?'
  e 'When are you going to arrive at the party?'
  f 'Whose dog is that? It seems to be lost.'
  g 'Why are humans on Earth?'
  h 'Where do you go to school?'

Exercise 114

1 a You must go, mustn't you?
  b I may not go, may I?
  c He will believe me, won't he?
  d They do not know how to play soccer, do they?
2 a George will want coffee, won't he?
  b The learners do not understand algebra, do they?
3 a George will want coffee, right?/George will want coffee, or am I wrong?
  b The learners do not understand algebra, right?/The learners do not understand algebra, or am I wrong?

Exercise 115

1 a I looked at <u>myself</u> in the mirror.
  b She cannot control <u>herself</u> when she has drunk alcohol.
  c You are acting strangely tonight; you are not <u>yourself</u>.
  d If we do not understand <u>ourselves</u>, how can we understand the people around us?

Exercise 116

1 a If he does his homework, she will make him some dessert.
  b If you make your bed, I will give you your pocket money.
  c If I am not tired, I will play cards with you.
  d If you do not make your bed, I will not give you your pocket money.
  e If he does not do his homework, she will not make him any dessert.
2 a It will all go horribly wrong if he says anything to her.
  b He will struggle with the car repayments every month if he buys this car.
  c I will not let you in my room if you are rude.
3 If you strike a woman, you will strike a rock.

Exercise 117

1 a If you studied for five hours, I would let you watch a television programme.
  b If he did a double somersault from the diving board, he would win the prize.
  c If she did not say anything, people would not call her rude.
2 a If you gave me a lift to town, I would be very appreciative.
  b If you drove the car, I could relax in the passenger seat.
  c If you read the story, I could close my eyes and just listen.

Exercise 118

1 a If she had kept my secret, I would have kept hers.
  b If you had asked me to the dance, I would have been the happiest girl in the world.

c If the leader had promised the soldiers enough weapons, they would have found energy to continue fighting.

d If I had worn that dress, I would not have seemed slim.

e If I had told you the truth, you would not have gone on holiday with them.

2 a first conditional sentence

b second conditional sentence

c third conditional sentence

3 a If Chippa continues to play in the PSL, he will be happy.

b If Chippa played for a team in the United Kingdom's Premier Leaugue, he would be very rich.

c If, at age fifteen, Chippa had played for a team in the United Kingdom's Premier League, he would have been very surprised.

Exercise 119

1 a Will someone open the door if you knock?

b Will we all die if that bomb explodes?

2 a Would someone open that door if you knocked?

b Would we all die if that bomb exploded?

c Would Chippa be very rich if he played for a team in the United Kingdom's Premier League?

3 a Would someone have opened that door if you had knocked?

b Would we all have died if that bomb had exploded?

c Would Chippa have been very surprised if, at age fifteen, he had played for a team in the United Kingdom's Premier League?

Exercise 120

1 a <u>It</u> is important to study for your examinations.

b <u>It</u> is a long way to Lilongwe.

c <u>It</u> was not the dog that was hurt; it was the driver.

2 a There is a girl in our soccer team.

b There is sugar in the tin.

c There are stars in the sky.

d There is not answer.

e There is no milk in the fridge.

3 a Is it raining?

b Is there no sugar in my coffee?

c Is it not far to go?

d Does there seem to be no explanation?

e Is there going to be trouble?

Activity L

1 They are stage directions.

2 a We are

b She is, She has

3 figuratively

4 a She told me that I would find the one.

b What truth must/should I try to realize?

c I will be right with you.

d They smell good, don't they?

e What vase should I not worry about?

f Who likes me?

g You are not too bright though.

5 a A question mark was put at the end of the sentence in the place of a full stop, to indicate the speaker should use a rising/questioning tone.

b The auxiliary verb 'did' has been inserted, the core verb has been changed into its base form, the word order has been changed and a question mark has been inserted in the place of a full stop.

c The question tag 'right' and a question mark have been inserted. The full stop has been deleted.

6 A/the spoon does not exist.

7 capital letter, apostrophe, ellipsis marks, full stop

8 a a third conditional

b The sentence as a whole is a statement.

9 a yourself

b It makes the sentence sound deep and meaningful.

10 a present tense, simple aspect

b present tense, progressive aspect

11 Sentence a uses the present simple in the future mode./Sentence a uses the auxiliary verb 'will' with a base verb.

Sentence b uses the present progressive to refer to the future.

12 The determiner refers to one of two people.

13 She is contrasting two things.

Exercise 121

1 a Learners are being compared to plants.

b It is used in more than one sentence.

2 a a hand grenade

b It emphasises the fact that this perfume is a strong scent.

Exercise 122

1 a In the past the land in France was divided up between the nobles, so most of the other people farmed on the nobles' land and had to obey them.

b Grégoire Ponceludon de Malavoy was a kind nobleman, therefore he wanted to help the people in his community.

c Dombes was in a flat area in France, therefore when it rained the water did not flow away in rivers.

d Mosquitoes, which breed in water, bred easily in Dombes, because the rainwater formed swamps.

e People in Dombes often died of malaria, because mosquitoes gave them this disease.

f De Malavoy did not want people in his community to get malaria, therefore he wanted to drain the water out of the swamps.

g De Malavoy designed a way of draining the swamps, but he did not have enough money to make his invention work, therefore he became very frustrated.

h De Malavoy went to the Palace of Versailles, because he wanted to meet the King of France.

i The King of France had lots of money, because he charged the ordinary French people high taxes.

j The king gave money to witty nobles who amused him, so De Malavoy tried to make a clever joke in front of the king.

2 a sentences 1 a, b, c, f, g, i, j

b so, therefore

Exercise 123

1 subject

2 a pun

b subject

c two

d says

e and

Exercise 124

1 a My brother is going to the navy (which means I will have my own bedroom).

b Knowing my father was going to lose his temper (and not wanting to be there when he did) I slipped off quietly after supper.

c The rosy glow of sunset flatters everyone. (This time of day is sometimes called 'the hour of the beautiful people'.)

2 a to clarify the meaning of the abbreviation 'MVP'

b They have been added to the existing text.

Exercise 125

1 a The results are accepted by the husband and wife.

b That dog is liked by us.

c John's girlfriend is met by him.

d The hair gel is enriched by the silicone.

2 a Breakfast is eaten by me.

b Breakfast is being eaten by me.

c Breakfast has been eaten by me.

3 a is

b are

c has

Exercise 126

1 a The book was translated by me.

b The aeroplane was flown by you.

c The packet was torn by Miranda.

d Out cool drinks were spilled by us.

e I was invited to the party by you./I was invited by you to the party.

f The seagulls at the beach were seen by the children./The seagulls were seen by the children at the beach.

2 a Breakfast was eaten by me.

b Breakfast was being eaten by me.

c Breakfast had been eaten by me.

3 a simple aspect: My sister was liked by him.

b simple aspect: The ball was thrown by Kayleigh.

c progressive aspect: The money was being spent by my mother.

d progressive aspect: The play was being enjoyed by us.

e perfect aspect: The test had been passed by all the learners.

f perfect aspect: His chocolate had been eaten by him.

g progressive aspect: The clothes were being washed by her.

h perfect aspect: Bad news had been expected by them.

4 a The naughty boy gave a long explanation.

b The sun had dried the clothes.

c My grandmother expected good behaviour.

d The school requires full attendance.

5 a

subject	passive auxiliary verb	passive participle	adverbial phrase
The ball	is	kicked	by the players.

b

subject	passive auxiliary verb	progressive participle	passive participle	adverbial phrase
The ball	was	being	kicked	by the players.

Exercise 127

1 a The rugby ball was dropped.
  b The sheet was torn.
  c The keys were lost yesterday.
  d The competition has been won already.
2 a The juice was spilled on the chair.
  b Mistakes had been made.
  c The taxes have been raised.
  d A packet of sweets was stolen from the shop.
3 sentence b

Exercise 128

1 a A useful resource is the *Cambridge Advanced Learner's Dictionary*. This dictionary is used by learners of English throughout the world.
  b Tashiana is now five years old. She was born on 4 July 2005 by her mother.
2 Tashiana is now five years old. She was born on 4 July 2005.

Exercise 129

1 a I must do my homework now.
   I should do my homework now.
   I have to do my homework now.
  b We must brush our teeth before bedtime.
   We should brush our teeth before bedtime.
   We have to brush our teeth before bedtime.
2 a I must stay in bed if I feel sick.
   I have to stay in bed if I feel sick.
  b He must wear a seatbelt when driving a car.
   He has to wear a seatbelt when driving a car.
3 a I must not make a mess.
   I should not make a mess.
   I ought not to make a mess.
  b She should not drink so much of the juice.
   She ought not to drink so much of the juice.
   She must not drink so much of the juice.

4 a Learners are required to wear black shoes and white socks.
  b All swimmers are required to wear a swimming cap.
  c Drivers are required to show their driver's licences at the road block.
  d Script writers are required to write stage directions in italics.
5 a I am obliged to support my parents in their old age.
  b I am obliged to pay for the things that I damaged.
6 a was required to/was obliged to/had to
  b bought to have/should have

Exercise 130

1 very grateful, much appreciated, with sincere thanks

Activity M

1 a a negative sentence
  b I must be understood figuratively. You cannot eat freedom, therefore 'a hunger to be free' is a metaphor.
  c the passive voice
2 d a, b and c are true.
3 He saw that the black people were not free.
4 a nun
5 d a participle showing that the sentence is in the passive voice.
6 a only
7 no
8 Mandela writes, 'Some say [my mission to liberate the oppressed and the oppressor both] has now been achieved.'/Mandela writes, 'Some say [the liberation of the oppressed and the oppressor] has now been achieved.'
9 a an extended metaphor
10 This metaphor shows that Mandela thinks there is still lot of work to do before South Africans will be really free.

English First Additional Language P1 Exemplar 2007

NATIONAL SENIOR CERTIFICATE
Grade 11
Marks: 75
Time: 2 hours

Instructions and information

1 This question paper consists of THREE sections, namely SECTION A,
   - SECTION B and SECTION C.
   - SECTION A: Comprehension   (30 marks)
   - SECTION B: Summary   (10 marks)
   - SECTION C: Language in context   (35 marks)
2 Answer ALL the questions.
3 Start each section on a NEW page and rule off across the page on completion of EACH section.
4 Leave a line after EACH answer.
5 Write neatly and legibly.
6 Follow the instructions carefully.
7 Number the answers correctly according to the numbering system used in this question paper.
8 Pay special attention to spelling and sentence construction.

Section A: Comprehension

Question 1

Read the following passage and answer the questions. In the case of multiple-choice questions, write down only the question number and the letter corresponding with the answer.

1 Now 54, Sabina Khoza started her working life as a salesperson. Then the company she was working for shut down and sold their delivery vans to staff members.

2 'I managed to buy eight of the kombis,' says Sabina. That was the start of her taxi fleet – which eventually grew to 17 vehicles. But crime forced her to abandon her budding taxi business. In fact, sick of the hijackings and violence, Sabina decided she needed a break from township life altogether.

3 And she didn't have to go far! A farm was for sale in Zuurbekom, on the outskirts of Soweto. 'It was strange,' she recalls. 'I'd just moved from Mofolo in Soweto and started off loading my furniture when a group of people came to help.

4 'Once the work had been done, they disappeared without as much as asking for a cent. This surprised me. Township people do not do any work without being paid. 'On the fourth day I saw these people again. I asked where they were staying. It turned out they were living on my farm. When they realised I was the new owner, they begged me not to evict them.'

5 Sabina was sympathetic to their predicament, and realised she'd have to find a way to make the best of the situation. The opportunity came when her tenants approached her about breeding chickens.

6 'I had never come close to a live chicken in my life,' laughs Sabina. 'As a matter of fact, I was rather afraid of chickens.'

7 Still, she bought 10 chickens and a feeder – and waited for the eggs to come. And waited. And waited.

8 'Then one day a visitor told us we were actually rearing cocks without hens,' laughs Sabina. This setback didn't discourage her, though. Soon she had her hens and had also received training in how to raise chickens. 'I remembered that when I stayed in Soweto, I could only get chickens in Kliptown,' she says. 'So I went and spoke to people in the area. Then one of my tenants went there to sell the birds. We'd spent R11,20 on each chicken and sold them at R20 each. In less than a week, we'd sold our birds.'

9 'Since then, we've been getting chicks regularly from a supplier and we're currently producing 150 000 birds a year. We also supply supermarkets with vegetables.'

10 Khoza's successful farming venture incorporates the latest technology and farming methods, and additional community projects include vegetable and maize production, as well as a guest house, which accommodates trainee farmers.

11 'I train members of the community and offer them opportunities as partners, not just as employees,' says Sabina, who has won numerous awards, including the Department of Agriculture's Female Farmer of the Year in 2003 and the 2004 Shoprite Checkers Woman of the Year Award.

12 'During the festive season, when people go on holiday, I stay at home and make money from all the Christmas bonuses people have been paid. And when all the holidaymakers have returned home, I take leave and book myself into a luxurious hotel, glad to have missed the peak season,' laughs Sabina.

[Adapted from *Bona Magazine*]

Questions

1.1 Why did Sabina not continue working as a salesperson? (2)

1.2 Quote a phrase of not more than six words which tells you why Sabina had left the township. (1)

1.3 Refer to paragraph 2. Three of the following are likely kinds of 'crime' in this context. Which ONE is the exception?
A Hijacking
B Passengers robbed at gunpoint
C Cash in transit heists
D Intimidation from rival fleet owners (2)

1.4 The word 'budding' (paragraph 2) implies that her taxi business at this time ...
A was in the early stages of development.
B seemed headed for success.
C seemed headed for collapse.
D Both A and B (2)

1.5 When Sabina said, 'It was strange' (paragraph 3), she meant that it was strange that ...
A she didn't have to go far.
B the place was called Zuurbekom (instead of, say, Soetbekom).
C you could buy a farm so close to Soweto.
D the people who helped her didn't ask for any money. (2)

1.6 What difference did Sabina observe between township people and the people on the farm? Quote a suitable sentence from paragraph 4 to support your answer. (3)

1.7 The 'predicament' referred to in paragraph 5, is most probably that the tenants ...
A were prepared to help off-load furniture without expecting to be paid for it.
B had been unaware that Sabina was the new owner.

C had nowhere to go if Sabina evicted them.

D were all unemployed. (2)

1.8 Explain in your own words why Sabina's first attempt at breeding chickens was unsuccessful. (3)

1.9 Explain the meaning of the following expression as used in the passage:
'... abandon her budding taxi business' (2)

1.10 Suggest TWO reasons that Shoprite Checkers probably had for naming Sabina their 2004 Woman of the Year. (1½ + 1½) (3)

1.11 What aspects of Sabina's story are surprising, considering that she is a woman? (2)

1.12 Describe any TWO incidents from this passage which show you that Sabina does not give up easily (4)

1.13 In NOT more than 7 words, provide a title for this article which draws attention to Sabina's achievements. (2)

Total Section A: 30

Section B: Summary

Question 2

Imagine that you are preparing an essay on 'Dieting and Eating Disorders'. Read the article below and extract SEVEN important points to include in your essay.

Instructions:

1 Write your points in full sentences using NOT more than 70 words.

2 Number your sentences from 1 to 7 and write only ONE fact per line.

3 Write in correct sentences and use your own words as far as possible.

4 Indicate the number of words you have used in brackets at the end of your summary.

Note that you will be penalised if you ignore these instructions.

There is a constant deadly battle between what teenagers want to look like and what they will do to get there. Teenagers fear that the weight that they've gained during puberty and teenage years is permanent.

They panic and desperately try to lose it. Once they start losing weight, people might compliment them, which makes them feel good. They may start to believe that losing weight will make them happier, but no matter how much weight is lost, it is never enough, and they are never happy.

Teenagers spend a lot of time worrying about what others think and they desperately try to conform to society's unattainable 'ideal' body image. They are lead to believe that if they are thin, they will be accepted. Many of them are constantly exposed to images of thin models appearing on television and in magazines. This only reinforces their belief that in order to be happy, successful and accepted, they must be thin. These factors lead to many teenagers going overboard with dieting, which can then result in eating disorders.

Dieting is about losing weight gradually in a healthy way. Eating disorders are about trying to make your whole life better through eating or not eating food. Sufferers seek approval and acceptance from others and believe life won't be good until a bit (or a lot) of weight is lost, without any concern for the damage done to their bodies.

Anorexia nervosa and bulimia nervosa are two common eating disorders. Anorexia is when someone experiences a significant weight loss resulting from excessive dieting. Anorexics consider themselves to be fat, no matter what their actual weight is. Often they don't realise that they are underweight. They avoid food and taking in calories at all costs, which can result in death. Bulimia is characterised by a cycle of over-eating and vomiting. A sure sign is regular bathroom visits after eating so as to induce vomiting.

[Adapted from: *Teen Zone*]

Total Section B: 10

Section C: Language In Context

Question 3: Visual Literacy

3.1 Analysing a cartoon
Study the following cartoon and answer the questions that follow:

By permission of Stephen Bentley and Creators Syndicate, Inc

3.1.1 Where does the conversation between the two women in the cartoon take place? (1)

3.1.2 Why are certain words (perfect, lose, gain and hate) in bold print? (2)

3.1.3 Refer to Frame 1. Describe the speaker's facial expression, stating what it reveals about her feelings. (2)

3.1.4 Refer to frame 4. Explain why the speaker says 'I **HATE** HER!' (2)

3.2 Analysing an advertisement
Study the advertisement below and answer the questions.

3.2.1 State TWO ways in which the advertiser attempts to attract the readers' attention. (2)

3.2.2 Explain why the advertiser has used the word 'overnight' in the headline. (2)

3.2.3 Do the dots below the word 'overnight' serve any purpose? Give a reason for your answer. (2)

3.2.4 Do you consider the name of the product, Clean & Clear, appropriate? Give a reason for your answer. (2)

[15]

Question 4: Language and editing skills

The article which follows, contains a number of deliberate errors in grammar and punctuation, as well as words within brackets which indicate the writer's uncertainty about which word to use. Read it carefully and answer the following questions:

Dome – The DK patriot

1 Inspired by *TKZEE*, Dome (has started/started) his music career in Grade Ten as the production half of kwaito group, *Rossmoda*. The crew soon dissolved and he formed a new one known as *Scrybe*. He continued doing music as a hobby until he, at The National School Of The Arts, met up with former *Skwatta Kamp* member, Master Sip, widely known as Ngwenya, as well as a huge community of hip hop artists. '(Here's/Heres) were I cut my teeth,' Dome says, 'because the level of competition was so high.'

2 Dome started making tracks at the old *Skwatta Kamp* studio in Leondale. He simply (couldn't/can't) aford the rates and got hold of a sampler that had belonged to Jo'burg beat legend, Iko. Connecting Iko's sampler to his father's hi-fi, Dome was able to produce at the alarming rate of a hundred and fifty beats a week.

3 Dome says, 'I got into the circle of current hot properties from Soweto and I was able to assemble a host of artists for my first production series, Domestic Violins'.

4 'I sold the album out of my backpack and with the money I made, I bought my studio,' says Dome.

5 Dome continues to single-handedly direct the musical score of the South Western Townships. To a number of artists, his music has proved to be the key to massive airplay. To us, the DK patriot (holds/hold) the key to the future of Soweto hip hop.

[Adapted from: *Hype Magazine*]

4.1 Choose the correct word from those in brackets. Write only your answer next to the question number (4.1.1 – 4.1.3) in the answer book.
    4.1.1 'Inspired by *TKZEE*, Dome (has started/started) his music career in Grade Ten as the production half of kwaito group, *Rossmoda*.' (1)
    4.1.2 '(Here's/Heres) were I cut my teeth,' Dome says. (1)
    4.1.3 To us, the DK patriot (holds/hold) the key to the future of Soweto hip hop.' (1)

4.2 Explain why *TKZEE, Rossmoda, Scrybe* and *Skwatta Kamp* are written in italics. (2)

4.3 The word 'were' (line 6) has been used incorrectly. Replace it with the correct word. (1)

4.4 Give the correct spelling of the word 'aford' in paragraph 2 (line 9). (1)

4.5 Provide the correct form of the word within brackets in the following sentence: Dome is a (success) artist in South Africa. (1)

4.6 Provide a synonym (word similar in meaning) from the passage for the word 'began'. (1)

4.7 Choose the correct word from within brackets.
My dad thinks rap music is the (worse/worst) kind of music he has ever heard. (1)

4.8 Complete the following sentences by choosing the correct preposition from the list given below. Write only the question number (4.8.1 – 4.8.2) and the answer. by; of; with; for
    4.8.1 Dome was influenced ... *Skwatta Kamp*. (1)
    4.8.2 I am a gread admirer ... Dome. (1)

4.9 Identify the parts of speech of the underlined words in the following sentence:
Dome said, 'I sold the album out of my backpack.' (1)

4.10 Change the following statement to a question to which the underlined part would be the answer:
Dome said that he was going to perform in Durban. (1)

4.11 Give the antonyms (words opposite in meaning) of the underlined words in the following sentence:
Dome has <u>sold</u> <u>many</u> albums in this country. (1)

4.12 Give the opposite gender of the underlined word in the following sentence:
He met the <u>manager</u> of the studio. (1)

4.13 Write down the plural form of the underlined word in the following sentence:
Dome met a huge <u>community</u> of hip-hop artists. (1)

4.14 Replace the underlined phrase with a single word:
The award for the best hip-hop artist is presented <u>once a year</u>. (1)

4.15 Fill in the missing word in the following sentence:
I love Dome's music. He is my ... artist. (1)

4.16 Rewrite the following sentence in reported speech:
Dome said: 'I sold the album out of my backpack.' (1)

Total Section C: 20
Grand Total: 75
Source: Department of Education

Answers

Secton A: Comprehension

Question 1
1.1 The company she worked for closed down. (2)
1.2 'sick of the hijackings and violence' (1)
OR
'crime forced her' (1)
1.3 C (2)
1.4 D (2)
1.5 D (2)
1.6 She found that people in the township wanted to be paid for everything that they did, whilst the people on the farm did not expect money for any favours.
'Township people do not do any work without being paid'
OR
'Once the work had been done, they disappeared without so much as asking for a cent' (3)
1.7 C (2)
1.8 She did not have the necessary experience. The chicks she had bought all turned out to be cocks. (3)
1.9 She had to give up her growing taxi business. (2)
1.10 Any TWO of the following:
her successful activities; the number of people benefiting from her business; her emphasis on community upliftment and not personal profit only (3)
1.11 Not many women choose careers in farming or the taxi industry. Men are usually more successful in these fields. (2)
1.12 She managed to build her taxi fleet from 8 to 17 despite the crime problem. She was not discouraged by setbacks; when she found out that she had no hens, she addressed the problem and now produces 150 000 birds a year. (4)
1.13 Any suitable answer, for example: Successful Sabina. (2)

Section B: Summary writing

Question 2

Important points

1 Many teenagers are obsessed with losing weight.
2 Weight loss does not always bring happiness.
3 Media images of thin models cause teenagers to diet.
4 Dieting is about healthy weight loss, but eating disorders are about poor self-esteem.
5 Many teenagers are concerned about weight loss, not the damage it can cause.
6 Anorexics avoid food because they believe that they are fat.
7 Bulimics overeat and then vomit.

(65 words)

Note:

* Give one mark for each fact per line – ignore other facts.
* If written in paragraph format, treat one sentence as one fact.
* Give one mark for the number of words that are indicated correctly.
* Give two marks for correct language usage.
* You must rewrite the main points in your OWN WORDS as far as possible.
* Subtract ½ mark for each of the following:
  Words over the 70 word limit (½ mark for every multiple of 5 words beyond 75.)
  Summary in paragraph form.
  Language usage: Deduct 1 mark for every 5 language errors.

Section C: Language in context

Question 3: Visual Literacy

3.1 Analysing a cartoon
    3.1.1 The conversation takes place in a gym or health club. (1)
    3.1.2 The bold print emphasises the words.
         The bold words were expressed louder than the others. (2)
    3.1.3 She is smiling and her eyes are wide open. She looks happy and
         pleased with herself because she has lost weight and is close to
         attaining her goal weight.
         (Give 1 mark for description and 1 mark for feelings.) (2)
    3.1.4 She says that she hates her because she is envious of her. The speaker is
         battling to lose weight while the other woman doesn't have to lose weight.
(2)
(7)

3.2 Analysing an advertisment
    3.2.1 Uses a large font.
         Uses an illustration (2)
    3.2.2 This word highlights how effective the product is since it can get rid of
         spots very quickly. This will encourage the reader to buy the product. (2)

3.2.3 Yes. The dots represent skin spots or pimples. The decreasing size of the dots indicates how the size of the spots will decrease when this product is used. (2)

3.2.4 Yes. The product is meant to make the skin clean and clear as suggested by the name. (2)

(8)

(15)

Question 4: Language and editing

4.1.1 Started (1)
4.1.2 Here's (1)
4.1.3 Holds (1)
4.2 The italics indicate that these are names of groups. (1)
4.3 where (1)
4.4 afford (1)
4.5 successful (1)
4.6 started (1)
4.7 worst (1)
4.8.1 by (1)
4.8.2 of (1)
4.9 I – (personal) pronoun (½)
sold - verb (½)
4.10 Where was Dome going to perform? (2)
OR
In which place/city was Dome going to perform?
4.11 sold – bought (½)
many – few (½)
4.12 manageress (1)
4.13 communities (1)
4.14 annually (1)
4.15 favourite/favorite (1)
4.16 Dome said that he had sold the album out of his backpack.
(½ mark for each of the underlined changes.) (2)

[20]

Acknowledgements

We'd like to thank the following for permission to use their material in either the original or adapted form:
Pages 26–27: 'You can't deny death, you can't fear it', © Hila Bouzaglou, first published in the *Mail & Guardian*. Page 41: 'One perfect rose', *The Norton Anthology of Poetry*. 3rd edition. page 1038. New York – London, 1983. Page 44: *Cambridge Advanced Learner's Dictionary*, Cambridge University Press, 2005. Page 45 King Features Syndicate. Page 56: http://en.wikipedia.org/wiki/Statue_of_Liberty. Page 73: http://en.wikipedia.org/wiki/Stereotype. Page 77: 'The struggle continues', by Lucy Jamieson, *Mail & Guardian*, Friday 27 October to 2 November 2006, page 10. Pages 92–93: 'Fit for a bling', by Oliver Roberts, *Style Magazine*, March 2006, pages 50–53. Page 95: *Cheaper by the dozen*. Page 3. Frank and Ernestine Gilbreth Carey. Heinemann. 1951. *Cloven Hooves*, Megan Lindholm. 1991. Bantam: Spectra. *Fillets of Plaice*, by Gerald Durrell. Fontana/Collins, 1977, page 137. Page 96: *The Witches*, by Roald Dahl, Jonathan Cape Ltd & Penguin Books Ltd. Illustration by Quentin Blake. Page 103: *True Love sMagazine*, December 2006, No. 334, page 31. Page 106: www.CartoonStock.com. Page 108: Easy Waves, *DRUM Magazine*, 26 October 2006, #737, page 31. Page 109: 'Heart + sole', *Touch Magazine*, February 2006, Volume 3 # 033. Page 181: 'The Wasteland', by T.S. Eliot. Page 120: 'Al-Qa'eda brings terror to the heart of London', Telegraph online. www.telegraph.co.uk. Page 123: 'We were like sardines in there, just waiting to die' 08/07/2005, by Sally Pook, Catriona Davies and Duncan Gardham. Page 125: 'The British Muslim Fanatic Who Plotted to Kill Thousands', Telegraph online, by Duncan Gardham. www.telegraph.co.uk. Page 137–138: *Juggling truths* by Unity Dow, 2004, Double Storey Books (Juta & Co.), pages 43-45. Page 152: 'Dynamite', by Thomas Setshogo, *Style Magazine*, March 2006, page 82. Page 156–157: 'Eyes on the future', IMAGES24.co.za/DRUM. Page 170: 'I have a dream', reprinted by arrangement with The Heirs to the Estate of Martin Luther King Jr., c/o Writers House as agent for the proprietor New York, NY. Copyright 1963 Martin Luther King, Jr.; copyright renewed 1991 Coretta Scott King. Page 188: 'Judging others, Ask, Seek, Knock', *Holy Bible: Good News Edition*. Page 189: Matthew Chapter 7, verses 1–12, *The King James Bible*, first published in 1611. Page 205–207: *The matrix*. Page 208: 'Highly explosive', *Style Magazine*, March 2006, page 77. Page 220: *Bloomsbury Thesaurus*, 1993, page 1493. Page 221: *Bloomsbury Thesaurus*, 1993, page 860. Page 222–223: *Long Walk to Freedom*, Nelson Mandela, Abacus, an imprint of Little, Brown and Company. Page 232–232: 'Stripped of my Powers', by Dwayn Daniels, a learner at St George's Grammar School. Page 234–235: 'Football disregards the borders between nations', by Wayne Stynder, a learner at Settlers' High School. Page 236–237: 'Do the advantages of technology outweigh the disadvantages?', by Lana Jacobs, a learner at St George's Grammar School. Page 238: Woza Albert!, Percy Mtwa, Mbongeni Ngema, Barney Simon.Methuen , London, 1983. Page 240: 'Nigerian air crash kills 97', *Cape Sun*, front page, 30 October 2006. Page 241: 'A noble profession', by Grace Khuzwayo, *BONA Magazine*, June 2006, page 64 and 65. Page 242: 'Mother Teresa dead at 87', www.cnn.com/WORLD/9709/05/mother.teresa/ Page 243: IMAGES24.co.za/DRUM. Page 246: *New African Magazine*. Pages 284–289: Department of Education. Page 287: Stephen Bentley and Creators Syndicate, Inc.

We are grateful to the following for permission to reproduce photographs:
Page 10: IMAGES24.co.za/Drum. Page 11: Topfoto/Inpra. Page 27 Richard Young/Rex Features. Page 56: Rex Features. Page 77: Photograph ©Ruphin Coudyzer FPPSA – www.ruphin.com. Page 92 (l): Online images. Page 93: John Pierce / Rex Features. Page 97 Jussi Nukari / Rex Features. Page 100 (l): Bridgeman Art Library. Page 100 (r): Topfoto. Page 101 (tl): Bridgeman Art Library. Page 101 (tr, bl, br): Topfoto. Page 102: Gary Childs / Rex Features. Page 103: *True Love Magazine*. Page 109: The Bigger Picture/Reuters. Page 112: Jeanne Maclay-Mayers. Page 120: Thomas Brandi / Rex Features. Page 123: The Bigger Picture/Reuters. Page 125 John Miller / Robert Harding / Rex Features. Page 152: The Bigger Picture/Alamy. Page 153: Rex Features. Page 156: IMAGES24.co.za/DRUM. Page 157: IMAGES24.co.za/Beeld/Felix Dlangamandla. Page 165: Online Images. Page 170: Topfoto/Inpra. Page 210 The Movie Company. Page 222 Drum Social Histories / Baileys African History Archive / africanpictures.net. Page 223 Drum Social Histories / Baileys African History Archive / africanpictures.net. Page 241: *BONA Magazine*, June 2006, page 64 and 65. Page 243: Rex Features. Page 246: Greatstock/Corbis.